Democratic Politics in the European Parliament

With the European Parliament comprising politicians from many different countries, cultures, languages, national parties and institutional backgrounds, one might expect politics in the Parliament to be highly fragmented and unpredictable. By studying more than 15,000 recorded votes between 1979 and 2004 this book establishes that the opposite is in fact true: transnational parties in the European Parliament are highly cohesive and the classic 'left-right' dimension dominates voting behaviour. Furthermore, the cohesion of parties in the European Parliament has increased as the powers of the Parliament have increased. The authors suggest that the main reason for these developments is that like-minded members of the European Parliament (MEPs) have incentives to form stable transnational party organizations and to use these organizations to compete over European Union (EU) policies. They suggest that this is a positive development for the future of democratic accountability in the EU.

Simon Hix is Professor of European and Comparative Politics in the Department of Government at the London School of Economics and Political Science.

Abdul G. Noury is Associate Professor in the Department of Economics and the Institute for European Studies at the Université Libre de Bruxelles.

Gérard Roland is Professor in the Departments of Economics and Political Science at the University of California, Berkeley.

Themes in European Governance

Series Editor
Andreas Føllesdal

Editorial Board
Stefano Bartolini, Ulrich Preuss, Helen Wallace
Beate Kohler-Koch, Thomas Risse, Albert Weale
Percy Lehning, Fritz W. Scharpf, J. H. H. Weiler
Andrew Moravcsik, Philip Schlesinger

The evolving European systems of governance, in particular the European
Union, challenge and transform the state, the most important locus of
governance and political identity and loyalty over the past 200 years. The series
Themes in European Governance aims to publish the best theoretical and
analytical scholarship on the impact of European governance on the core
institutions, policies and identities of nation states. It focuses upon the
implications for issues such as citizenship, welfare, political decision-making,
and economic, monetary and fiscal policies. An initiative of Cambridge
University Press and the Programme on Advanced Research on the European-
isation in the Nation-State (ARENA), Norway, the series includes theoretically
informed studies analysing key issues at the European level and within European
states. Volumes in the series will be of interest to scholars and students of
Europe both within Europe and worldwide. They will be of particular relevance
to those interested in the development of sovereignty and governance of
European states and in the issues raised by multi-level governance and multinational integration throughout the world.

Other books in the series:

Michael Zürn and Christian Joerges (eds.) *Law and Governance in Postnational Europe: Compliance beyond the Nation-State*

Gerda Falkner et al (eds.) *Complying with Europe: EU Harmonisation and Soft Law in the Member Status*

Jonas Tallberg *Leadership and Nagotiation in the European Union*

Rachel A. Cichowski *The European Court and Civil Society: Litigation, Mobilization and Governance*

Democratic Politics in the European Parliament

Simon Hix

London School of Economics and Political Science

Abdul G. Noury

Free University of Brussels

Gérard Roland

University of California, Berkeley

CAMBRIDGE UNIVERSITY PRESS
Cambridge, New York, Melbourne, Madrid, Cape Town, Singapore, São Paulo

Cambridge University Press
The Edinburgh Building, Cambridge CB2 8RU, UK

Published in the United States of America by Cambridge University Press,
New York

www.cambridge.org
Information on this title: www.cambridge.org/9780521694605

First published 2007

Printed in the United Kingdom at the University Press, Cambridge

A catalogue record for this book is available from the British Library

Library of Congress Cataloging in Publication data

Hix, Simon
　Democratic politics in the European Parliament / by Simon Hix, Abdul
Noury, Gérard Roland.
　p. cm.
Includes bibliographical references and index.
ISBN-13 978-0-521-87288-1 (hardback : alk. paper)
ISBN-13 978-0-521-69460-5 (pbk. : alk. paper)
　1. European Union. 2. European Parliament. 3. Legislative power –
European Union countries. 4. Legislators – European Union countries.
I. Noury, Abdul II. Roland, Gérard, 1954 – III. Title.

JN36.H53 2007
328.4–dc22
　　　　　　　　　　　　　　　　　　　　　　　　　　　　2006034601
ISBN 978-0-521-87288-1 hardback
ISBN 978-0-521-69460-5 paperback

List of Contents

List of figures

List of tables

List of boxes

Acknowledgements

Independently of each other, Simon in London and Gérard and Abdul in Brussels began collecting the voting records of the Members of the European Parliament (MEP) in 1998. Abdul and Simon then 'discovered' each other at the American Political Science Association conference in Washington, DC in September 2000, when they presented almost identical papers analysing the dimensions of voting in the European Parliament. We quickly decided to pool our efforts, and started working on collecting the full set of roll-call voting data from July 1979 to June 2004. This proved more difficult than we had originally anticipated. The voting records from the first three parliaments had to be entered from hard copies of the annexes to the minutes of the European Parliament's plenary sessions. This involved scanning each page and applying a specially written piece of software to transform the text files into a database. For the fourth and fifth parliaments, we were able to gain access to the original electronic files from the European Parliament.

This research would not have been possible without the support of several people. Georges Destrée, from the Centre de Calcul at the Université Libre de Bruxelles (ULB), wrote the computer code, which enabled us to transform kilometres of text into lines of numerical code. Giacomo Benedetto coordinated the scanning of the files for the first two parliaments and entered a huge amount of data on each MEP and each vote. Vincenzo Verardi scanned the voting records for the third and fourth parliaments. Bjorn Hoyland entered the information about each vote in the first and fifth parliaments. Elsa Roland helped integrate the databases from the third and fourth parliaments. Michiel van Hulten provided us with access to the electronic files from the fifth parliament, and Michiel's assistant, Ruud Verschuur, provided invaluable support in sending us the files. Maria Elvira Traccitto, from the European Parliament, provided us with extensive data on each individual MEP. Pat Cox, who was President of the European Parliament between 2002 and 2004, invited us to present the research in the European Parliament in 2003. Without the help of these people this research would not have been possible.

Financial support for the research was provided by the Economic and Social Research Council of the United Kingdom (No: L213 25 2019), the Nuffield Foundation (No: SGS/00387/G), the Leverhulme Trust (No: RG/8/2000/0042), an ACE grant from the European Commission and an ARC grant from the Communauté française de Belgique (No: 00/05-252). Additionally, we were very fortunate to be able to spend most of the 2004–2005 academic year together at the University of California, Berkeley, to complete the book. We would like to thank Bruce Cain, Heddy Riss and Liz Wiener, at the Berkeley Institute of Governmental Studies, for helping in organising Simon and Abdul's visit. To enable them to visit Berkeley for the year, Simon received a Distinguished Fellow award from the US–UK Fulbright Commission and Abdul received a Belgian–American Education Foundation fellowship. We gratefully acknowledge the generous support of these institutions and people.

We would also like to acknowledge the following people who have commented on various aspects of the research and the book manuscript: John Carey, Micael Castanheira, Richard Corbett MEP, Christophe Crombez, David Farrell, Matt Gabel, Bjorn Hoyland, Simon Hug, Amie Kreppel, Charles Lees, Chris Lord, Iain McLean, Keith Poole, Tapio Raunio, Howard Rosenthal, Michael Shackleton, Roger Scully, Erik Voeten and Helen Wallace.

Simon, Abdul and Gérard

Introduction

'I have come to the conclusion that if a vote were to take place today, the outcome would not be positive for the European institutions or for the European project. In these circumstances I have decided not to submit a new Commission for your approval today. I need more time to look at this issue, to consult with the Council and to consult further with you, so that we can have strong support for the new Commission. ... These last few days have demonstrated that the European Union is a strong political construction and that this Parliament, elected by popular vote across all our member states, has a vital role to play in the governance of Europe.' *José Manuel Durão Barroso, Commission President designate*

'Today this House on the river Rhine has grown in stature. Its will was tested, its will has prevailed. ... Mr Barroso, you suggested yesterday that it was anti-European to vote against your Commission. ... [but] today, Euroscepticism loses because the voice of democracy in Europe has risen by an octave and has made itself heard in every national capital and beyond.' *Graham Watson, Leader of the Alliance of Liberals and Democrats for Europe (the liberal party in the European Parliament)*

On 27 October 2004 the European Parliament refused to elect the new Commission, the European Union (EU) executive. There was no vote, as 10 minutes before the vote the Commission President designate, José Manuel Durão Barroso, announced that he was withdrawing his team of Commissioners. He simply did not have the numbers: the Party of European Socialists, the second largest party in the Parliament after the June 2004 elections, was backed in its opposition to the proposed Commission by the smaller liberal, green, and radical-left parties. This coalition, with a combined force of 371 out of the 732 Members of the European Parliament (MEPs), was easily larger than the pro-Commission bloc of the European People's Party (EPP), with 268 seats, and the small conservative national party to its right, with 27 seats.

If it was so clear that the Parliament would reject the Commission, why did Barroso not withdraw his team earlier? It had been known for

1

some time that many liberal, socialist and green MEPs were unhappy with the nomination for the justice and home affairs portfolio of Rocco Buttiglione, a devout Catholic with ultra-conservative views on immigration, women's rights and homosexuality.

Barroso and the governments thought that they could railroad the Parliament. The governments expected the Parliament to support a Commission that was composed of politicians nominated by the twenty-five governments of the EU member states, as it had always done before. The Parliament does not have the right to reject individual Commissioners, but only to reject the whole team, and rejecting the whole team was thought of as the 'nuclear option'. Moreover, a cross-party coalition in the Parliament had voted for Barroso in July, and the proposed Commission contained a reasonable balance of conservatives, social democrats and liberals. Above all, Barroso did not place Buttiglione in another portfolio or force the Italian government to nominate someone else, because the governments were convinced that they could force 'their' MEPs to support the Commission.

This time, however, the European Parliament did not bend to the will of the governments. Only the night before the vote did it become clear that the overwhelming majority of MEPs would side with the leaders of their supranational parties in the Parliament rather than with their national party leaders, who were lobbying them heavily to support the Commission. It was now too late to reshuffle the team. Barroso hence decided that delaying the vote was the only option.

The media heralded this climb down by Barroso and the governments as a founding moment for democracy at the European level.[1] A coalition of supranational political parties was able to rally their troops in the Parliament to block the will of the supposedly sovereign governments of twenty-five nation-states. With cohesive parties that are independent from national government pressures, the formal powers of the European Parliament, to amend legislation and the budget and to elect and censure the Commission, were now a reality. Democratic politics had finally arrived in the EU.

Most commentators failed to realise, however, that parties and politics inside the European Parliament had been developing for some time.

---

[1] For example, Wolfgang Munchau in *The Financial Times* declared that it was 'a great day for European democracy' (28 October 2004, p. 17). Adrian Hamilton in *The Independent* wrote: 'Europe's leaders ... cannot just continue taking the Union's institutions or its voters for granted ... But the other great lesson of this week may well prove more beneficent in the long term ... we are seeing in [the European Parliament's] manoeuvrings the beginnings of cross-national parties and Europe-wide politics' (28 October 2004, p. 41).

Since the first direct elections in 1979, beyond the attention of the mass media and the voters, and even off the radar screens of most of the EU's governments, the MEPs had gradually fashioned a well organised and highly competitive party system at the European level. What actually happened in October 2004 was that Europe's political class was finally forced to wake up to the new reality, where supranational party politics is a key aspect of policy-making in the emerging European polity.

What we do in this book is explain how this process developed: why MEPs chose to organise as supranational parties in the European Parliament in the first place, why these parties then evolved as powerful agenda-setting actors, why voting along supranational party lines gradually replaced voting along national party lines as the dominant form of behaviour in the Parliament, and ultimately how democratic politics emerged in the only directly elected institution at the European level.

We argue that increases in the power of the European Parliament have played a crucial role in shaping supranational parties in the European Parliament.[2] In a rather short space of time, a matter of decades rather than centuries, the European Parliament has evolved from an unelected consultative body to one of the most powerful elected assemblies in the world. Today, a large proportion of social and economic legislation applied in the member states of the EU is adopted at the European rather than the national level. The European Parliament not only has the power to amend and reject most EU laws but also influences the make-up and political direction of the body that initiates these laws: the European Commission. We argue that this increase in powers has made the European Parliament look increasingly like a normal parliament with cohesive parties who compete to dominate legislative outcomes and who form coalitions with other party groups for that purpose.

Summary of the argument and the main findings

We analyse all of the nearly 15,000 recorded votes by individual MEPs (roll-call votes) in the first five elected European Parliaments, covering the 25-year period between 1979 and 2004. We show that voting in the European Parliament has become increasingly structured. Contrary to a widespread popular perception, this structure is based around the transnational European parties, and not nationality. A German conservative is more likely to vote with a Portuguese conservative than with

---

[2] For a survey of the explanations for the development of the powers of the European Parliament, see, in particular, Rittberger (2005).

a German social democrat or a German green. The voting behaviour of MEPs is thus based on party rather than nationality.

We build a theory to explain why this is the case in the European Parliament and also in other democracies. Our argument is based on the idea that in a democracy political conflicts (over redistribution, legislation, and so on) inside a parliament between representatives of different territorial units are best solved by federalism; in other words, by the appropriate devolution of power to the territorial units themselves, when these conflicts are important. The costs of devolution can then be minimised by keeping some powers centralised, such as jurisdiction over free trade and other areas (some key environmental competences, for example) where externalities between territorial units are important and would have a negative effect under decentralisation. We argue that it is more difficult and less efficient to organise the devolution of powers to socio-professional groups or economic sectors, or other functional interests in the economy, because this would entail potentially very negative economic consequences. If conflicts between territorial units can be solved more easily by devolution of powers than conflicts between socio-economic groups, then it follows quite naturally that the conflicts one ends up observing in national parliaments or federal legislatures are conflicts between socio-economic groups. This explains why parties form along the left–right axis and not along territorial lines. The theory applies to other advanced democracies as well as to the European Parliament.

We show that party cohesion has increased as the powers of the European Parliament have steadily increased. This suggests that higher stakes in decision-making have given MEPs with similar policy preferences the right incentives to solve their collective action problems inside the parliament, to form European-wide parties, to delegate increasing powers to the leaders of these organisations, to come up with unified positions to compete with the other European parties and to discipline their members into voting with the European party line. We show, for example, that cohesiveness of parties does not decrease in the long run even when the parties become more ideologically heterogeneous. However, higher fragmentation of the European parties is associated with a somewhat lower cohesion. In other words, when the European parties are composed mostly of many small national party delegations, they have a harder time to agree on a common position than when the European parties are composed of some large national delegations and some smaller ones.

The cohesion of European parties is quite surprising for several reasons. First, the degree of agenda control by the European party leaders is more limited than in most national parliaments. Indeed, the European Commission has the exclusive right of initiative of nearly all EU legislation. Hence, legislation that comes on the floor of the European Parliament emanates from outside the parliament and not from a majority coalition inside the parliament. This inability to control the agenda should reduce party cohesion, as the leaders of the parties in the parliament cannot filter out proposals on which their members have divergent political opinions. We do find some evidence of lower cohesion due to the lack of agenda control – for example, the parties are slightly more cohesive on non-legislative issues, which are initiated internally in the parliament, than on legislative issues, which are initiated externally. However, we also find evidence suggesting that the European parties are able to overcome the lack of agenda control and vote cohesively. For example, we find that a European party is as cohesive in a vote on a 'hostile amendment' (where an amendment is proposed by another party on a bill where a member of the first party is the *rapporteur*) as in all other votes.

A second reason why cohesiveness should be lower in the European Parliament is that European parties do not have many instruments to discipline their members. They do not control the selection of candidates in European Parliament elections, as this is controlled by the national parties who make up the European parties. The European parties also have no control over the future career of MEPs, as it is again the national parties who control the allocation of ministerial portfolios and other jobs in the domestic arena and the selection of European Commissioners. The only instruments European parties have to discipline their members are the allocation of membership of legislative committees, rapporteurships and other positions of influence within the European Parliament. These instruments are relatively weak in terms of their disciplining power. They are definitely weaker than the ones available to parties in parliamentary regimes. However, to the extent that it is national parties that develop common positions in their European parties, it is national parties that play a key role in enforcing European party discipline. Individual MEPs nearly always vote with their national party delegation, independently of their own preferences. If one adds this to the fact that it is rare that a national party votes against its European party, one understands that national parties play a key role in determining the cohesion of the European parties. European parties are able to mobilise their members to participate more in votes that are expected to be closer and the outcome more competitive.

We consequently argue that the incentive to form and maintain powerful transnational party organisations is fundamentally related to political competition inside the European Parliament to secure policy outcomes from the EU that are as close as possible to the ideological (left–right) preferences of the MEPs and national parties. It pays to be cohesive because this increases a party's chance of being on the winning side of a vote and thus to influence its final outcome. It is thus natural that the increases in the powers of the European Parliament have led to a stronger and more democratic structure of politics in the European Parliament, based around left–right competition between genuine European parties.

Outline of the book

Chapter 1 provides some essential background material on the development of the powers of and parties in the European Parliament. Chapters 2 and 3 then present the two basic elements of our theory: that political parties are essential for the functioning of democratic politics, and that these political organisations are more likely to emerge around ideological (left–right) divisions than territorial divisions.

The remainder of the book contains a series of empirical tests of our ideas, using a unique dataset of all roll-call votes in the European Parliament between 1979 and 2004. Chapter 4 starts the analysis by looking at the increasing participation of MEPs in roll-call votes and how participation varies with the powers of the European Parliament on the issue of the vote. We find growing levels of participation, more growth in more organised parties, and more participation where the Parliament has more power.

The next three chapters focus on partisan politics inside the Parliament. Chapter 5 looks at the 'cohesion' of the political parties. We introduce a cohesion index for measuring the cohesion of parties and national delegations. We show that while voting along transnational party lines has increased, voting along national lines has decreased. We then investigate the determinants of party cohesion, and find that the transnational parties are increasingly cohesive despite growing internal ideological and national diversity.

We then investigate two possible explanations of growing partisan politics in the European Parliament. Chapter 6 focuses on whether the parties in the European Parliament can enforce party discipline by controlling the agenda. We find that parties are more likely to be cohesive where they have some control over the agenda, on non-legislative resolutions, for example. Because agenda-setting rights are shared amongst the parties and because legislation is initiated externally by the Commission, this limited agenda control in the European Parliament should lead to a lower cohesion than what we observe. We also show that parties are not less cohesive when facing hostile amendments on bills they sponsor. There is thus strong suggestive evidence that European political groups are able to discipline the voting behaviour of their members even when they do not control the agenda.

Chapter 7 focuses on whether national parties or the European political groups have more control on the MEPs. We find that MEPs are less likely to vote against their national parties than their European political groups. On balance, one-third of an MEP's voting behaviour is determined by his or her European political group and two-thirds is determined by his or her national party. Hence, growing transnational party politics in the European Parliament must be explained via national political parties. Despite continued policy differences between the member parties in each European political group, national parties have decided to form increasingly powerful transnational political parties and to endow these organisations with leadership and agenda-setting powers.

The next two chapters then look at the ideological structure of politics in the European Parliament, within and between the European parties. Chapter 8 focuses on coalition formation between the European parties. We look at the proportion of times the majority in each political group voted the same way as a majority in another political group. We show that coalitions in the European Parliament are increasingly along left–right lines. We also investigate the determinants of coalition formation, and find that the left–right ideological distance between any two political groups is the strongest predictor of whether they vote together in a given period and over time.

Chapter 9 then looks at the dimensions of voting in the Parliament. We apply a scaling method to the roll-call votes and find that the classic left–right conflict is the main dimension of voting in the European Parliament, between as well as inside the European parties. In other words, the further an MEP is from the average left–right preferences of his or her European party, the more likely he or she will vote differently from the other members of the party. We also find that, although less salient, the second dimension captures MEPs' preferences on European integration as well as conflicts between the parties in the European Parliament and the parties represented in the Council and Commission.

The next two chapters supplement the aggregate analyses in the previous empirical chapters with two detailed case studies. Chapter 10 investigates the parliament's executive-control powers, by analysing MEP behaviour in four key votes in the fourth parliament (1994–1999) on the investiture and censure of the Santer Commission. We find the emergence of 'government-opposition' politics in the European Parliament: where the European parties who dominate the Commission tend to support the Commission, while the parties who are either not represented in the Commission or who are marginalised in this institution tend to oppose the Commission. From this perspective, at the start of the Barroso Commission in 2005, there was 'unified government' in the EU, where a centre-right coalition controlled the Commission, the European Parliament, and the Council.

Chapter 11 turns to the parliament's legislative powers, by investigating MEP behaviour in the fifth parliament (1999–2004) on the Takeover Directive. We find that even when the political stakes are extremely high, European parties and left–right preferences have a significant influence on MEP behaviour. Where an issue is highly salient for a particular member state in a vote, the MEPs from this state may vote together and against their European parties. However, because this only affects one or two member states in any vote (as was the case with German MEPs on the Takeover Directive), and because this only occurs in a small number of votes on any bill, European parties' positions and left–right preferences of MEPs are the main determinants of legislative outcomes in the European Parliament.

Finally, Chapter 12 concludes by drawing out the implications of our argument and findings as well as discussing avenues for future research.

Lessons for political science and European politics

The research presented in this book contains insights both for political science in general and for the sub-field of European politics. We spell them out briefly here but will come back to these issues throughout the book.

From the point of view of political science, our book contributes to the study of legislative behaviour in a comparative perspective. A first important question refers to the role of parties in democracies. Why do we generally observe party formation in democracies? Along what lines do they form? What is the effect of party systems in legislative decision-making? In Chapter 2, we provide a synthesis of these questions and provide a systematic analysis of the advantages of strong party systems in democracies relative to weak and fragmented party systems. We distinguish between the role of parties in solving collective action problems *external* and *internal* to the elected legislature. Collective action problems external to the legislature refer to electoral politics. Parties play a crucial role in mobilising the electorate to vote, a key question in political science. They also provide brand names with well-known and recognisable platforms and a reputation that has value with voters and is therefore valuable to preserve, which enhances the reliability of politicians. Collective action problems internal to the legislature refer to legislative politics. Cohesive parties reduce the volatility and increase the predictability of legislative decisions. They allow for specialisation of parliamentarians in specific issues, which improves the quality of bills. They increase the efficiency of policy-making by screening out inefficient programmes that only bring benefits to small groups and costs to the general public. They also reduce the dimensionality of politics by creating correlations between the different dimensions of politics.

We contribute to the theory of parties by proposing a theory, briefly summarised above, for why parties in stable democracies form mainly along the left–right axis and not along territorial lines. Our theory is a complement to the 'cleavage theory' of Lipset and Rokkan. The cleavage theory does not ask why parties do not generally form on a territorial basis, except in countries where the borders and the territorial organisation of the state remain contested. In the context of the European Parliament, it is especially important to ask that question. On the other hand, the cleavage theory gives content to our notion that parties form on a functional and not on a territorial basis.

Political scientists have made much progress in recent years in trying to understand what causes voting behaviour inside elected legislatures. The European Parliament is an especially interesting institution to verify political science theories. With members from multiple nation-states, who are organised into national as well as transnational political parties, and with dramatic changes in the powers of the institution, the European Parliament is a unique laboratory for testing general theories of political parties and legislative behaviour. Most political science theories of parties and legislative politics have been developed in very particular institutional contexts, such as the US Congress or the British House of Commons. If these theories are truly generalisable, however, they should also hold in the European Parliament. Different theories highlight different causes of party cohesion. Many traditional theories emphasise the 'carrots and sticks' used by party leadership to discipline their representatives to toe the party line. One alternative theory, associated mostly with Keith Krehbiel, emphasises the preferences of the members of a party. Cohesion in voting is related to closeness in political and ideological preferences. Politicians sort themselves into parties on the basis of their preferences, and it is this sorting that fundamentally creates cohesion. Another theory, put forward in a recent book by Gary Cox and Mathew McCubbins, emphasises the role of agenda control in explaining party cohesion. Parties use their control over the legislative agenda to only put forward bills on which there is strong support from their party in the parliament.

In this book, we find that ideology alone cannot explain party cohesion. While European parties tend to form coalitions on the basis of ideological closeness, variation in cohesion within the European parties is not related to variation in ideological preferences in the European parties. Similarly, compared with other legislatures, European parties have relatively little control over the agenda. Nevertheless, cohesion is relatively strong. Overall, it is impossible to escape the conclusion that the European parties are able to discipline their representatives in the European Parliament. However, our findings suggest that this happens mostly via the influence of national parties, which voluntarily choose to form European parties to promote their own policy goals, and then act collectively to secure these goals.

From the point of view of European politics, our work builds on the research of scholars in this field in the last decade. Scholars not only have been closely observing the functioning of the European Parliament, but have also collected samples of voting data to try to understand better the patterns of voting behaviour. By putting together and making available the complete population of roll-call data in the history of the European Parliament, we hope to contribute to bringing the level of research on the European Parliament to the level of existing research in American politics, where roll-call data from the whole history of the US Congress are used in a standard way to analyse issues of American politics.

Our research shows that the European Parliament cannot be understood as a unitary actor engaged in strategic games with the Commission and the Council. It shows how and why cohesion of the European parties has changed over time. It shows that left–right politics is the main dimension of contestation in the European Parliament, but a second dimension has also emerged, which relates to the speed and nature of European integration and battles between the European Parliament and the Council and Commission.

More broadly, the European Parliament is fundamentally important for the future of the EU and democratic governance in Europe. The EU was probably the most significant institutional innovation in the organisation of politics and the state anywhere in the world in the second half of the twentieth century. At the beginning of the twenty-first century, however, there is growing concern about how viable this organisation is in the long term if it cannot be made more democratically accountable. The European Parliament is uniquely placed, as the only directly elected institution at the European level, to operate as the voice of the people in the EU governance system. If democratic politics does not exist in the European Parliament, then the future of the EU may be bleak. However, if democratic politics has begun to emerge inside the European Parliament, in terms of being based around political parties that articulate the classic ideological divisions of democratic politics, then perhaps democracy beyond the nation-state is possible after all.

This is all the more important in the light of the constitutional fiasco triggered by the failed referendums on the European Constitution project in France and the Netherlands. Opposing arguments have been voiced that the Constitution went too far or not far enough in the European integration process. It is doubtful, however, that a new constitutional project would gain more support within the European population if it does not strengthen the democratic accountability of European institutions. The European Parliament is the only directly elected body in the EU. While being often criticised or vilified by some national politicians and national media, one should not forget that it is also the European institution that is most trusted by European citizens. In the Eurobarometer opinion poll survey in the Autumn of 2004, 57 per cent of respondents in the 25 EU member states said that they trusted the European Parliament, while only 52 per cent said that they trusted the European Commission, and 45 per cent said that they trusted the European Council – which is composed of the heads of government of member states. One can argue that these figures are relatively low, but our research shows that there are good reasons for citizens to trust the European Parliament! The European Parliament is a real parliament, with real parties and real democratic politics.

1 Development of the European Parliament

In this chapter, our aim is to provide some essential background material for understanding the argument and evidence we present in the rest of the book.[1] We focus on three aspects of the story of the European Parliament: (1) the main powers of the institution and how these have changed; (2) how the political parties and the party system in the European Parliament have evolved; and (3) why the 'electoral connection' from citizens to MEPs remains rather weak despite six rounds of European Parliament elections. The chapter concludes with a discussion of 'roll-call votes' in the European Parliament, which is the data we use in the rest of the book to understand how politics inside the European Parliament has changed. Roll-call votes are votes where the voting decision of each MEP is recorded. The roll-call voting records are published in the annexes to the minutes of the plenary sessions of the European Parliament. Nowadays, they can also be found on the website of the European Parliament.[2]

1.1 Powers of the European Parliament

The precursor to the modern European Parliament was the 'Assembly' of the European Coal and Steel Community, which held its first meeting on 10 September 1952. With the launch of the European Economic Community (EEC) in 1958, the assembly chose to refer to itself as the 'European Parliament', a moniker that was grudgingly accepted by the then six EEC member states (Belgium, France, Germany, Italy, Luxembourg and the Netherlands) and was officially endorsed in the Single European Act (SEA) in 1985.

---

[1] A very useful tool for understanding the functioning of the European Parliament is the detailed and comprehensive book by Corbett, Jacobs and Shackleton (2005).

[2] The website of the European Parliament is www.europarl.europa.eu. Under the 'plenary sessions' part of the site one can click on the minutes (by date), then click on a given date, and then look at the roll-call voting records in either MS Word or pdf format.

Until 1979 the European Parliament was composed of delegates from national parliaments. In the early 1970s as part of a plan to reinvigorate European integration the governments decided that the European Parliament should be elected directly by the citizens. The first 'direct elections' were held in June 1979 and elections have been held every five years since, with the sixth elections taking place between 10 and 13 June 2004.

The size of the parliament has changed dramatically. It started with 78 members; grew to 142 in 1958; reached 198 with the accession of the United Kingdom, Ireland and Denmark; and grew to 410 members in 1979. The parliament then expanded with each successive enlargement of the EU: to 434 members after the accession of the Greece in 1981; 518 after the accession of Portugal and Spain in 1986; 567 after the unification of Germany in 1994; 626 after the accession of Austria, Finland and Sweden; and 732 after the accession of the Czech Republic, Cyprus, Estonia, Hungary, Latvia, Lithuania, Malta, Poland, Slovakia and Slovenia in 2004.

The development of the powers of the European Parliament has been no less dramatic. For most of its history the parliament was a purely consultative institution. But, since the mid-1980s the parliament has gained increasing power in the two traditional areas of authority of elected assemblies: to control the executive, and to make legislation. The main changes in these two areas are summarised in Table 1.1.

1.1.1   Power to control the executive: a hybrid model

Executive power in the EU, in terms of the right to set the policy agenda, is split between the European Council and the Commission. Whereas the European Council, which brings together the heads of government of the member states, sets the long-term policy agenda, the Commission sets the short-term agenda, via a formal monopoly on the right to initiate legislation. The European Parliament has very little power to influence the behaviour of the European Council. However, since the Treaty of Rome in 1958, the European Parliament has had the power to sack the Commission by passing a vote of censure in the Commission as a whole. This first power of the European Parliament was consciously modelled on the way government worked at the national level in Europe, where one of the main powers of parliaments is to remove the government (Rittberger, 2003). But the European Parliament's power over the EU executive is not exactly as in a parliamentary model, where a parliamentary majority can 'hire and fire' the executive. The Commission is not elected by a majority in the European Parliament even though since

Table 1.1. *Main changes in the powers of the European Parliament*

Event (date)	Control of the executive	Making legislation
Treaty of Rome (1958)	*Commission censure procedure.* EP can remove Commission by a 'double-majority': an absolute majority of MEPs plus two-thirds of votes cast	*Consultation procedure.* Council must consult EP before passing most legislation
Budgetary Treaties (1970 & 1975)		*New budgetary procedure.* EP can reject EU budget and can amend certain budget lines (mainly excluding agriculture and regional spending)
First EP Elections (1979)	*EP has a source of legitimacy that is independent from national governments and national parliaments*	
Single European Act (1987)		*Cooperation procedure introduced.* EP has two readings of bills before Council passes law (for most single-market legislation)
Maastricht Treaty (1993)	*New Commission investiture procedure.* European Council must 'consult' EP on nominee for Commission President *Commission term of office reformed* to coincide with EP's five-year term	*Co-decision procedure introduced.* 'Conciliation committee' convened if EP and Council disagree, but Council can make a new proposal if still no agreement (replacing cooperation procedure)
Opening session of Fourth Parliament (July 1994)	*EP votes on Commission President.* EP votes for Jacques Santer (260 in favour vs. 238 against), setting the precedent that the EP can vote on the governments' nominee for Commission President	*EP rejects Voice Telephony Directive.* EP rejects a piece of EU legislation for the first time, setting the precedent hat the Council cannot act unilaterally under the co-decision procedure
Censure of Commission (March 1999)	*Commission resigns.* Whole Santer Commission resigns after an EP report criticising the Commission and before an EP censure vote that is likely to pass	
Amsterdam Treaty (1999)	*Investiture procedure reformed.* EP has vote on European Council's nominee for Commission President and on the Commission as a whole	*Co-decision procedure reformed.* Establishes a genuine bicameral system between the EP and Council (covers most socio-economic policies)
Nice Treaty (2003)	*Investiture procedure reformed.* European Council chooses Commission President and	

Table 1.1. (*Cont.*)

Event (date)	Control of the executive	Making legislation
	whole Commission by qualified-majority (instead of unanimity), which increases EP influence in the process	
Rejection of Commission (October 2004)	*Team of Commissioners withdrawn.* Barroso withdraws proposed Commission on day of EP investiture vote because the EP is likely to reject the Commission	

the Maastricht Treaty the Commission must be approved by a majority in the European Parliament. The European Parliament has genuine powers to fire the Commission, but this requires a two-thirds majority, which makes it difficult to use a 'vote-of-confidence'-like procedure to censure the Commission. Let us develop these points in more detail.

Under the Treaty of Rome, the Commission President was chosen by unanimity amongst the heads of government of the member states in the European Council. The other members of the Commission were then nominated by each government and approved by a unanimous vote of the European Council. The European Parliament had no formal role in this process. But, after the first direct elections, the parliament decided to hold an informal 'vote of confidence' on each incoming Commission. This practice was formalised by the Maastricht Treaty, which allowed the European Parliament to be 'consulted' on the choice of Commission President, introduced a right of the parliament to veto the Commission as a whole, and changed the Commission's term of office to five years to correspond with the European Parliament's term.

The European Parliament went a stage further, by interpreting its right to be 'consulted' on the choice of Commission President as a formal right of veto (Hix, 2002a). The European Parliament introduced a public vote on the Commission President designate. The governments could ignore the outcome of this vote. But when the first such vote was taken, in July 1994, the nominee for Commission President (Jacques Santer) acknowledged that if the parliament voted him down he would withdraw his candidacy because a Commission President would not be able to govern effectively without the support of the parliament. This *de facto* right of the European Parliament to veto the choice of Commission President was then formalised in the Amsterdam Treaty, which came into force in 1999.

Following the Maastricht Treaty, the European Parliament also introduced committee hearings of the nominees for the members of the Commission. These hearings were consciously modelled on the US Senate hearings of nominees to the US President's cabinet. However, unlike the US Senate, the European Parliament does not have the power to reject individual Commissioners, but only the Commission as a whole.

Under the Amsterdam Treaty, because the Commission President and the Commission as a whole were still proposed by unanimity in the European Council, the European Parliament's power to influence the election of the Commission was limited. In practice, if the prime ministers who backed the Commission in the European Council could persuade the MEPs from their parties to back the Commission in the parliament, then unanimous agreement in the European Council would almost certainly mean majority support for the Council's proposed President and team of Commissioners in the parliament. For example, in July 1994, despite opposition amongst most socialist, liberal, green and radical-left MEPs to his nomination, Jacques Santer (a centre-right politician from Luxembourg) won the vote in the parliament by 260 to 238 because he was supported by all the MEPs on the centre-right plus almost all of the MEPs from the socialist parties in government, whose leaders had supported Santer in the European Council (Gabel and Hix, 2002a).

The Nice Treaty changed this in February 2003 by introducing qualified-majority voting in the European Council for electing the Commission President and the Commission as a whole. This significantly increased the power of the European Parliament to influence the make-up of the Commission. Because a qualified-majority coalition in the European Council is smaller than a unanimous coalition, the European Council is now less able to impose its choice of Commission President or the Commission as a whole on the Parliament.

This was immediately apparent in the battle to succeed Romano Prodi as Commission President. Many of the good candidates seemed to be from the centre-left or the liberals. However, the newly elected parliament in June 2004 had a centre-right majority, and Hans-Gert Poettering, the leader of the largest group (the European People's Party), insisted that the governments must propose a candidate from the centre-right, in line with standard practices in parliamentary government. Also, a Franco-German deal to choose Guy Verhofstadt, the liberal Belgian Prime Minister, was rejected by the other member states. A qualified-majority of governments eventually supported José Manuel Durão Barroso, the conservative Portuguese Prime Minister, presumably against the wishes of France and Germany. Barroso was duly backed by a centre-right/liberal coalition in the European Parliament. But, as we discussed in the Introduction, the European Parliament was then prepared to reject the proposed team of Commissioners. This was a credible threat at least partly because the German socialist and French conservative MEPs, whose party leaders had been in the losing minority in the European Council, had no incentive to support the Commission in the vote.

The Constitutional Treaty proposed to introduce an ambiguous clause whereby the European Council would 'take into account the results of the European elections' when nominating a Commission president. This could be interpreted not only as a continuation of current practices but also along the lines of a more standard model of parliamentary government, where the head of state, such as the Dutch or Belgian monarch, or the German or Italian president, officially 'nominates' the leader of the party that won the election as the *formateur* of the government.

While there thus has been some movement towards the parliamentary model in the choice of the Commission President, the latter has very little leeway in the choice of the other members of the Commission. These are usually proposed by the incumbent national governments and accepted by the newly elected Commission President. The Barroso episode related in the Introduction was the first time in the history of EU institutions that the European Parliament forced a Commission President to withdraw a Commissioner whom the European Parliament considered to be inappropriate. The will of the European Parliament thus prevailed against the will of the Italian government.

While only a majority vote is needed in the European Parliament to approve the Commission, it is much more difficult for the European Parliament to sack the Commission. The existing rules for passing a 'censure' motion make it difficult for such a motion to pass simply because the majority in the Parliament no longer supports the policies of the Commission. A censure vote requires a 'double majority': a two-thirds majority in the vote, which must also be an 'absolute majority' (50 per cent plus 1) of all MEPs. Given the arithmetic of party composition in the European Parliament, this double-majority threshold can in practice be reached only if the main parties on the left and right vote together, which they will only do for non-policy reasons, such as corruption, mismanagement or serious incompetence. Hence, this is closer to the power of the US Congress to impeach the US President for what the US Constitution calls 'high crimes and misdemeanours' than the power of the majority in a domestic parliament in Europe to withdraw its support for the government. While this threshold is quite high, an argument can be made against a lower threshold. If it is too easy to vote down an executive in a parliament, this can trigger unnecessary government crises and long periods of vacuum of power. This is avoided in some countries such as Germany by a 'constructive vote of confidence', whereby the executive can be sacked by a majority in the parliament only if an alternative government is elected by the parliament to replace it.

Not surprisingly, given the very high threshold to censure the Commission, no censure motion has ever been passed, despite several attempts to do so. The closest the European Parliament came to doing this was in March 1999, when the Commission led by Jacques Santer resigned *en masse* before a censure vote that was likely to go against the Commission. Also, this case fits the idea that the European Parliament can censure the Commission only for non-partisan reasons, because the accusations of mismanagement and nepotism in the Santer administration were the most serious ever aimed at the Commission, and so led to a large cross-party coalition in favour of censuring the Commission, as we show in Chapter 10.

In other words, the relationship between the European Parliament and the Commission is a hybrid form of government. As in a parliamentary model of government, the European Parliament has an increasingly influential say in the election of the Commission, retains the sole right to sack the Commission as a whole, and does not have the power to reject or remove individual Commissioners. However, as in a separation-of-powers model of government, the Commission cannot dissolve the European Parliament and so threaten the MEPs with new elections if they refuse to back a key legislative proposal, and because a double majority is required to remove the Commission, once installed the Commission is unlikely to be removed before the end of its term.

1.1.2 *Power to make legislation: from a lobbyist to a co-legislator*

The European Parliament initially only had the power to be consulted on legislation. By the end of the 1990s, however, in most important areas of legislation, the European Parliament had equal power with the government ministers in the Council.

The Treaty of Rome established that the Commission has the sole right to initiate legislation in all areas. As far as the European Parliament is concerned, the Treaty of Rome established the so-called 'consultation procedure', whereby the European Parliament is required to be consulted on the Commission's proposed legislation before it is adopted by the Council. If the European Parliament proposes amendments to legislation, there is no obligation on either the Commission or the Council to accept these amendments. A ruling of the Court of Justice in 1980 confirmed that the Council could not adopt legislation without the European Parliament issuing an opinion, which enabled the parliament to exercise some influence by threatening to delay issuing an opinion. But, in practice, under the consultation procedure, the European Parliament is no more than a 'lobbyist' of the Commission and the Council.

The first major development in the European Parliament's legislative powers was the introduction in 1970 and 1975 of a new procedure for adopting the annual budget of the then European Community. The limit on the revenue available to the Community was fixed by the member states. But, within this overall limit, annual expenditure would be determined jointly by the European Parliament and the Council. The European Parliament now had the power to reject the budget as a whole, to increase or reduce expenditure within certain limits, and to redistribute revenues between the lines in the budget.

However, these budgetary amendment powers applied only to the 'non-compulsory expenditure' part of the budget, which excludes the main items of the EU spending on the agricultural price support and regional development. Also, the size of the EU budget is small relative to national government budgets, constituting about 1 per cent of EU GDP, which is approximately 3 per cent of the total public expenditure in the EU. In other words, compared with national parliaments, the formal powers of the European Parliament to tax and spend remain limited.

Nevertheless, the legislative powers of the European Parliament were substantially extended by treaty reforms in the 1980s and 1990s. In 1987 the SEA introduced the 'cooperation procedure'. This procedure gave the European Parliament two readings of legislation and reduced the ability of the Council to overturn amendments proposed by the Parliament. For the first time the European Parliament had some legislative agenda-setting power, even if this power was conditional on securing support from the Commission for the amendments and finding a majority in the Council to support the parliament's proposals (Tsebelis, 1994). The cooperation procedure only applied to ten articles in the treaty, but these included most areas of the single-market programme, specific research programmes, certain decisions relating to the structural funds and some social and environmental regulation.

In 1993 the Maastricht Treaty then effectively replaced the cooperation procedure with the 'co-decision procedure'. Under the co-decision procedure, if the European Parliament and Council disagree after two readings in each institution, a conciliation committee is convened, composed of an equal number of representatives from the European Parliament and Council. An agreement in the conciliation committee is then subject to ratification without amendment in a third reading in the European Parliament and Council.

However, under the Maastricht Treaty version of the co-decision procedure, if the European Parliament and Council failed to reach an agreement in the conciliation committee, the Council was able to re-propose the text agreed to by the governments before conciliation. If this happened, the European Parliament could then only accept or reject the new proposal. This provision was inserted by the governments to allow them to maintain a dominant position, since faced with a 'take-it-or-leave-it' proposal from the Council the European Parliament would be more likely to back new EU legislation rather than to veto it, especially if the legislation would promote European integration (Tsebelis, 1996; cf. Scully, 1997b). The co-decision procedure originally applied to most areas of single-market legislation that had been covered by the cooperation procedure and several new areas introduced by the Maastricht Treaty, such as public health, consumer protection, education and culture.

Nevertheless, the first time that the European Parliament and the Council failed to reach an agreement in the conciliation committee and the Council duly re-proposed the agreement reached by the governments at an earlier stage, the European Parliament voted immediately to reject the draft bill rather than accept that the Council could act unilaterally (on a directive on Open Network Provision in Voice Telephony). This was the first time that the European Parliament had successfully blocked a piece of EU legislation, and established the precedent that the co-decision procedure in practice finished if a joint text could not be agreed upon in the conciliation committee (Hix, 2002a). Consequently, in 1999 the governments reformed the co-decision procedure, effectively bringing the Treaty rules into line with the now-established practice: that legislation could not be passed without the positive consent of a qualified-majority in the Council and a simple majority in the European Parliament. The Amsterdam Treaty also extended the co-decision procedure to cover almost all regulation of the EU single market (such as environment policy, health and safety, social policy and harmonisation of standards) and some areas of policy on the free movement of persons, immigration and asylum. As a result of these reforms, the main EU legislative procedure is now a genuine bicameral procedure, under which the Council and the European Parliament have equal power (cf. Crombez, 2001). The Constitutional Treaty that was rejected in the French and Dutch referendum proposed to generalise the co-decision procedure as the main legislative procedure in the EU.

Given the new legislative powers of the European Parliament, it is not surprising that there are increasing battles between the parliament and the Council in the adoption of EU legislation. However, without an inbuilt government majority in the European Parliament, which can force its 'backbenchers' in the parliament to support it, coalitions in the European Parliament shift from issue to issue. For example, in the adoption of the End-of-Life Vehicles Directive in 2000, which introduced rules on the recycling of cars, a centre-right majority in the fifth parliament (1999–2004) watered down the draft legislation supported by the 'red–green' majorities in the Council and Commission. Meanwhile, in 2001, a centre-left coalition in the same parliament rejected the deal in the Council on the Takeover Directive, which would have liberalised rules on hostile takeover bids, as we show in Chapter 11.

In sum, the European Parliament has developed significant independent legislative amendment and agenda-setting powers. Despite the Commission's exclusive right of initiative, the European Parliament is an elected body that is independent of the executive and shows this independence. It has also repeatedly shown its independence from the Council. The European Parliament is clearly not simply a rubber stamp for an executive with a parliamentary majority. At the domestic level in Europe, where governments usually command a parliamentary majority, legislation is rarely amended by parliaments against the wishes of the executive. In contrast, approximately 50 per cent of legislative amendments proposed by the European Parliament become law (cf. Tsebelis et al., 2001; Kreppel, 2002a). In fact, because the majority in the European Parliament is not forced to support everything the Commission or the Council proposes, it is not unreasonable to say that the European Parliament is one of the most powerful legislative chambers in the world.

1.2   Political parties in the European Parliament: a 'two-plus-several' party system

The European Parliament's internal rules and procedures have evolved in response to these changing executive-control and legislative powers (esp. Kreppel, 2002b; Corbett et al., 2005). Specifically, the European Parliament has developed an elaborate internal division of labour. The work of scrutinising legislation and proposing amendments is divided between standing committees. Similarly, the work of organising the agenda is divided between a number of leadership organs, such as the

Bureau, which is composed of the President of the Parliament, the fourteen Vice-Presidents and the five Quaestors (who act as spokespersons for the individual MEPs and protect their interests).

However, by far the most important division-of-labour organizations in the European Parliament are the 'political groups' (cf. Hix et al., 2003). These groups control who is elected as the President of the Parliament, who will become a committee chair, which MEP writes which legislative report, who can speak in the plenary debates and for how long, which way the MEPs vote in each issue, and just about every other important issue in the European Parliament. As such, the political groups in the European Parliament are similar to parliamentary parties in national parliaments in Europe, and are probably more powerful than the Democratic and Republican caucuses in the US Congress.

When the Common Assembly of the European Coal and Steel Community first convened on 10 September 1952 there were no ideologically based political groups. Following the tradition of other international assemblies, such as the Consultative Assembly of the Council of Europe, the members of the Assembly sat in alphabetical order. Also, during the constituent meeting of the Common Assembly there were a number of decisions that suggested that the new Assembly would be organised around national rather than ideological or partisan affiliations. It was decided, for example, that there should be five Vice-Presidents so that every member state could have a representative as either President or a Vice-President on the Executive Bureau of the new Assembly.

The first formal recognition of the existence of transnational party divisions within the Assembly did not occur until January 1953. During the discussion and debate over the new Assembly's Rules of Procedure it was suggested that the nomination of members to committees attempt to balance *both* representation of the various member states and 'the various political traditions'. This was a watershed, and by March 1953 there was a *de facto* division into three political party groupings: Christian Democrat, Socialist, and Liberal. These were the primary party families of continental Western Europe at the time. This *de facto* existence of the political groups led the new Rules Committee to conduct a study on the implications of political party group formation and suggest courses of action.

The report from the Rules Committee, which was adopted in June 1953, emphasised the crucial role of political parties in the internal organisation of the assembly. The report noted that the groups had, in practice, already formed and all that was needed was to establish some form of formal recognition. This recognition took the form of an addition to the Rules of Procedure, which stated that members of the assembly could form groups according to 'political persuasion'. All that was required to form a group was a declaration of formation including the name of the group, its executive and the signatures of its members. The only restrictions were, first, that groups be politically and not nationally based; second, that they have at least nine members; and third, that no individual could belong to more than one group.

From this point forward the political groups developed as the main aggregate organisational entities in the European Parliament. The groups were given financial support. Each group organised independent secretariats and was given office space within the European Parliament's buildings in Strasbourg and later in Brussels. Debates in the parliament also began to be organised on the basis of official group positions instead of individual members' statements. By the time the first European elections were held in 1979, the political groups dominated all aspects of the parliament's work, from deciding who is elected to be the parliament's president, to assigning committee positions, to organizing the agenda of the plenary.

Regarding the balance of power between the political groups, as Table 1.2 shows, since the first European elections there have been a large number of groups, and the membership and names of these groups have continuously changed. Nevertheless, there are six main political 'families' that have remained relatively consistent across all six elected parliaments:

- *Social democrats* – the Socialist Group, which in 1992 became the Group of the Party of European Socialists (PES), incorporates all the main socialist, social democratic and labour parties in Europe and has had the most consistent membership of all the groups.

- *Centre-right* – in contrast to the unity of the social democrats, the centre-right has been split into several Christian democratic, conservative and nationalist groups, but by 1999 (in the fifth parliament) most of these parties had joined the European People's Party-European Democrats (EPP-ED), with only a small number of conservatives and nationalists staying in the Union for a Europe of Nations (UEN).

- *Liberals* – between these two main forces, the third main political party, which in its latest incarnation is called the Alliance of Liberals and Democrats for Europe (ALDE), brings together the various liberal, centrist and democratic parties in Europe.

- *Radical-left* – to the left of the social democrats, the various left-socialist, ex-communist and other radical-left forces were originally divided between two groups but since the fourth parliament they have

Table 1.2. *Political parties in the elected European Parliament*

Description (party groups)	First Parliament (July 1979)		Second Parliament (July 1984)		Third Parliament (July 1989)		Fourth Parliament (July 1994)		Fifth Parliament (July 1999)		Sixth Parliament (July 2004)	
	Seats	%	Seats	%	Seats	%	Seats	%	Seats	%	Seats	%
Social Democrats (SOC, PES)	113	27.6	130	30.0	180	34.7	198	34.9	180	28.8	200	27.3
Christian Democrats and Conservatives (EPP, EPP-ED)	107	26.1	110	25.3	121	23.4	157	27.7	233	37.2	268	36.6
Gaullists and Allies (EDA, UFE, UEN)	22	5.4	29	6.7	20	3.9	26	4.6	30	4.8	27	3.7
British Conservatives and Allies (EDG)	64	15.6	50	11.5	34	6.6						
Italian Conservatives (FE)							27	4.8				
Liberals (ELD, ELDR, ALDE)	40	9.8	31	7.1	49	9.5	43	7.6	51	8.1	88	12.0
Communists and Allies (COM, LU, EUL/NGL)	44	10.7	43	9.9	14	2.7	28	4.9	42	6.7	41	5.6
Italian Communists and Allies (EUL)					28	5.4						
Greens and Allies (G, G/EFA)					30	5.8	23	4.1	48	7.7	42	5.7
Regionalists and Allies (RBW, ERA)	11	2.7	19	4.4	13	2.5	19	3.4				
Anti-Europeans (EN, EDD, IND/DEM)							19	3.4	16	2.6	37	5.1
Extreme Right (ER)			16	3.7	17	3.3						
Independents (TGI)									18	2.9		
Non-attached MEPs	9	2.2	6	1.4	12	2.3	27	4.8	8	1.3	29	4.0
Total MEPs	410		434		518		567		626		732	

Party Group Abbreviations:

Social Democrats

SOC	Socialist Group
PES	Party of European Socialists

Christian Democrats and Conservatives

EPP	European People's Party
EPP-ED	European People's Party–European Democrats
EDA	European Democratic Alliance
UFE	Union for Europe
UEN	Union for a Europe of Nations
EDG	European Democrats Group
FE	Forza Europa

Liberals

ELD	European Liberals and Democrats
ELDR	European Liberal, Democratic and Reform Party
ALDE	Alliance of Liberals and Democrats for Europe

Radical-Left

COM	Communist Group
LU	Left Unity
EUL	European United Left
EUL/NGL	European United Left/Nordic Green Left

Greens and Regionalists

G	Greens
G/EFA	Greens/European Free Alliance
RBW	Rainbow Group
ERA	European Radical Alliance

Anti-Europeans, Extreme Right and Independents

EN	Europe of Nations
EDD	Europe of Democracies and Diversities
IND/DEM	Independence/Democracy
ER	European Right
TGI	Technical Group of Independents

been united in a single party, the European United Left/Nordic Green Left (EUL/NGL).

- *Greens and regionalists* – the green and ecologist parties have usually chosen to ally with the centre-left regionalist and sub-state nationalist parties, and currently form the Greens/European Free Alliance (G/EFA).
- *Anti-Europeans and extreme right* – finally, there has always been a collection of 'protest' parties, the two main elements of which are the anti-Europeans (from both the left and right), who currently form the Independence/Democracy group (IND/DEM), and the extreme right, who currently do not have enough seats to form a party group and so remain as 'non-attached' members.

Essentially, the party system in the European Parliament can be thought of as a 'two-plus-several' party system. The two main groups, the socialists and the EPP,[3] have each held between 30 and 35 per cent of the seats, while several smaller groups have each held between 3 and 10 per cent of the seats. As a result, the two main parties have dominated politics inside the European Parliament, but neither party has held an outright majority. In a way, the composition of the European Parliament is similar to that of the German Bundestag, which has a large Christian democratic and social democratic party and a small liberal party often allied with the Christian democrats as well as a small green party, which is usually allied with the social democrats.

1.3   The electoral disconnection

In a famous book, the American political scientist David Mayhew argued that the driving force behind politics in the US Congress was the 'electoral connection' between voters and their elected representatives (Mayhew, 1974). In comparison, despite the growing executive-control and legislative powers of the European Parliament, and despite the emergence of a transnational party system inside the European Parliament, the connection between EU citizens and their representatives in the European Parliament is extremely weak.

Few citizens seem aware of the significance of the European Parliament or understand how it works. Ninety-two per cent of EU citizens claim that they have 'heard of the European Parliament'.[4] And, 57 per cent

---

[3] We use the term EPP rather than Christian democrats/conservatives throughout the book.

[4] Eurobarometer No. 58, October–November 2002.

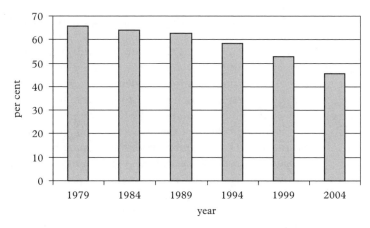

Figure 1.1. Voter participation in European Parliament elections

of citizens say that they 'trust' the European Parliament, which compares favourably with the proportion of citizens who trust their national parliaments.[5] However, these seemingly positive attitudes towards the European Parliament have not translated into political action. When it comes to voting in European Parliament elections, most voters are not motivated by what happens in the European Parliament. Turnout in European elections is very low compared with national elections and has fallen dramatically. About 25 per cent fewer citizens voted in the European elections in June 2004 compared with the last national general election in their member state. Figure 1.1 shows voter participation in European elections over time.

Traditionally, many commentators have argued that the problem of the so-called 'democratic deficit' in the EU could be solved by increasing the powers of the European Parliament (e.g. Williams, 1991). However, while the powers of the European Parliament have steadily increased over the last twenty years, the involvement of citizens in European elections – the only directly democratic element of the EU political system – has declined. Hence, many leading scholars now claim that the issue of the democratic deficit cannot be, and indeed should not be, resolved via the European Parliament (e.g. Majone, 2002; Moravcsik, 2002).

However, the reason people do not vote in European elections has very little to do with the powers of the European Parliament or a lack of awareness of the differences between the political parties in the

[5] Eurobarometer No. 62, October–November 2004.

European Parliament. Because the focus of domestic party leaders and the domestic media is on the battle to win national government office, European elections are simply mid-term, or 'second-order', national contests (Reif and Schmitt, 1980; van der Eijk and Franklin, 1996). There is much more at stake in national general elections than in European elections, which do not currently lead to the formation of an 'EU government' or have the potential of dramatically changing the direction of the EU policy agenda, because of the checks and balances in the EU system. This has two effects. First, many voters stay home from the polls because they regard European elections as relatively unimportant. Second, a large proportion of the people who do vote in European elections use the elections as an opportunity to protest against the party or parties in government at the domestic level rather than to express their views on who should be the largest party in the European Parliament. This was as true in the first elections in 1979 as it was in the sixth elections in 2004.

The absence of a clear electoral connection means that political developments inside the European Parliament, such as the evolution of the transnational political groups, cannot be explained by external collective interests of the MEPs. Because European Parliament elections are fought by national parties rather than the transnational political parties in the European Parliament, the MEPs in a particular European political group are unlikely to be rewarded by voters in the next election if they acted collectively to secure their previous manifesto promises. Equally, the MEPs or transnational parties are unlikely to be punished for failing to act on previous electoral promises.

Without an external motivation, political behaviour in the European Parliament is primarily driven by considerations internal to the institution and the EU policy process. For example, MEPs are motivated by personal career development, such as promotion inside the European Parliament or within their national political system, and by the desire to make good legislation. Above all, like all politicians, MEPs aim to secure policy outcomes that are as close as possible to their personal or their parties' policy preferences. Hence, even without a clear electoral connection, there are significant reasons for MEPs to want to organise with each other into political parties to promote their individual or collective policy goals. This is all the more true if the decisions in the European Parliament make a difference. This was not the case in the early years, when the European Parliament had a purely consultative role. But the European Parliament has acquired more and more power to influence the EU executive (the Commission) and shape EU legislation. Hence, these policy motivations mean that, even without a direct connection to the voters, the European Parliament has the potential to be the main arena for democratic politics in the EU.

European Parliament elections have not established a connection between EU citizens and the EU policy-making process. However, if politics inside the European Parliament is already democratic, then allowing more to be at stake in European elections would further increase the accountability of the EU. For example, if the member-state governments allowed a battle between rival personalities for the Commission President, and the outcome of European Parliament's elections determined which of these figures would take over the highest political office in the EU, then the political parties in the European Parliament would have an incentive to declare their candidate for the Commission Presidency before the elections and then campaign for these candidates. This would give the European Parliament's elections a more clearly European character and promote a contest about which of the main European parties would be able to set the EU's legislative agenda for the next five years.

1.4   The dataset: roll-call votes in the European Parliament

The voting behaviour of the members of a parliament can reveal a lot about how a parliament works, such as whether voting is along territorial lines or party lines, what types of coalitions form, what are the main dimensions of political conflict and whether parties are able to control the behaviour of their members.

Studying voting in the European Parliament is not quite as straightforward as in some other parliaments, where all votes are recorded. There are in fact three types of votes in the European Parliament. First, there are 'show of hands' votes, where the chair of the session simply observes which side has won the vote. Second, there are 'electronic votes', where MEPs press the Yes, No or Abstain buttons on their desks and the result of the vote is flashed on the screen at the front of the chamber, but how each MEP voted is not recorded. Third, there are 'roll-call votes', where the voting decision of each MEP is reported in the minutes. Under the European Parliament's rules, only certain votes are required to be taken by roll-call. However, a 'political group' or approximately a fifth of all MEPs can request any vote to be taken by roll-call. In practice, roughly a third of votes are by roll-call.

In other words, we are only able to study in detail MEPs' behaviour in one-third of the votes in the European Parliament. Also, because roll-call votes in the European Parliament are requested by political parties, political parties presumably decide which votes they would like to have by roll-call for strategic reasons – for example, to demonstrate their position on a particular issue, or to reveal that they are more united than another political group. This presents a potential problem of 'selection bias', in that the MEP behaviour we observe in roll-call votes may not be representative of their behaviour in all votes in the European Parliament. Indeed, Carrubba et al. (2006) find that in the fifth parliament roll-call votes were held on some issues more than on others and were called by some political groups more than others.

Nevertheless, because the political groups are more likely to request a roll-call vote on issues that are important to them, it is reasonable to assume that roll-call votes are used for the more important decisions in the European Parliament. For example, the number of roll-call votes has increased as the powers of the European Parliament have increased. There were 886 roll-call votes in the first directly elected parliament (1979–1984), 2135 in the second parliament (1984–1989), 2733 in the third (1989–1994), 3739 in the fourth (1994–1999) and 5265 in the fifth (1999–2004). Presumably, citizens are more interested in their elected representative's behaviour on important issues rather than on less important issues.

In addition, studying roll-call votes allows us to understand how MEPs vote when votes are held in public. When votes are taken in public, the media, governments, interest groups and citizens can look at how the MEPs have voted. Hence, even if roll-call votes are not an accurate sample of all votes in the European Parliament, the voting behaviour of MEPs in roll-call votes is interesting in and of itself.

We have collected the total population of roll-call votes since the first vote in the first plenary session of the first directly elected parliament, in July 1979, to the last vote in the last plenary session of the fifth directly elected parliament, in May 2004. This is a total of almost 15,000 votes by over 2,000 MEPs. To analyse the votes, we collected three types of information.

First, one of six codes was entered for each MEP in each vote: a Yes vote, a No vote, an Abstain vote, being 'present but not voting' (if the MEP signed the daily attendance register but did not participate in the vote), being absent from the parliament on the day of the vote, or not being an MEP at the time of the vote (MEPs are sometimes replaced during their mandate by a substitute). The voting data from the early parliaments was entered either by scanning the paper voting records or by downloading the voting records from the parliament's website and then applying specially developed software to read the data from either the scanned files or the Internet documents. The data for the fourth and fifth parliaments was entered directly from the electronic voting records that we obtained from the European Parliament.

Second, we collected information about each MEP. This included the MEP's member state, national party affiliation, European political group affiliation, date of birth, and the year he or she entered the European Parliament. These data were put together from the files on each individual MEP that are maintained by the European Parliament's Secretariat.

Third, we collected information about each vote. This included, among other things, the date of the vote, the legislative procedure of the vote, the voting rule (whether a simple majority or an absolute majority was required for the vote to pass), the rapporteur of the report, which political group requested the roll-call vote and the main policy issues of the vote. These data were collected from the minutes of the European Parliament's plenary sessions, which are published in the C-Series of the Official Journal of the European Union.

1.5   Conclusion

With this unique and rich dataset we are able to analyse exactly how politics inside the European Parliament has evolved since the first direct elections in 1979. We are also able to use the data to explain how and why political behaviour and organisation have changed in the European Parliament. Our book is certainly not the final word on this subject and we hope that our data will be used by future generations of scholars who are interested in parliamentary voting behaviour, in general, or politics in the European Parliament, in particular.

In the meantime, we shall now explain why normal democratic politics exists in the European Parliament before analysing how it has emerged and evolved over the last two and a half decades.

2 Democracy, transaction costs and political parties

Early social scientists, like Moisei Ostrogoski, Robert Michels, Lord Bryce and Max Weber, became interested in the relationship between democracy and political parties with the onset of democratic politics in Europe at the start of the twentieth century. It would be impossible and inappropriate for us to review all the work done on this subject in the ensuing century. As a short-cut, we start the discussion in this chapter by identifying two contemporary accounts of democratic politics that have very different conceptions about the role of political parties. The comparison of these two views will help in presenting our positions.

A first view emphasises that elected representatives mainly defend their constituencies' interests. In this view, a parliament is likely to be fragmented into the many constituencies that are represented within its walls. The smaller the size of the constituencies (the electoral districts) the better it is for democracy since smaller and more homogeneous groups can be better defended by their representatives. According to the same logic, the position of the elected representatives should be as close as possible to their constituencies' interests. Parties should, on the contrary, be seen with suspicion because they tend to create a distance between elected representatives and the citizens. We call this view 'citizen-delegate democracy'.

The second view considers that strong parties are fundamental for the good functioning of democracy. Parties are the natural intermediary between voters and the democratic decision-making process. Parties aggregate and clarify policy positions and facilitate efficient compromises between the different groups represented inside the party. They create predictability and stability, and altogether increase efficiency in policy-making. We call this view 'party-based democracy'.

These conceptions are, of course, gross oversimplifications of a vast literature on parties and democracy. They, nonetheless, illustrate two starkly different conceptions of the role and purpose of political parties and have direct relevance to how we understand democracy in general and the development of politics and parties in the European Parliament in particular.

2.1   Citizen-delegate democracy

The main emphasis of the citizen-delegate view is that democracy should be as representative as possible. This means that the positions expressed by representatives in parliament should be as close as possible to the preferences of their constituencies. The implicit view is that constituencies are homogeneous and have similar preferences, or at least that variation in preferences is stronger across constituencies than inside constituencies. Where this is the case it makes sense to see the elected representative as a delegate of his or her constituency.

In this view, the main problem to solve is how to make sure the elected representatives do not deviate, or deviate minimally, from the preferences of their constituencies. In other words, one should focus on the principal-agent problem that exists between the voters and their elected representatives (e.g. Ferejohn, 1986; Fearon, 1999; Bergman et al., 2000). The voters delegate to their representative the task of defending their interests, but the latter may have interests of his or her own that deviate from that of the voters. Voters would obviously punish a representative who fails to defend their interest by not voting him or her back to office. However, many of the actions taken by representatives might not be observed by voters. The more room there is for secretive actions, the less easy it is for voters to monitor and punish representatives who misbehave. Hence, transparency is important. Voting behaviour and other actions, such as presence in the parliament and participation in different committees and subcommittees, should be made easily observable. This information should be easily accessible to the public and could be used in election campaigns in order to reward or punish a legislator.

From the citizen-delegate point of view, parties and party formation are viewed with suspicion. Parties are seen as a collusion device that create distance between voters and their representatives. Parties are thus seen as exacerbating the principal-agent problems. The party becomes another principal of the elected representative and its objectives may conflict with those of voters in different constituencies, and perhaps even in most constituencies. Things get even worse if parties have control over the selection of candidates and the order of candidates on electoral lists. In multi-member districts, for example, if a party has a chance of getting three to four seats, the candidate who is the first on the list is nearly guaranteed to be elected. However, if that candidate is not popular with the voters, then voters have lost their ability to oust this candidate. Overall, there is not much positive to be said for parties if one follows the citizen-candidate view.

A strand of democratic thought follows the citizen-delegate theory of democracy and argues that parties should not be strong, as they would undermine the ability of voters to hold their elected representatives individually accountable. Sartori argues, for example, that 'parties' are, by definition, anathema to the formation of democratic will, as they try to promote the interests of one 'part' of the community rather than the good of the community as a whole (Sartori, 1976: 1–18). These ideas have a long history. As democracy began to flower in Britain in the eighteenth century, Henry St. John Bolingbroke (1971 [1738]: 102) asserted that: 'Governing by party ... must always end in the government of a faction. ... Party is a political evil, and faction is the worst of all parties'. Similarly, James Madison's design of the US Constitution, with its checks and balances and candidate-centred elections (for the President and US Congress), can be read as a Bolingbroke-inspired anti-party design (Dahl, 1956: 4–33). Related to these views, in David Mayhew's (1974) path-breaking theory of American government, it is the 'electoral connection' between an individual member of Congress and the voters in his or her district that drives (and should drive) political behaviour in Washington, and not broader political ideologies or party interests.

The citizen-delegate view is simple to understand. It has much logical appeal if one reasons within a framework of one representative and one constituency. However, in reality parliaments consist of several hundreds of representatives. In many cases, decisions are *indivisible*, which means that the same decision applies to all districts. In other words, if a decision must be taken on say the national healthcare budget or on whether to send troops to a foreign country, that decision may have different consequences in the different constituencies but the same decision will apply to all. There will not be separate decisions for the different constituencies. Therefore, in a legislature with several hundred representatives, it is logically impossible for a decision to always produce the closest possible outcome to the preferences of every voting district. Rather, the opposite is true. It is not very likely in a typical legislature that a representative picked at random will prove to be pivotal in a legislative vote. Even if he or she insists on obtaining a decision that is optimal for his or her constituency, it is irrelevant for the final decision taken by the majority. This will be all the more true in larger parliaments with a big number of representatives and many small electoral districts.

With the citizen-delegate view, the question remains open of how individual votes are aggregated; in other words, how the position of each representative leads to a final decision for the parliament. The question of the aggregation of preferences seems to be a difficult one, but it turns out that political science has found an answer. It is a simple but provocative answer: a voting decision by a parliament will normally correspond to the decision preferred by the median member of that parliament. In other words, if you rank all members of a parliament on how they stand on an issue (say from very strongly opposed to very strongly in favour), the median voter will be the one exactly in the middle, that is, the one who will make the difference between just over 50 per cent and just less than 50 per cent. This is the celebrated 'median voter theorem' developed first by Hotelling (1929) and Black (1958). The median voter theorem is very surprising. Indeed, one would think that in democratic decision-making, everybody's opinion should carry some weight. The median voter theorem says the opposite. Only the preferences of the median voter count; the distribution of preferences of other voters do not count at all. It is as if the median voter were chosen to be a dictator. It is thus not *a priori* easy to reconcile the median voter theorem and the popular conception of democracy. On the other hand, if we were asked to answer the following question: 'In an ideal democracy, how should decisions be taken?', there is a good chance that the answer we would formulate would be close to the median voter theorem. The most important reason would probably be that it avoids extreme decisions. If one cares a lot about the discomfort or the disutility caused by a decision, that is the disutility of the voter who is the farthest away from a given decision, then the choices of the median voter are always those that minimise this disutility. Avoiding extremism is clearly an important goal one would associate with democracy, and trusting choices to the median voter precisely allows this. So, on second thoughts, the median voter theorem is less shocking than it initially appears.

However, the median voter theorem holds only under very special circumstances that are rarely fulfilled in the real world. The most restrictive one is that there should only be one dimension of conflict. For example, in the case of the European Parliament, where there are ideological as well as national interests, it would be hard to imagine that only one dimension is present, though we investigate this issue in Chapter 9. If there is more than one dimension, the citizen-delegate view has no answer as to how decisions should be taken in a parliament. The rather unrealistic prediction of the theory is that a voting equilibrium does not exist (cf. Arrow, 1951; Mckelvey, 1976).

The reason is as follows. Imagine that a bill is put to the floor of the parliament. Then, if there is more than one dimension, even if the first bill is proposed at the position of the median voter on that dimension, an amendment can be proposed that will move the position of the bill along a second dimension, and create a new majority in favour of the amended bill. However, if this happens, the amended bill is likely to be defeated by a new bill and so on. The decision-making process would then cycle on and on and no definitive decision would be taken. The reason this might happen as soon as one has more than one policy dimension is that it is less easy to rank preferences in a consistent and unambiguous way because different voters trade off policies along the two dimensions in different ways.

To illustrate, assume there are two dimensions of policy: preferences over the level of economic redistribution, and preferences over the level of social conservatism or social liberalism. The decision process might start off with a package involving large redistribution and a very liberal social agenda. This might be defeated by a more conservative agenda with less redistribution where conservative pro-redistribution forces are ready to give up some redistribution in favour of a more conservative agenda. This might then be defeated by a more conservative agenda with more redistribution, where liberal voters who favour redistribution are persuaded to change camps. The latter might now be defeated by a socially liberal agenda with a low amount of redistribution. Here, anti-conservative voters might give up redistribution in order to prevent a conservative agenda. This might then be defeated by a socially liberal agenda with more redistribution. We are thus back to the starting point, and so on.

An important assumption behind the median voter theorem (and also one of the reasons equilibria are so fragile) is that the agenda is assumed to be very competitive. In other words, any imaginable proposal can be put on the table without cost or restriction. There is no real description of the process by which proposals are generated. It is as if proposals could be generated instantaneously without any cost both in preparing a proposal and in discussing it in parliament. In reality, both of these costs are important. These can be seen as some of the fundamental transaction costs in political activity. Just like standard neoclassical general equilibrium theory has tended to neglect transaction costs, the median voter theory ignores the transaction costs of political decision-making. These transaction costs are arguably even more important than economic transaction costs.

Preparing a legislative proposal is costly because one needs to think through many implications of the proposal one is putting on the table. One must also think about alternatives to see which ones are the most suitable to satisfy the objective one wants to pursue with the legislative proposal. The quality of a proposal depends crucially on the amount of time invested in preparing it. This does not mean that the proposal is uncontroversial. It may hurt some interests and benefit others. However, much thinking is necessary in designing a proposal so that it benefits a majority while being less costly than alternative proposals.[1]

The discussion of legislative proposals in plenary sessions in a parliament is also costly as it takes up the collective time of several hundreds of representatives, even taking into account a possibly high rate of absenteeism. Time is scarce, and therefore only limited time can be devoted to the discussion of bills put on the floor. For the same reason, an important gate-keeping function must be performed: proposals that are deemed frivolous or not worthy of being considered by the parliament are usually filtered out.

As a result of the costs of preparing and discussing proposals, the agenda is not as competitive as the citizen-delegate view assumes. All legislatures devise rules for deciding how proposals are put on the agenda of parliaments.

If one accepts the view that there are substantial transaction costs involved in preparing and discussing legislative proposals in parliaments and that agendas are not as competitive as in the citizen-delegate view, then one can see that there is a role for parties. When we acknowledge that transaction costs are an important variable in policy-making, we see not only that parties play a positive role in democracies but also that a strong party system is preferable to a weak party system with fragmented representation, which would lead to instability and inefficiency.

2.2   Party-based democracy

A starkly opposing perspective to the citizen-delegate model is that parties are essential for the operation of democracy. The early theorists of parties argued that parties were desirable because they fulfilled essential 'functions', such as structuring the popular vote, integrating and mobilising the masses, aggregating diverse interests, recruiting leaders for public office and formulating public policy (cf. Neumann, 1956; King, 1969). More recently, however, political scientists have focused on why citizens, candidates and parliamentarians voluntarily decide to form and sustain parties (e.g. Schlesinger, 1984; Cox, 1987; Strøm, 1990; Cox and McCubbins, 1993; Aldrich, 1995).

---

[1] Efficiency is not always present. Special interests often manage to change bills in their favour even when the costs to society are larger than the benefits to them.

Before talking about the role of parties, it is useful to define what we mean by parties. There is an important difference between parties and coalitions. Coalitions can be of two types. They can form on a vote-by-vote basis, which is often the case in presidential systems, or they can take the form of a government coalition where different parties share ministerial portfolios and share agenda-setting powers. Members of a coalition in a parliamentary democracy tend to vote cohesively because they have a secret weapon that keeps the coalition together: the vote of confidence. In case of a disagreement within the coalition, it is always possible to associate a vote of confidence with a bill. The deviating partner thus risks being punished by the collapse of the coalition if it wants to go against its coalition partner on a given bill. Government collapse is in general a negative outcome for the members of the coalition because they lose precious agenda-setting powers and government portfolios. The only reason they might welcome a government collapse is if they expect a better position in the next government, which happens sometimes. This will be the case, for example, if a government collapse will trigger early elections that will favour the party triggering the crisis. Parties who are part of a government coalition know that voters can reward or punish them for what they deliver to their constituencies inside the coalition. At times, it might be electorally more costly to stay inside the coalition than to leave it and trigger a government collapse. The loyalty to the coalition only goes as far as the rational interests of the party leaders.

Coalition discipline, even in a parliamentary government, is always less strong than party discipline. When politicians join a party, they are expected to be active within the party, contribute to its policies and electoral campaigns and also to follow party discipline, in particular when voting in the parliament. Parties have a number of sticks and carrots to ensure this discipline. Party whips monitor attendance and voting behaviour of members of parliament. Parties often control which candidates stand in elections (in proportional elections as in the Netherlands and also in plurality elections as in the United Kingdom). This is a powerful tool to discipline representatives who deviate from party discipline in the parliament since the party can put them in a place on the list where they have no chance of being re-elected. Party lists are emphasised, and rightly so, as a disciplining device in the political science literature, but they are not the only tools available for disciplining members. Parties allocate committee presidencies and membership in parliament. More importantly, parties allocate ministerial positions and executive responsibilities. In effect, parties in democracies tend to be the most cohesive collective machines for mobilising voters as well as for adopting and implementing policies.

For our discussion, it is useful to distinguish between the role parties play in *electoral* politics and *legislative* politics. Electoral politics is about how politicians manage to overcome what is often called the 'external collective action problem' of politics. Indeed, democracy cannot work without the massive participation of voters, but an individual voter does not have any special incentive to vote because he or she can free-ride on the vote of others. This collective action problem is not only about turnout; it is also about punishing bad incumbents or electing promising reformers. Parties play a fundamental role in mobilising voters and in competing for votes on political platforms.

Legislative politics, on the other hand, refers to another collective action problem, that of elected representatives in the parliament itself. An individual representative in parliament faces similar problems to the one an individual voter faces in elections. His or her probability of being pivotal in any single vote is quite small and he or she can also free-ride on the legislative activity of others. Here, parties also play a fundamental role in solving the 'internal collective action problem' of politics.

The distinction between these two roles of parties is useful because, as we discussed in Chapter 1, European parties play virtually no role in European Parliament *electoral* politics. However, parties play a big role in European Parliament *legislative* politics. Studying the European Parliament allows us to understand the 'pure' role of parties in solving the internal collective action of politics, separate from the external problem. We first discuss the former, and then the latter.

2.2.1 Parties in legislative politics and the making of public policy

The first modern political parties emerged in the early nineteenth century, long before universal suffrage and the development of mass electoral politics (LaPalombara and Weiner, 1966). Like the Federalists and Republicans in the early US Congresses, early 'parliamentary parties' in Europe included the Whigs and Tories in the British House of Commons, the National Liberals and Progressives in the German Reichstag, and the Conservative and Left (Venstre) parties in the Scandinavian parliaments. These parties were formed by groups of 'notables', to enable politicians with similar aims to organise together to promote their interests and ideas (esp. Weber, 1946 [1918]; Duverger, 1954 [1951]). For example, while the early liberal parties campaigned for basic political freedoms, free trade and extension of the suffrage, early conservative parties sought to defend the interests of the state, the church and the landed aristocracy. Only with the gradual extension of the suffrage in the late eighteenth century did these parties begin to set up local party organisations with the aim of recruiting party members and coordinating electoral campaigns. In other words, the earliest political parties were formed 'internally' in representative assemblies, most of which (or the successors of which) are still major parties today. The socialist parties, who formed throughout Europe around the time of the extension of the suffrage to the working class, were the first parties in Europe to emerge 'externally', via the mass mobilisation of the electorate.

If we abstract from mass electoral politics, there are four complementary reasons for why party systems are desirable in legislative politics.

First, parties reduce the volatility of policy and thus increase the predictability of politics (cf. Riker, 1980; Aldrich, 1995). If there is more than one dimension, then policy can be unstable, as we explained earlier when discussing citizen-delegate democracy. However, this instability can be overcome by delegating agenda-setting power to a particular legislator or group of legislators.

Why parties reduce the volatility of policy is explained in Box 2.1, where instead of assuming a very competitive agenda, one assumes that a legislator has agenda-setting powers. In other words, for each bill, a legislator is given the right to formulate the proposal that will be voted on. For simplicity, it is assumed that the agenda-setter can propose his or her preferred policy and find a majority in favour. This will be the case if the status quo, which is obtained if the proposal is rejected, is worse for a majority. It is well known that the worse the status quo the easier it is for an agenda-setter to manipulate the agenda in his or her favour (McKelvey, 1976; Romer and Rosenthal, 1978). The other assumption is that the probability of being agenda-setter is proportional to the size of a party in parliament, an assumption that is usually made in political science models and that has some empirical backing (see, for example, the discussion in Diermeier and Merlo, 2000). In this case, fragmentation of the parliament will lead to the dispersion of agenda-setting powers. This might seem good at first glance because many representatives then have a small chance of setting the agenda. However, this leads to a high volatility in the policy. Since anyone can become an agenda-setter, policies may vary widely. This creates uncertainty in terms of policy choice. As can be seen from Box 2.1, when representatives get together and form a party, not only do they have a higher chance of setting the agenda but also the policy they will propose will be a compromise between their bliss points. Party formation thus reduces uncertainty and avoids extreme policies. This logic of reducing uncertainty leads to the formation of a small number of large parties.

Box 2.1 Parties and the reduction of policy volatility

To understand the role of parties when there are transaction costs in setting up the legislative agenda, assume that legislative proposals are drafted by an agenda-setter. Assume also that agenda-setting power is allocated randomly and in proportion to a party's strength in the parliament. This means that if a party has twice the size of another party, its probability of being the agenda-setter is twice as large. Then assume that each representative has Euclidean preferences: that is, the utility from a policy is a negative function of the quadratic distance between the policy chosen x_i and the policy-maker's 'bliss point' x_i^0: $-(x_i - x_i^0)^2$. Also assume that the status quo for each vote is very undesirable, so that the agenda-setter can always get a majority for his or her own bliss point. Finally, to illustrate the role of parties, assume that there are only six representatives: 1 to 6, whose bliss points correspond to their number.

Starting with a situation where there are no parties, each representative has a one-sixth probability of becoming the agenda-setter. The expected utility of each representative is in the second column of the table. As an illustration, we show the calculation for representative 1: $-1/6(0^2 + 1^2 + 2^2 + 3^2 + 4^2 + 5^2) = -55/6$. As one can see the representatives with the more extreme bliss points have the lowest expected utility. This is because of the quadratic distance and the fact that they suffer most when policy is at the other extreme.

Expected utility of	Six parties (1, 2, 3, 4, 5, 6)	Five parties (12, 3, 4, 5, 6)	Four parties (12, 3, 4, 56)	Three parties (12, 34, 56)	Three parties (123, 4, 56)	Two parties (123, 456)
Representative 1	−55/6	−54.5/6	−54/6	−53.5/6	−52.5/6	−51/6
Representative 2	−31/6	−30.5/6	−30/6	−29.6/6	−28.5/6	−27/6
Representative 3	−19/6	−18.5/6	−18/6	−17.5/6	−16.5/6	−15/6
Representative 4	−19/6	−18.5/6	−18/6	−17.5/6	−16.5/6	−15/6
Representative 5	−31/6	−30.5/6	−30/6	−29.5/6	−28.5/6	−27/6
Representative 6	−55/6	−54.5/6	−54/6	−53.5/6	−52.5/6	−51/6

Now assume that the policy of a party with several representatives is the average of the bliss points of the representatives. If representatives 1 and 2 form a party together while the others remain separated the pay-off to representatives 1 and 2 is improved but so is the pay-off for the other representatives, as shown in column three. The next three columns look at other scenarios with four and three parties. Finally, the last column looks at a situation where 1, 2 and 3 form one party and 4, 5 and 6 form another party. As one can see, the pay-off of all players is improved under a two-party system. The reason is that parties reduce the volatility of decision-making, which is valuable when agents are risk-averse.

The expectation that parties facilitate stable public policies is as old as the formation of parliamentary parties themselves. For example, Edmund Burke, who was a member of the British House of Commons in the late eighteenth century, saw parliamentary party organisations as 'the proper means [for politicians] to carry their common plans into execution, with all the power and authority of the state' (Burke, 1839 [1770]: 425–6). Burke was certainly not a radical democrat. However, he was probably the first to argue that government only works effectively if there are stable parliamentary parties, rather than regarding parties as a threat to political stability and consensus (Sartori, 1976).

A second advantage associated with the formation of parties in parliaments is that parliamentary parties provide advantages of specialisation (esp. Rohde, 1991; Kiewiet and McCubbins, 1991; Cox and McCubbins, 1993). We assume above that agenda-setters can, at no cost, pick a policy proposal that corresponds to their preferences. However, this is not a realistic assumption. A great deal of work is needed to understand and evaluate different policy options. Elected representatives, like other individuals, lack the expertise to have detailed knowledge of all policy areas. Moreover, they lack the time, the resources and the attention span to acquire such knowledge. It is here that the advantages from specialisation step in. Just like Adam Smith's pin factory workers, politicians gain from having a division of labour amongst themselves. Some will invest in finding out what is the best environmental policy for their party, others will invest in thinking about education policy, and so on. Without parties, individual representatives would struggle to understand the stakes of a given vote, then struggle again to understand the issue at hand in the next vote, and so on. Most likely, they would end up voting randomly on some issues because of a lack of time to understand what is at stake. Such politicians would almost certainly end up voting against the interests of their voters or supporting interest groups. This might go unnoticed, but there is a reasonable chance that this would be discovered and come to haunt them one day.

The gains from specialisation allow parliamentarians to overcome this problem. Each individual representative specialises in some policy issues on which he or she develops valuable expertise for his or her party. The members of the party specialise in an issue and formulate the party position on that issue with the help of specialised staff who work full time for that purpose. The party position is then adopted by party representatives who are not specialised but who trust their party members to have the best interests of the party in mind. Specialisation thus helps in improving the preparation of policy positions. However, specialisation also creates an agency problem between party members. How can a representative be sure that the policy proposed by the party experts is the best for the party.

How can a representative prevent those who specialise in an issue from biasing the party position towards their own interests?

Box 2.2 Parties and general versus local public goods

Consider again a situation where there are six representatives. Assume first a situation where with the given budgetary resources the agenda-setter could secure a pay-off of 100 for his or her constituency and 5 to two other constituencies to form a majority. Consider another budgetary allocation where the first three representatives each get a pay-off of 50. In both cases, the opposition gets a pay-off of zero. Assume for simplicity that only these two policy options are available.

	Represen- tative 1	Represen- tative 2	Represen- tative 3	Represen- tative 4	Represen- tative 5	Represen- tative 6	Total value	Expected value
Policy package without parties	100	5	5	0	0	0	110	18 1/3
Policy package with parties	50	50	50	0	0	0	150	25

First of all, in a situation without parties, the agenda-setter always prefers the first policy package because he or she can secure a pay-off of 100 for his or her constituency. However, the total value of that package is equal to 110, which is lower than the pay-off of 150 from the second policy package. Note that from an *ex ante* point of view, the second policy package is better because it gives each representative an expected pay-off of 25 against 18 and one-third for the first one. However, given that the agenda-setter has monopoly rights over the agenda, he or she would always prefer the first package, once chosen as agenda-setter.

On the other hand, if representatives 1, 2 and 3 form a party, it is clear that the party would prefer to propose the second policy package, which gives higher total and expected value. The reason is that the party internalises the interests of a broader constituency compared with the case where there are no parties. This affects its choices as agenda-setter and leads to more efficient outcomes in terms of public good provision.

This is likely to be difficult if the interests of the party representatives are too far apart. Commonality of interests is an important force that can allow party members to benefit from the gains from specialisation. If interests are too far apart, then it is difficult and costly to monitor the policy choices of party experts. Agency costs might partially or even to a great extent outweigh the gains from specialisation. Agency problems within a party are thus a factor that limits the size of a party.

A third advantage of party systems is that parties can be better advocates in parliaments of what are called 'general public goods' as opposed to 'local public goods' (cf. Schattschneider, 1960). General public goods are public goods that benefit a large segment of the population. This is the case, for example, of defence, by protection of the environment, national social security programmes and education programmes. Local public goods, on the contrary, benefit narrow local communities. This would be the case, for example, of local schools, local police or a bridge that would be used mostly by local citizens.

To illustrate the point consider the example in Box 2.2. Assume that the status quo is equal to zero. Without parties, if the agenda-setter is chosen randomly among the different representatives, we can imagine a political outcome where the agenda-setter proposes a policy package where (1) his or her constituency gets a local public good that has a huge value, (2) he or she puts together a majority with representatives receiving local public goods each with a very small value (though strictly positive) and (3) the minority gets nothing. This policy package would have a lower value to the electorate as a whole than one where more general public goods benefiting a large majority of constituencies were proposed. However, if the latter package has a lower value to the agenda-setter than the one just outlined, the general public goods would not be proposed and the result is an inefficient policy package that benefits mostly the agenda-setter but not all other representatives. In such a situation, *all* representatives are worse off from an *ex ante* point of view because they only face a small probability of being the agenda-setters. Representatives also have an incentive to form parties that would propose general public goods that benefit all constituencies from the party, and possibly beyond. How well parties would internalise all their internal constituencies obviously depends on their internal rules, but it is not unreasonable to think that a party representing about half the seats of parliament would be better at proposing general public goods than an isolated representative who has only the narrow interests of his or her constituency in mind. If parties can propose a better set of public goods and make voters *ex ante* better off by proposing more general public goods that enhance expected welfare, then this can allow them to obtain an electoral advantage over candidates who are not part of parties. We should thus see parties being more electorally successful because of their better ability at delivering public goods that benefit broader categories of the population.

This conclusion is more general than it seems. It goes beyond the example of local and general public goods. It implies that parties can increase efficiency of decision-making by internalising broad and stable categories of interests. This is an important property because it implies that parties can increase efficiency of decision-making compared with more fragmented parliaments. One way of seeing this is to think of the role of interest groups in a strong versus a weak party system. In a weak party system, interest groups will attempt to lobby individual representatives to convince or bribe them (by legal or illegal means) into voting a certain way. The United States' system of government is perhaps the best example of this. With weak parliamentary parties, lobbyists target individual Congressmen to influence the majority on a given bill. In a strong party system, in contrast, lobbying individual representatives does not make sense, since they will tend to follow the voting instructions of their party leaders. In this case, lobbyists must target the party leadership in order to convince them to take a stance on any particular issue. Party leaders are thus approached by a large number of lobbies. There is a reasonable probability that the demands of the different lobbies are jointly inconsistent. Party leaders must thus take into account a great number of conflicting demands when taking a position. This forces them to internalise a broader number of interests than would be the case for an individual lobbyist who could be pivotal on one issue but not on others. Strong parties hence increase efficiency of decision-making in a very general way.

Fourth, parties help in reducing the dimensionality of politics. As we have just discussed, when politics has more than one dimension, the median voter theorem breaks down. There is no voting equilibrium and there is cycling in decision-making. This is one of the biggest weaknesses of the citizen-delegate view. As we have seen, once we introduce transaction costs, the problem of cycling ceases to be relevant since voting follows more the logic of agenda-setting theory in which cycling disappears because the agenda-setter is always able to make legislative proposals. Even when no legislative proposal can be successful, the status quo is then the outcome but no cycling occurs because the agenda is not competitive. Note, however, that in a fragmented parliament with diffused agenda-setting powers, the dimensionality of politics can remain high. Is that necessarily a bad thing? It might be. Assume a situation where each representative cares only for one dimension of politics and is completely indifferent to all other dimensions. This is of course an extreme example but it helps to clarify the argument. In this case, each agenda-setter would care only for his or her own dimension and might propose policies in other dimensions that could be improved upon by communication and deliberation with other representatives. This would entail a lot of randomness and inefficiency and not contribute to enhancing the predictability of decision-making.

On the other hand, parties help to reduce the dimensionality of politics. They do so by taking positions on particular policy issues and sticking to them. There is no logical link between views on redistribution and views on abortion, for example. However, when there are a small number of political parties and a new issue arises, each party tries to figure out what its position should be on that issue. That way, positions get correlated in a systematic way. This correlation reduces the dimensionality. Thus, while positions on redistribution and abortion are quite separate dimensions, a positive attitude towards redistribution gets correlated with a pro-choice view and vice versa. They are correlated because the whole party takes a position and party members follow the party position in their voting behaviour. The party must of course be able to enforce a certain party discipline because some representatives will disagree with some of the party positions. This reduction in dimensionality enhances the predictability of democratic decision-making and hence increases efficiency.

Do these advantages of party systems automatically imply that we should observe strong party systems in legislatures? Not necessarily. This will depend a lot on the incentives of politicians and the institutional rules within which they operate. Such incentives will nevertheless generally be present. By behaving cohesively over time, groups of politicians who have broadly shared preferences and goals can be more decisive than groups of unorganised politicians or cliquish fractions.

2.2.2   Parties and electoral politics

Mass democratic elections work better with parties for two main reasons. First, parties provide the equivalent for politicians and voters of 'brand names' for large firms and consumers (cf. Downs, 1957). Without parties, voters have a hard time recognising serious and competent candidates from less serious and competent ones. Voters face the same problem with candidates as with products appearing on the market for the first time. Recognising the quality of a candidate is a serious concern for voters just as recognising the quality of a car, a computer or a camera is a serious issue for consumers. Just as brand names act as a form of guarantee of quality, parties can act as a guarantee of the quality of candidates in elections. Parties have their reputation at stake when sponsoring candidates who carry the party label.

In addition to guaranteeing the quality and honesty of politicians, party labels provide voters with a short-hand description of the likely policy positions of the politicians who belong to the party. Parties will only sponsor candidates whose ideological positions are broadly aligned with those of the party. Without parties, voters would have to find out, and politicians would have to supply, a huge amount of information about where each politician stands on the important issues of the day. In contrast, with established party labels, the information costs for voters and politicians are considerably reduced. Once party brands have been established, voters are often reluctant to exchange their favourite brand for another untried or untested one. This partly explains what is known as 'party identification' (cf. Campbell et al., 1960). This also explains why electoral volatility is often very high in new democracies, where voters have very little information about the previous behaviour and preferences of the parties standing in the elections, and so decide to switch their vote in the next election once they have learned the meaning of the various party labels.

Second, parties have an advantage compared with independent candidates in their capacity to mobilise the electorate. Voters need to be mobilised to achieve turnout. Max Weber was one of the first to mention the voter mobilisation role of parties in the context of universal suffrage: 'These modern forms are the children of democracy, of mass franchise, of the necessity to woo and organise the masses, and develop the utmost unity of direction and the strictest discipline' (Weber, 1946 [1918]: 102). The theory of voting participation tells us that each voter has only a tiny probability of being pivotal, which makes the expected benefit from voting very small, even with large stakes. Voters thus do not in general have a rational incentive to bear the costs of voting, however small, given such a tiny expected benefit (Tullock, 1967). Candidates thus need to spend a large amount of resources to attract the attention of voters and to convince them to go to the polls.

We do not really have a good theory of voter mobilisation, but in practice it appears to play an important role in elections. For example, Aldrich (1995: 97–125) explains how mobilisation substantially increased voter turnout in the 1828 presidential election in the United States. In 1827, Martin Van Buren, a New York politician who later became the eighth US President (1837–1841), launched an initiative to create a mass party, the Democratic Party, to mobilise support for the candidacy of Andrew Jackson. He built a large coalition, called the National Alliance, building on support from local political networks with its main goal to get Jackson elected. There was explicitly no political platform associated to the Jackson candidacy because of the difficulty of agreeing on such a platform with the various networks composing the Alliance. This was the first time a formidable organisational apparatus was put together to mobilise for a presidential election in the United States. The objective was for the campaign to penetrate as much as possible the electorate and to reach out widely to voters in support of Jackson. The results were spectacular. Participation in the 1824 presidential election was 27 per cent and it increased to 56 per cent in the 1828 presidential election. This marked the birth of modern mass parties in the United States, which eventually spread to all democracies.

In sum, we have identified six reasons why strong parties are good for democracy. First, parties have 'brand names' and a reputation they need to protect for their long-term interests. This offers voters a better guarantee of the quality and competence of candidates and a good approximation of the policy positions of politicians on all the major issues of the day. Fragmented parliaments have less guarantees to offer voters and less power of commitment.

Second, parties can exploit economies of scale in the mobilisation of voters. Fragmented parliaments with weak parties are associated with elections with a lower participation rate and less voter mobilisation.

Third, parties reduce volatility and increase predictibility in the making of public policy. Fragmented parliaments tend to increase volatility of decision-making, making it possibly quite chaotic, meaning that decision-making can be paralysed.

Fourth, parties allow parliamentarians to benefit from specialisation, which improves the quality of policies being debated in parliaments. Fragmented parliaments tend to have a lower quality of decision-making due to reduced specialisation.

Fifth, parties increase the efficiency of policy-making. Parties internalise the benefits and costs of public programmes for large groups of the population and screen out inefficient programmes that may benefit small groups at the expense of larger groups. In fragmented parliaments, coalitions are built on a case-by-case basis. Higher transaction costs for building coalitions often allow powerful lobbies, representing concentrated interests, to gain rents at the expense of diffuse public interests.

Sixth, parties reduce the dimensionality of politics by creating correlations between the various dimensions of politics. Fragmented parliaments will tend to exhibit higher dimensionality, which makes it difficult to create stable majorities and govern effectively.

We thus conclude that if one takes the transaction costs of democratic politics seriously, a well-functioning democracy requires strong political parties. The idealised citizen-delegate model of democracy, which ignores transaction costs, should lead to a dysfunctional democracy.

2.3   Parliaments without strong parties: a history of failure

The historical experience gives various examples of the negative effects of weak party systems in different historical contexts. We briefly review two such experiences: the United States Congress in the early nineteenth century, and the French Fourth Republic in the middle of the twentieth century.

Aldrich (1995) describes the effects of party formation on voting in the early US Congress. In the First (1789–1791) and Second Congress (1791–1793), when stable parties had not yet formed, voting was unstable and chaotic (Grant, 1977). One typically observed factional groupings around each issue even though two camps started to emerge: the Federalists and the Jeffersonians. Some votes were along partisan lines, and others were along geographical lines. Not only was voting highly factionalised, but many bills were proposed several times with different voting outcomes, such as the assumption of the debt of the states by the federal government.[2] Without coherent and cohesive parties, legislation was difficult to pass and representatives had to engage in protracted negotiations to organise vote-trades, which often failed to materialise owing to limited commitment. Applying a scaling technology to all votes in the US Congress (which we apply to the European Parliament in Chapter 9), Poole and Rosenthal (1997) observe that the partisan dimension of politics in the First Congress was weak, but this dimension strengthened substantially in the Third Congress (Aldrich, 1995: 86–92). To put things in perspective, only two out of ten votes in the First Congress were party votes (votes where a majority of one party voted against the majority of the other party), whereas eight out of ten votes in the Third Congress were party votes. In the First Congress, Alexander Hamilton, the leader of the Federalists used his agenda-setting power to coordinate the voting behaviour of his partisans and

---

[2] States had accumulated large debts in the early history of the United States. Alexander Hamilton put forward a plan for debt assumption with the objective of strengthening the power of the central government.

achieved increasing legislative success for pro-Federalist bills. In response, Thomas Jefferson and James Madison organised a united opposition, the Republicans. In the Third Congress, the Federalists and Republicans became quite structured legislative parties.

In parliamentary systems, unstable parties have a negative influence on government stability. This negatively affects legislative activity since governments typically have agenda-setting powers. When governments fall, legislative activity is generally stalled until a new government is found. The introduction of bills is delayed until a new coalition is found. The French Fourth Republic is a good example of how unstable parties produce unstable governments. The French Fourth Republic lasted from early 1947 until early 1958. It had twenty-one governments, all coalition governments. Governments thus lasted, on average, six months. The membership of the parliamentary parties was also very unstable. At least 20 per cent of parliamentarians changed parties at least once during the French Fourth Republic (cf. MacRae, 1967). With weak parties, voting in the National Assembly was highly dimensional and fragmented (Rosenthal and Voeten, 2004). This was in stark contrast to most other parliamentary systems in Western Europe in the post-war period, where single-party or coalition governments were relatively stable, and parties were able to enforce party discipline and hence enable governments to push through important reforms. Weak parties in France also had a major negative influence on policy-making. For example, inflation was a bigger problem in France in the 1950s than in most other countries in Western Europe. Also, successive French governments were unable to deal effectively with the decolonisation process in Vietnam and Algeria.

2.4   Implications for the European Parliament

The European Parliament has the potential to be the most fragmented parliament in the world. It has elected representatives from twenty-five countries who speak more than twenty different languages. There are over 150 national parties represented in the European Parliament. If there is one parliament that has the conditions to come the closest to the 'citizen-delegate' model, it is the European Parliament. The view one takes on the desirability of strong parties or, on the contrary, of party fragmentation will thus affect one's judgement of the European Parliament. If one takes the citizen-delegate view, then one should be critical of the formation of transnational parties in the European Parliament. If one accepts the party-based view of democracy, however, one should welcome the emergence of such organisations, especially given the heterogeneity of preferences in this very large and diverse parliament.

Scholars have studied the development of transnational parties in the European Parliament since they started to emerge in the early years of what was then the Common Assembly of the European Coal and Steel Community (esp. Van Oudenhove, 1965). Research on the organisation and behaviour of these organisations then exploded immediately before and after the first direct elections to the European Parliament in 1979 (e.g. Fitzmaurice, 1975; Claeys and Loeb-Mayer, 1979; Henig, 1979; Pridham and Pridham, 1981; Niedermeyer, 1983; Bourguignon-Wittke et al., 1985). The prevailing view amongst researchers and commentators at that time was generally one of optimism about the development of genuine transnational parties in the wake of direct elections. For example, Walter Hallstein, the former President of the European Commission, stated that he expected that European-wide elections of the parliament would 'give candidates who emerged victorious from such a campaign a truly European mandate from their electors; and it would encourage the emergence of truly European political parties' (Hallstein, 1972: 74). In a similar vein, David Marquand (1978) argued that as a result of elections to the European Parliament, gradually a *Europe des patries* (a 'Europe of nation-states') would be replaced by a *Europe des partis* (a 'Europe of transnational parties').

In a short period the general mood changed to one of pessimism. European Parliament elections did not produce coherent transnational parties, which were capable of mobilising voters to campaign for and support particular European-wide policy platforms. Instead, the general pattern across Europe was that these elections were little more than 'second-order national contests', about national rather than European issues, and on the performance of national rather than European-wide parties, as we described in the previous chapter (e.g. Reif and Schmitt, 1980; van der Eijk and Franklin, 1996). The main problem for transnational parties was that national parties already played the two main roles of parties in the electoral arena that we highlighted earlier. Voters already understood and identified with national party 'brand labels' and so were understandably reluctant to replace these names with new and unknown European-wide party labels. And national parties already had sophisticated campaigning machines to mobilise their supporters.

Nevertheless, in the early 1990s political scientists began to turn their attention to the evolution of political parties inside the European Parliament. And, for the first time, researchers started collecting data about the organisation and behaviour of these parties, using sophisticated methods to understand and discover new facts, and relate their findings to the general study of parties in legislatures. For example, Fulvio Attinà (1990, 1992) was the first to systematically collect roll-call voting data from the European Parliament and to develop an index to measure the voting cohesion of the transnational political groups (cf. Zellentin, 1967; Quanjel and Wolters, 1993; Brzinski, 1995). We build directly on this work in Chapter 5. Similarly, as part of a major international project on the organisation of political parties in democracies, Luciano Bardi (1992, 1994) systematically catalogued the internal organisational and decision-making structures of the political groups in the European Parliament and established that these groups are almost identical to parliamentary parties in other democratic parliaments.

More recently, two book-length manuscripts have applied some of the general theoretical ideas about why parties form in legislatures to the European Parliament and, in so doing, have established the study of political behaviour and organisation in the European Parliament as part of the mainstream research in comparative politics. First, Tapio Raunio (1997) looked at party and MEP behaviour in the third parliament (1989–1994), analysing the internal division of labour in the parties, party cohesion and coalition behaviour in roll-call votes, and written questions by MEPs to the European Commission. Raunio concluded that the parties in the European Parliament are coherent organisations, which have defined policy goals and are able to shape the behaviour of their members.

Second, Amie Kreppel (2002b) focussed on the impact of increased legislative power of the European Parliament on the political groups. She analysed the internal organisation of the parties, the influence of the parties on EU legislation, the evolution of the parliament's rules of procedure particularly as they apply to political parties, and MEP behaviour and partisan coalitions in roll-call votes (using a similar scaling method to the one we use in Chapter 9). Overall, Kreppel concluded that increased legislative influence of the parliament led to growing centralisation in the political groups and growing ideological compromise, as the parties were forced to 'get things done'.

Our analysis builds directly on previous research on the European Parliament, which has observed and explained the evolution of politics and parties in this institution. Unlike previous scholars, however, we have been fortunate enough to collect the whole population of roll-call votes in the European Parliament since the first direct elections in 1979, and are hence able to study in detail how politics and parties have evolved in this increasingly important assembly. As a result of being able to explore this long time series, some of our findings are quite different from the existing research. For example, we find growing party competition rather than cooperation.

2.5   Conclusion

Democratic governance without political parties would be possible only if the conduct of elections and policy-making was completely costless. There are, however, significant informational and other transaction costs in the electoral process and the making of public policy. The historical experience shows that parliaments without strong parties have suffered from instability, inefficiency and decision-making paralysis. We thus agree with Schattschneider's (1942: 1) famous dictum that 'democracy is unthinkable save in terms of political parties'.

Politics in the European Parliament is no exception. Even without strong external electoral incentives to form transnational parties (for the reasons we explained in Chapter 1), political parties are desirable inside the European Parliament because MEPs face a chaotic, uncertain and costly world if they act alone.

3   Ideological not territorial politics

In the previous chapter we argued that when there are transaction costs to policy-making it is better to have strong parties. The discussion was silent, however, about the dimensions along which these parties should form. In democratic systems we are used to thinking of parties as located along a left–right axis, though other dimensions sometimes play a minor role. But we did not discuss why parties should necessarily form along the left–right dimension.

Parties could conceivably form around any set of policy issues or societal interests. Parties could, for example, form along territorial lines instead of socio-economic lines. In the case of the European Parliament, parties based on the national/territorial divisions between the EU member states might even seem more natural than parties based on transnational ideological interests or values. Uninformed outsiders often assume that voting in the parliament follows national lines, for example with the French conservatives voting more with the French socialists than with the Scandinavian conservatives. Indeed, the dominant public perception is that EU politics is about conflicts between countries: for example, 'Britain' opposes qualified-majority voting on taxation, 'France' opposes further reductions in agricultural spending and 'Denmark' wants higher environmental standards. This perception is largely based on debates in the European Council, where only the heads of state and government are represented, which means that any differences of positions necessarily appear to be between member states rather than ideologies.

If EU politics is essentially driven by national/territorial divisions rather than ideological divisions, parties in the European Parliament would then have to be stable coalitions of MEPs from each member state (the French party, the English party, etc.) or from blocs of states (the Scandinavian party, the Mediterranean party, etc.). As we demonstrate in later chapters, this is not the case. Politics in the European Parliament is primarily about left–right divisions rather than territorial divisions, and is hence like most other democratic parliaments. One obvious question, then, is: why should parties form along ideological lines rather than along territorial lines?

This question is more general than it seems. We are not used to raising this question because in most democracies, and even in large and geographically dispersed polities (such as the United States or India), parties are primarily formed and they compete along ideological lines, with territorial conflicts playing only a minor role. If we understand why this is the case, we might understand why we observe the same phenomenon in the European Parliament where one would *a priori* think that the main lines of conflict are territorial.

The basic argument we develop in this chapter is that political conflicts between regions or territorial entities can often be solved by finding an adequate devolution of power to territorial entities. We argue that while there can be much scope for decentralisation of powers between territorial entities there is much less scope for a similar decentralisation of powers between sectoral and professional interests. In advanced democracies, once countries have found an adequate mix of centralisation and decentralisation, most conflicts one should observe at the central level should be conflicts between sectoral and professional interests. Parties would thus form according to those interest constellations, which correspond mainly to the usual left–right divide.

In Section 3.1 we put forward some concepts that are useful for understanding this problem: indivisibilities, externalities and redistribution. In Section 3.2 using those concepts, we develop our argument. In Section 3.3, we compare our argument with the traditional cleavage theory of party formation. In Section 3.4, we draw the implications of our analysis for the European Parliament.

3.1   Political conflict, indivisibilities, externalities and redistribution

Political conflicts usually involve indivisibilities, externalities and redistribution. These are three economic concepts that play an important role in public economics and political science.

We already introduced the concept of indivisibilities in the previous chapter. Indivisibilities in political decisions are present when a political decision *applies to all* or when it is *difficult to exclude individuals from the application of a decision*. Indivisibilities are related to two factors: (1) the indivisibility of a vote and (2) indivisibilities related to the decisions themselves. The indivisibility of a vote is easy to understand. It relates to the fact that when a bill is brought to the floor of a legislative assembly, it is either adopted or rejected. The decision is one and indivisible whether one has voted in favour or against. The indivisibilities related to a decision are a different matter. Not all legislative decisions necessarily imply indivisibilities. The decision to target budgetary expenditures to a given region involves few indivisibilities. To take an extreme example that clarifies this idea, imagine that a parliament decides to build a bridge across a river that runs in the middle of a given town and assume that only citizens of that town will cross the bridge and benefit from it. Imagine further that while the bridge benefits the citizens of the town, it benefits only them and that the economic benefit to the town has no impact on the economy outside that town. If the costs of the bridge are borne only by the citizens of the town in question, the decision to build the bridge concerns only the citizens of the town and is of no concern to outside citizens. However, if the bridge has no tolls or barriers of any kind, it is difficult to prevent any citizen from other towns from crossing the bridge. In this specific case, the decision to build the bridge involves an indivisibility with respect to the citizens of the town in question but no indivisibility with respect to citizens of other towns.

Indivisibilities are usually related to the 'public good' character of expenditures. A public good is a good or service that is both 'non-excludable' and 'non-rival'. A good is non-rival when its consumption or usage by somebody does not prevent others from consuming or using it. Most goods are rival: foods, cars, and so on. However, many goods are non-rival. This is the case of the bridge in the above example. It is also the case of roads and many other goods, such as swimming pools, parks, air and water purity, security and defence. The same is true for information, which plays an increasingly important role in post-industrial economies. The sale of information by one person to another does not prevent the seller from selling the information again.

Pure public goods are goods that are both non-rival and non-excludable. One cannot prevent people from breathing clean air nor from benefiting from common defence and security services, for example. However, one can prevent people from crossing a bridge unless they pay a toll. One can keep information secret and exclude others from enjoying it unless they pay a price. In general, pure public goods are not well allocated by the market system because non-excludability makes people unwilling to pay voluntarily for goods, and therefore creates a problem of who pays for these goods.

While indivisibilities tend to be naturally associated with public goods, indivisibilities can be artificially created by legislative decisions. Thus, for example, a decision to give a subsidy of a certain amount to all farmers is indivisible in the sense that it concerns all farmers. However, there is nothing intrinsically indivisible about it. Nothing prevents a legislative decision to subsidise only a single farmer with a known identity. Indivisibilities in legislative decisions are thus not necessarily associated to public goods. They may be associated to what is called 'publicly provided private goods'. Indivisibilities create the potential for conflict because decisions are proposed that apply to a large group of voters or possibly the whole population while the costs and benefits of that decision are not equally shared among voters. While the concept of public goods is well known in political science, the concept of indivisibility in political decisions is less well known.

We have discussed at length the concept of indivisibilities in legislative decisions. Two other concepts need to be clarified: externalities and redistribution.

Externalities can be seen as a form of indivisibility. Externalities are effects of a certain decision on others. Externalities can be positive or negative. An example of a 'negative externality' is the pollution resulting from industrial production, which is a huge problem in our societies. An example of a 'positive externality', in contrast, is the effect of construction highways on the neighbouring local economies.

One speaks of redistribution each time a political decision takes away resources or incomes or benefits from some groups to give it to others. Redistribution is generally a source of potential conflict unless it is associated with large increases in efficiency that benefit everybody.

Why are these concepts of indivisibility, externalities and redistribution relevant in our discussion of political party and democracy? As we will see, these concepts imply that parties should form and compete along ideological rather than territorial axes.

3.2   Solving political conflicts

Our first argument in this direction is that conflict can be minimised by minimising indivisibilities, in other words by making divisible what can be made divisible.

First, what do we mean by political conflict? We concentrate on political conflict in parliaments. A conflict is present whenever different coalitions of interest have opposing stakes in the outcome of a legislative vote: some benefit from a 'Yes' while others benefit from a 'No'. There is no conflict when all sides benefit from a given decision. We will use this narrow concept of conflict in what follows.

Redistributive transfers are a form of politically created indivisibility and usually involve conflicts since some are net recipients and others are net contributors. These conflicts would be absent without public transfers (which allocate resources directly) or regulations (which allocate resources indirectly). This should not be understood as an argument for eliminating existing public spending or regulation, since this would also create a conflict (some would benefit and others would lose from a change in the status quo). Rather, it implies nothing else than the positive statement that creating a new policy with redistributive effects is likely to generate political conflict.

However, even when there are real indivisibilities involved, one can minimise them in many ways. Take again the example of the local bridge. The bridge only involves indivisibilities for the local population. Unnecessary conflicts are thus created if the bridge is part of a national or European project because of the redistributive implications: the whole population is asked to contribute to a public good that only benefits the population in one locality. Such redistribution might be deemed desirable for redistribution's sake, but it is also likely to involve political conflict if a majority outside the locality is not willing to pay for the bridge. If the bridge benefits the locality only, one creates an unnecessary conflict by allocating a decision on that bridge to the higher level of government. The result might be inefficient in the sense that the bridge never gets built. Indeed, the locality would be the only net recipient whereas the rest of the society would be a net contributor. The project would thus be rejected in a majority vote of the society as a whole.

One consequently minimises indivisibilities by having the locality decide and pay for the bridge. If such local issues are allocated to the local level, efficient outcomes are more likely. Moreover, one reduces the potential for political conflict by minimising indivisibilities. Even then, it might be possible to further minimise indivisibilities by instituting tolls for crossing the bridge. In that way, those who benefit more from the bridge in the locality will pay more for it. Does this mean that one should dispense with public decisions on the bridge altogether and rely only on private firms? Such ideas were widespread in the eighties during the period of Thatcherism and Reaganism. This is not necessarily the case, however, because a private monopoly might charge monopoly prices for crossing the bridge. Moreover, it might use its economic powers to hold up the city government and make it adopt decisions in favour of the firm. This is called rent-seeking.

To summarise our argument so far, minimising indivisibilities can minimise conflicts. A natural implication of the earlier argument is that potential conflicts between regional entities are best resolved by finding the adequate level of decentralisation (cf. Oates, 1972; Alesina and Spoloare, 2003). So, why transfer policy competences to the European level where there are no strong natural indivisibilities or externalities across member states (Majone, 1996; Alesina et al., 2001)? One argument is that one may desire the redistributive effects of taking such decisions at the European level. Why not redistribute from the rich to the poor? A majority of poor may want that. Would they be able to impose such an outcome under majority voting?

Probably not. The reason is that in a democracy the option of secession may reduce the level of redistribution between regional entities (Bolton and Roland, 1997). To see why, imagine a situation in a polity where there is a majority of poor regions. The democratic process could lead to a majority vote in favour of large redistribution from the rich to the poor. However, the rich regions may threaten to secede (for example, the case of Lombardy in Italy). As a result, the poor regions have no power to impose redistribution.

However, secession may impose inefficiencies for the rich regions as well as for the poor regions. There might be fewer economies of scale in public good provision. Contract enforcement might be less efficient across separate countries. Regulations might be used to create forms of hidden protectionism, and so on. These conflicts and inefficiencies could therefore be avoided by a constitutional design that limits the power of the central government and creates a decentralised (federal) structure with the appropriate allocation of competences between the higher level and the lower level, a first order issue being to prevent any kind of protectionism between countries.

This argument on the adequate level of competences is especially valid in the European context. The EU is a decentralised system of governments. Although the continental-scale market is regulated at the European level, taxing and spending are overwhelmingly kept at the national level, and the EU budget is primarily used for compensating member states that gain least from market integration. The sovereignty of each member state is also preserved by imposing the requirement that the unanimity rule is used in the EU Council in areas where the states suspect that the result of qualified-majority voting would lead to a significant change in national/territorial redistribution. This is the case for taxation, for example, where if a qualified-majority were used the Council would probably vote to impose higher tax rates on the minority of states with lower tax rates.

This institutional design severely limits the power of the EU and also limits the extent of territorial conflicts between the member states. This does not mean that we should never observe redistribution between member states inside the EU. It implies that if we observe it it must be the result of a unanimous agreement, which serves to benefit all interests. For example, EU spending programmes are the result of 'package deals' where advances in European economic integration were associated with compensation packages for the likely losers of this economic integration in the form of Common Agricultural Policy or the Structural Funds (e.g. Moravcsik, 1991, 1998; Pollack, 1995). Apart from these package deals, there has not been any drive towards direct redistribution programmes at the European level. The total EU budget is approximately one per cent of the combined GDP of the member states.

If conflicts between regional entities are best solved by a quasi-federal constitutional design, then conflicts between regions and territorial entities are not likely to be the major source of political conflict in legislatures of advanced democracies where an adequate mix of centralisation and decentralisation has presumably developed over time. This does not mean at all that we should not observe conflicts between regions. Competences that remain centralised may entail conflicts between regions. Even in federal countries like Belgium, Canada, Spain, India or Brazil, conflicts over the competences of the federal level keep appearing. Our argument is simply that the possibility of devolution of powers makes it possible to reduce the level of political conflicts between regional entities by finding the appropriate mix of centralisation and decentralisation.

If one follows this argument, this implies that party formation is not very likely to occur along geographical lines in advanced democracies that have had time to develop satisfactory forms of federalism. Indeed, party formation concerns stable coalitions on different sides of major conflict areas in democratic legislatures. We should thus, as a rule, not see parties in democracies form along geographical lines.

This prediction is generally borne out in advanced industrialised democracies where despite the presence of small regionalist or secessionist parties party formation occurs usually along ideological lines. In contrast, in countries where decentralisation has not made enough progress and where regional interests are quite divergent, one should observe more often the emergence of regional parties (e.g. Chhibber, and Kollman, 2004; Brancati, 2007). However, there are a number of countries where the party system, if it exists, is based mainly on territorial or ethnic divisions. This is the case, for example, in many states in Africa (Cowen and Laakso, 2002). This does not contradict our argument. Most of those countries are young democracies and one can argue that the territorial organisation of the state and the geographical borders have not yet stabilised. Indeed, the borders of many African countries are artificial legacies of colonialism (Herbst, 2000). It is thus quite likely that the current situation is unstable. Many African countries may not keep democratic institutions. But those that do are likely to experience secessions or secessionist tensions that lead to devolution of powers of central government.

Another example is Belgium, where the growing social and economic conflict between the Dutch- and French-speaking communities in the 1960s and early 1970s led to the formation of two new territorial-based and ideologically broad parties: Volksunie (VU) in the Dutch-speaking part of the country, and the Front Démocratique des Francophones (FDF) in the French-speaking parts. These two parties together won more than twenty per cent of the votes in the 1971 and 1974 parliamentary elections in Belgium. However, following a reorganisation of the Belgian state along federal lines, and a decentralisation of a large amount of public spending to the regional level, the votes for these two parties declined as voters went back to supporting the old ideologically based parties. Eventually, by the 2003 election, VU and FDF had disappeared, with the VU members joining either the Flemish socialists or Christian democrats and most of the FDF members joining the French-speaking liberals. In other words, a territorial conflict emerged, cutting across the traditional left–right ideological division between the mainstream parties in Belgium. But decentralisation of policy-making effectively removed the need for political parties based purely around the territorial conflict.

We have argued so far that appropriate allocation of decision-making authority between central and local government is the best way to limit conflicts between territorial entities. If this is the case and if appropriate forms of federalism have developed, then regional conflicts should rarely appear in elections and parliaments at the central level of government. Therefore, there is little ground for parties to form on the basis of regional interests inside the central parliament. However, this does not automatically mean that parties should form along ideological lines. Is it not possible to invoke a similar argument about conflicts between socio-economic groups?

While it is easy to decentralise public decision-making to regional entities relative to matters that concern them, it is more difficult to decentralise decision-making powers to particular socio-economic groups. The immediate argument one may invoke is that enforcing excludability on the basis of locality is easier than enforcing it on the basis of socio-economic status. This does not, however, seem as convincing as it may appear at first sight. While it is possible to reserve education and health services to inhabitants of a given locality, why should it be more difficult to do so for professions such as doctors, teachers or taxi drivers?

A better argument seems to be that decentralising allocation of powers to professional groups and socio-economic categories would tend to stifle competition completely since one of the main aims of professional interest groups is to secure monopoly power and to eliminate the threat of competition. Another way of saying the same thing is that externalities across sectors and professions are very strong and that allocating autonomy of decision-making powers to sectors and professions therefore tends to lead to inefficient policy-making.

Does this mean that no externalities exist as a result of decentralising policy powers to territorial units? Not at all. There are all kinds of externalities between territorial units, the most obvious being related to management of the environment and to air and water pollution.

Perhaps one of the worst cross-territorial externalities is that territorial units tend to favour local protectionism and it is important to impose free trade across territorial entities in a centralised way. It is no coincidence that the success of American federalism was based to a great degree on the interstate commerce clause, whereby the federal government has authority to guarantee and regulate inter-state trade. Similarly, the success of the EU has been based on its ability to assure free trade in the EU single market and to overcome a long history of protectionism. This is also why the WTO is called upon to play a fundamental role in the global economy and why countries as powerful as the US should learn to submit to the authority of the WTO in matters of international trade.

Protectionism by territorial entities is a major source of inefficiency because it tends to promote local monopolies and leads to catastrophic contractions of output. Protectionism by sectors is also a major source of inefficiency and maybe an even worse one than protectionism between countries. Indeed, this would tend to create a sequential chain of monopolies. A sectoral chain of monopolies is the one thing worse than a single monopoly as we know from the 'double marginalisation' argument in the theory of industrial organisation. Indeed, a chain of monopolies tends to exacerbate the monopoly problem as an upstream monopoly does not take into account the effect of its monopoly behaviour on the downstream monopoly. A chain of monopolies leads to higher prices and lower output than an integrated monopoly (Tirole, 1989). Note that sectors and socio-professional groups do generally have self-regulatory powers, but these are much less extensive than those accorded to regional entities. And for good reason! Giving sectors and socio-professional groups more powers would lead to the major inefficiencies of double marginalisation.

Allocating power to legislate to specific socio-economic interests would potentially be even worse as it would produce completely inconsistent sets of laws and regulations. Imagine a situation where workers and business associations legislate separately on issues such as labour regulations. Since labour and capital are both needed in the production process, it is obviously impossible to have different sets of rules in the workplace. It would produce total chaos. These rules tend to be indivisible and cannot be legislated separately.

The foregoing reasoning shows that there is a non-negligible asymmetry between decentralising political powers to regional entities and decentralising them to sectors or socio-economic interests. This is particularly the case if one is able to prevent protectionism between territorial entities by free trade agreements. It is then quite clear that decentralising legislative powers to sectors creates more externalities than decentralising them to regions. The argument is sketched further in the Appendix to this chapter.

The implication of our argument is that one should see very little (or hardly any) allocation of legislative powers to sectors because of the inefficiencies it would imply.[1] Therefore, legislative decisions relative to sectoral and professional interests should be centralised. To the extent that such decisions create conflicts between different socio-economic groups, such conflicts should form a major dimension of conflict in central (or federal) parliaments. Voting blocs should thus form around these conflicts. This is why party formation should occur mostly along the dimension of socio-economic interests.

The theory outlined here uses arguments from the standard economic theory of fiscal federalism, but also addresses the question of what should be the main dimension of party formation. We thus combine a theory of state formation (the boundaries of states) and fiscal federalism with a theory of party formation.

3.3   The Cleavage theory of democratic politics

For much of the past forty years, the 'cleavage theory' has been the dominant explanation of conflicts in party systems, particularly in Europe. On first impression, one might assume that our understanding of socio-economic and territorial conflicts is at odds with this approach. However, this is not the case. Our theory should be seen as complementary to cleavage theory. Cleavage theory does not ask why territorial cleavages are absent from a party system. Our understanding of party formation is situated at a somewhat more abstract level than

---

[1] This argument is a bit of a shortcut because, as discussed in Chapter 2, inefficient institutions may exist and persist. Nevertheless, in this case, the inefficiencies would be so huge that it would be difficult to imagine how such a system could be viable even in the medium run.

cleavage theory. On the other hand, cleavage theory gives content to our claim about functional conflicts. Moreover, the empirical expectations of the two approaches are quite similar.

Seymour Martin Lipset and Stein Rokkan (1967) first set out their theory in a famous paper in the 1960s. They argued that political 'cleavages' between social groups were the result of 'critical junctures' in the historical development of a society. Three main junctures are worth highlighting. First, the experience of building a nation-state created territorial/ethnic conflicts between groups aligned to the new central institutions and groups aligned to sub-national institutions or ethnic structures. Second, the period of 'democratic revolution' and the resulting liberalisation of society and the state in the late eighteenth and early nineteenth centuries produced a conflict between the new mainly urban middle class and the traditional religious, state and landed interests. Third, the industrial revolution and the emergence of industrial society in the later part of the nineteenth century created a conflict between organised industrial labour and the owners of capital.

When universal suffrage was introduced at the beginning of the twentieth century, Lipset and Rokkan argued that these conflicts became 'frozen' in the resulting party systems. Mass political parties emerged for the first time to organise the new electoral campaigns, and these new parties sought to mobilise around the conflicts of interests and ideologies that existed in society. As a result, the 'latent' divisions within society became translated into 'manifest' conflicts in the party system and in the new democratic parliaments. So, conservative and Christian democratic parties defended the interests of the state, the landed aristocracy and the Church. Liberal parties promoted the interests of the middle classes and liberal professions. Socialist parties promoted the interests of the industrial working class. And various rural, regional and ethno-linguistic parties defended the interests of sub-national minorities who had been marginalised in the process of state formation.

This is not to say that nothing has changed in the past century. First, new social conflicts have appeared since the party systems were first frozen. For example, with the development of post-industrial society, green parties emerged to articulate the new 'post-materialist' values of the growing public sector middle class (Inglehart, 1977, 1990). Also, as many European countries became immigrant rather than emigrant societies, and as social democratic parties moved away from their traditional working class support-base to appeal to middle class voters, new extreme-right parties sprang up (Ignazi, 1992; Kitschelt, 1995). And with the development of European integration, and the consequent reorganisation of the state to a new level of government, a new 'critical juncture' is developing that pits groups aligned to the new European-level institutions against groups aligned to the old national institutions (Hix, 1999; Bartolini, 2005).

Second, there has been a gradual erosion of the traditional social cleavages as society has become more complex. The expansion of the public sector and the replacement of manufacturing-based economies with service-based economies has produced a growing private and public sector middle class and increasing social mobility (e.g. Bell, 1960). As a result, electoral volatility has increased, party identification amongst voters has declined and the classic cleavages identified by Lipset and Rokkan do not explain voting behaviour and party positions as well as they once did (e.g. Dalton et al., 1984; Franklin et al., 1992; Karvonen and Kuhnle, 2001).

Nevertheless, the classic 'party families' identified by Lipset and Rokkan still dominate all the main democratic party systems today, over one hundred years after the establishment of universal suffrage in most of these systems. This is partly due to the ability of parties, as organisations, to adapt to changing political circumstances. However, this is also due to the fact that many of these traditional conflicts are still with us today. For example, battles over tax rates, inflation rates, unemployment spending, social security and public healthcare provision are modern versions of the cleavage between the working class and the owners of capital (cf. Dahrendorf, 1959; Lipset, 1959). Similarly, battles over gender equality, abortion, environmental protection, multiculturalism, gay marriage and stem-cell research are modern versions of the cleavage between the urban middle class and the rural and land-based interests, who are more traditional and religious. As a result of these continued divisions, the balance of votes between the parties on the right and the parties on the left has remained remarkably stable for over a century (Bartolini and Mair, 1990). In fact, most electoral volatility has occurred within the left and right blocs (e.g. between the socialists and greens, or between the liberals and conservatives) rather than between these blocs.

As a result, the 'left–right' dimension has remained the dominant dimension of conflict in elections and parliaments throughout the democratic world (e.g. MacDonald et al., 1991; Budge et al., 2001; Benoit and Laver, 2005). This is partly explained by the malleability of the notion of the left–right axis that has been able to absorb new issues. However, the left–right conflict still has substantive meaning, and serves as an effective way of communicating the various policy positions associated with 'left' and 'right' to voters. The left–right conflict, in its contemporary variant, captures two sets of policy divisions: economic (state intervention vs. free market), and social (liberty vs. authority) (e.g. Kitschelt, 1994). Moreover, these two conflicts are both socio-economic, in that they divide groups in society along functional rather than territorial lines. Hence, the parties that emerged as a result of universal suffrage at the start of the twentieth century around two of the socio-economic 'cleavages' are still ideally situated to articulate the main positions on the modern left–right dimension (cf. Finer, 1987; Bobbio, 1996 [1995]). Also, the early mass political parties, whether socialists, liberals or conservatives, set up organisations to mobilise voters across geographic districts (e.g. Bartolini, 2000; Caramani, 2004). By definition, then, these parties have always defined themselves as promoting functional rather than non-territorial interests. Meanwhile, territorial conflicts, and the parties that articulate these conflicts, have not been subsumed in the modern left–right dimension.

Democratic politics, at least in polities with stabilised borders and stabilised allocation of powers between the local and the central level, is fundamentally about reconciling differences of interests that cross territorial units. It is not about conflicts between territorial units. Because the European Union has been created through unanimous voluntary agreement between the nation-states of Europe, potential territorial conflicts have been addressed in the basic constitutional architecture of the EU. As a result, national–territorial conflicts are present in EU constitutional and budgetary bargaining, but are kept 'off the table' in the day-to-day legislative business of the EU. As a result, politics at the European level, in the European Parliament and even throughout the whole EU policy-making process, is likely to be similar to politics at the national level in Europe, where the left–right dimension captures basic socio-economic interests and preferences.

3.4   Implications for the European Parliament

Our theory implies that the left–right dimension should be the main dimension of conflict in the European Parliament and also the main axis of party and coalition formation. It also implies that parties should form around this dimension and that competition and coalition formation between these parties should be along a left–right dimension rather than a national/territorial dimension (such as more or less economic and political integration in Europe). As we discussed in the previous chapter, existing research on the European Parliament suggests that this pattern of behaviour is beginning to emerge. There is also some evidence that left–right conflicts structure behaviour in the EU Council (Mattila and Lane, 2001; Mattila, 2004).

Nevertheless, the view that EU politics should be dominated by left–right politics is not the only view. We discuss existing theories of the dimensionality of EU politics in detail in Chapter 9, when we focus on measuring the dimensions of voting in the European Parliament. But the main claims of this work are worth summarising here, to highlight the contrasts with our propositions. Gary Marks and Marco Steenbergen (2002) identify several models of the structure of conflict in EU politics. The first model, which Marks and Steenbergen call the 'international relations' model, is the one that is most directly opposing to our view. In this model, EU politics is dominated by conflicts between the EU member states. These conflicts could be geopolitical, such as battles over national sovereignty and national interests (Hoffmann, 1966). Alternatively, they could be economic, such as battles over national budgetary contributions or which member states win or lose from the single market or economic and monetary union (Moravcsik, 1998). Either way, according to this view territorial conflicts are primary while trans-territorial socio-economic conflicts are secondary, or even non-existent.

The other models are not so directly opposing to our argument, but have some subtle differences. For example, Liesbet Hooghe and Gary Marks argue that the main dimension of conflict at the European level is between 'regulated capitalism' and 'neo-liberalism' (Hooghe and Marks, 1999). Similarly, Fritz Scharpf (1999) and George Tsebelis and Geoffrey Garrett (2000) predict that conflicts will be about the level of regulation in the single market, between actors who prefer high European-wide standards (such as consumer groups, socialist and green parties, and Scandinavian states) and actors who prefer low European-wide standards (such as business interests, liberal and conservative parties, and states like the United Kingdom). These models are similar to our argument, in that they both expect the dominant battles to be between competing socio-economic interests or value sets.

Somewhat differently, though, in the 'Hix–Lord model', the left–right dimension and the pro-/anti-European integration dimensions both exist at the European level (Hix and Lord, 1997; Hix, 1999). Moreover, these two dimensions are expected to be orthogonal, since there will be conflicts within both the left and right about the appropriate level of economic and political integration in the EU polity – rather like the mix of socio-economic and territorial conflicts in political systems like Belgium, Switzerland and Canada. On the one hand, this model is identical to our view, in that socio-economic and territorial conflicts are fundamentally different and so cannot be subsumed into a single dimension. On the other hand, whereas we expect the left–right dimension to be clearly dominant, in this model the two dimensions are expected to be more or less equal.

Finally, a rather different idea is that the institutional design of the EU might be the reason for left–right politics in the European Parliament rather than the inherent structure of interests and preferences of elected politicians at the European level (cf. Bindseil and Hantke, 1997). This explanation starts from the observation that the majority hurdle in the Council is higher than that in the parliament: a qualified-majority or unanimity in the Council compared with a simple majority in the parliament (most of the time). This is often the case in bicameral legislative systems, and invariably means that the chamber with the higher voting threshold can dominate the chamber with the lower threshold (Tsebelis and Money, 1997). Applied to the EU, once a deal has been reached in the Council, it is unlikely that the European Parliament will be able to change this deal very much. However, the European Parliament could alter the bargaining situation with the Council if it can add another dimension of conflict (cf. Riker, 1986). Since national governments are represented in the Council, the agreement in the Council is likely to be along a national–territorial dimension. Hence, it would be in the strategic interests of the European Parliament to differentiate itself from the position in the Council along a different dimension, such as the left–right, which would force the Council to bargain along this new dimension, and most likely shift the location of the original policy agreement in the Council.

However, as we demonstrate in the next chapters, this institutional-based explanation does not hold. This alternative explanation implies that for non-legislative decisions, such as own initiative resolutions (for example, on fighting AIDS in Africa or on opposing the Iraq war), MEPs should not vote strategically in the same way as they do on legislative issues, when they are negotiating with the Council. If their 'true' preferences are such that nationality matters more than ideology, then we should see MEPs voting along national lines on non-legislative resolutions. But, as we demonstrate, this is not the case. Member state, territory or nationality are not strong determinants of voting behaviour in the European Parliament. In contrast, there is overwhelming evidence that left–right preferences are the dominant determinants of MEP and party behaviour on all issues in the European Parliament.

3.5   Conclusion

In the previous chapter we explained why parties should form in the European Parliament, even if European elections do not provide a strong connection between MEP behaviour and voting behaviour in these elections. Then, in this chapter we have explained why these parties should be organised around socio-economic rather than national/territorial interests and why they should hence mainly compete along a left–right dimension rather than a pro-/anti-EU integration or other national-interest-based dimension. In the next chapters we test these ideas against the voting behaviour of MEPs in the last twenty-five years.

If our theoretical ideas are right, and we aim to convince the reader that they are, then there are significant implications for the position of the European Parliament in the EU and for the prospect of democracy at the European level. Our rather optimistic view is in contrast to both the unqualified optimism surrounding the birth of European elections as well as some of the recent sceptical views about the prospect of democratising the EU (e.g. Majone, 2002; Moravcsik, 2002). Genuine European-wide parties may not emerge in European elections for some time. However, competitive and cohesive parties have emerged inside the European Parliament and are likely to continue to strengthen. This is good not only for the functioning of EU policy-making but also for the democratic accountability of EU governance. We shall return to this issue in the concluding chapter.

Appendix: decentralised governance to territorial entities and sectors

We present here a simple example to illustrate one of the main points in our argument. Imagine a situation with two territorial entities A and B and two sectors 1 and 2. Think of the two sectors as, for example, steel industry and car industry or any two sectors where one sector buys from another. In reality, there are many exchanges between sectors but it is better to keep the analysis simple. Assume that the regions are completely symmetrical and have an equal endowment of sectors. Assume also that they are identical in all respects except for their location. Now compare two scenarios: one where legislative powers are decentralised to territorial entities and one where they are decentralised to each sector. We assume that the legislative authorities only take into account the interests of their constituencies.

Take first the scenario where legislative decisions are decentralised to regions. Region A has producers from sector 1 and sector 2. It obviously also has consumers. Since region A only takes into account its interests, it neglects externalities between regions. Suppose that the pollution from its industries crosses borders. In this case, it imposes a negative externality s on region B. Call $y_{A1}(D)$ and $y_{A2}(D)$ the output produced under these decentralised arrangements D in both sectors. If we use similar notation for B and use $\star$ for solutions under the socially optimal solution, we have that $y_{A1}(D) + y_{A2}(D) > y^\star_{A1} + y^\star_{A2}$ but $(y_{A1}(D) + y_{A2}(D)) - (y^\star_{A1} + y^\star_{A2}) < s$ and similar relations hold for region B. In other words, under decentralisation, output produced in the different industries is higher than what would be produced if the externalities were internalised. But the externality imposed on the other region is higher than the reduction in output to the optimum. Welfare in each region under decentralisation, as measured by output net of the externalities received from the other region, is thus lower than under the social optimum: $Y_A(D) = y_{A1}(D) + y_{A2}(D) - s < Y^\star_A = y^\star_{A1} + y^\star_{A2}$. The same, of course, holds for region B.

We could imagine a worse interpretation of the simple example, where the legislators of A also try to impose protectionist measures against region B and vice versa. In this case, s can be quite large. However, there are reasons for this not to be the case. Protection in the steel industry is likely to be rejected by producers in the car industry and by consumers. Protection in the car industry would be rejected by consumers but it is not clear that it would be rejected by the steel industry. Protection of both industries would clearly be supported by both industries even though it would be opposed by consumers. In any case, protectionism between territorial entities would entail huge economic costs.

Consider now the alternative scenario, where legislative decisions are decentralised to the steel industry and the car industry. In this case, each sector legislates in favour of its interests. Calling S the system of sectoral decentralisation, we have $y_{A1}(S) + y_{B1}(S)$ and $y_{A2}(S) + y_{B2}(S)$ as the output in each sector under this arrangement. Sector 1 will legislate to give itself monopoly power and sector 2 will legislate to give itself monopoly power. This will in itself reduce the output and increase the price in each sector compared with the social optimum as we know from elementary economic theory. Moreover, sector 1 imposes a strong externality on sector 2 by increasing its production costs. Total output is even lower than it would be under a single integrated monopoly (denoted by M) where the car industry and steel industry are vertically integrated:

$$Y > Y^\star(M) > (y_{A1}(S) + y_{B1}(S)) + (y_{A2}(S) + y_{B2}(S)) = Y(S).$$

It is plausible that $(y_{A1}(S) + y_{B1}(S)) + (y_{A2}(S) + y_{B2}(S)) < Y_A(D)$. In other words, the welfare effects of decentralising legislation to sectors are worse than from decentralising to regions.

We have not so far compared these two scenarios with the one we would have under full centralisation of legislative decisions. Assume that there are transaction costs associated to conflicts inside the central parliament related to legislation, as we discussed in the previous chapter. Without going into much detail, suppose that the cost of conflict is K and that decisions under centralisation lead to output level $Y^* - K$. If $K > s$, then it is preferable to decentralise legislative decisions to the territorial entities and it is also efficient, in terms of second best. It is thus quite possible to have $Y^*-s > Y^*-K > Y(S)$. In this case, geographical conflicts will have been avoided by an efficient (constrained second best) decentralisation to territorial entities while inefficient decentralisation to sectors will have been prevented. Only conflicts between sectors will now be debated in the central legislature.

The main point of this simple example is that if decentralisation of legislative decision-making to territorial entities is a not-too-costly way of solving territorial conflicts, decentralising legislative power to trans-regional interest groups such as sectors is much more costly in terms of efficiency losses. Therefore, if these efficiency considerations are taken into account in deciding the mix of centralisation and decentralisation of powers, conflicts between transregional sectoral or functional interests remain in legislatures, which means that political parties will tend to be based around affinity of interests and preferences of sectoral or functional rather than territorial groups. We should thus observe party formation not along territorial lines but along socio-economic lines.

4   Participation

A common misconception is that MEPs are 'part-time' politicians who are highly paid but rarely show up at plenary sessions. Part of this misconception stems from the fact that the European Parliament's plenary sessions only last for one week each month. However, MEPs do much more than speak and vote in plenary sessions. The average month of an MEP involves a week of committee meetings in Brussels, a week of party meetings in Brussels, a plenary week in Strasbourg or Brussels debating and voting on legislation and resolutions, and a week 'back home' dealing with constituency and other local political business. Shuttling between Brussels, Strasbourg and home, MEPs 'live out of a suitcase'. Moreover, the constant shuttles of the MEPs are associated with moves of tons of documents that are needed for the normal operation of the European Parliament. Seen this way, it is as if MEPs are moving offices twice a month. It is thus not too surprising that most MEPs only serve for one five-year term.

Another aspect of this misconception stems from the common observation that even in the plenary sessions not all MEPs take part in all votes. However, like all elected politicians, MEPs have to make choices about how best to allocate their time: for example, whether to work on a committee report, prepare a speech, meet with interest groups or constituents, attend a party meeting, undertake research, attend a committee meeting, attend a plenary debate and speak in the plenary. With so many competing pressures, if MEPs are rational politicians, they will weigh up the costs and benefits of taking part in a vote, such as the opportunity cost of voting when this time could be spent doing something else. MEPs are no different from this point of view from other elected representatives in democracies throughout the world.

At one extreme, a vote could be on a key legislative issue that is crucial for the MEP's national and European parties and where the outcome of the vote is too close to call. In this situation, the MEP is likely to make every effort to take part in the vote. For example, 91 per cent of MEPs participated in the vote on 4 July 2001 on whether to accept or reject the Takeover Directive, which ended in a tie of 273 votes in favour to 273 votes against and 22 abstentions. At the other extreme, a vote could be on a largely irrelevant issue in an area where the parliament has no power and where the outcome of the vote is predetermined because there is overwhelming support or opposition to the issue. For example, only 62 per cent of MEPs participated in the vote on 22 April 2004 on a minor amendment to a non-binding resolution on transatlantic relations, which passed by 307 votes in favour to 75 votes against and 7 abstentions. In this situation, the MEP may well have better things to do than to vote. Again, in any normal democracy, elected representatives face such choices.

Another factor that influences participation rates in the European Parliament, and which is quite different from most other democratic assemblies, is the way that MEPs are paid. First, MEPs are not all paid the same, since the basic salary of each MEP is the same as the salary of national members of parliament in the MEP's member state. Second, MEPs 'top up' their salaries with a daily allowance, which they receive if they attend the business of the parliament in Brussels or Strasbourg. A change in the system of daily allowances in 1994 provided greater incentives for MEPs to participate in votes. An agreement on a common pay structure for all MEPs was reached in June 2005, whereby all MEPs would receive a salary of €7,000 (approximately $8,300) per month (corrected for inflation). However, the single MEP salary and the new system for reimbursing expenses will not come into effect until July 2009.

In this chapter, we demonstrate that participation in roll-call votes in the European Parliament is not random and can be explained by some simple assumptions about the motivations of MEPs. In Section 4.1, we discuss some general theories of participation in legislatures and how these apply to the European Parliament. In Section 4.2 we show how participation rates in the European Parliament vary systematically across time, by political group, and by member state. In Section 4.3 we undertake a statistical analysis to demonstrate that variations in voting participation in the European Parliament are to a large extent explained by the varying powers of the parliament over time and by issue area as well as by whether MEPs think their political group will be able to change the outcome of a vote. In other words, far from being lazy politicians, MEPs are highly active and highly motivated actors, just like their cousins in other democratic assemblies.

4.1   Participation in the European Parliament: the costs and benefits of voting

If one assumes that MEPs are strategic when deciding whether to participate in a vote, their behaviour is likely to be explained by a famous equation in political science (Downs, 1957; Riker and Ordeshook, 1968; cf. Ferejohn and Fiorina, 1974):

$$R = PB - C + D$$

Here, R is the net reward from voting, in terms of the total political benefit of taking part in a vote. B is the specific benefit of participating in a particular vote, in terms of the utility gained from being on the winning side, and P is the probability of being 'pivotal', in terms of changing a losing outcome into a winning outcome. C is the fixed cost of voting, such as the opportunity cost of voting rather than undertaking some other activity. And D is the fixed benefit of voting, such as the sense of 'duty'. A rational parliamentarian will participate in a vote if and only if $R > 0$.

This model was originally developed to explain turnout in mass elections. However, the model is equally applicable to participation in parliaments, such as the United States and the European Parliament (Poole and Rosenthal, 1997: 210–26; Noury, 2004). In the parliamentary context, the fixed costs and benefits of voting are quite different from the mass elections context. The fixed costs of voting in most parliaments are relatively low, since time is usually allocated in the plenary agenda for the specific activity of voting, and other activities (such as committee or party meetings) are avoided at such times. On the other hand, the fixed benefits of voting in most parliaments are usually high, since those members of parliament who show up to vote are likely to be rewarded by their party leaderships for 'good behaviour', such as promotion to positions of influence in the parliament or the party. If a party is cohesive in its voting behaviour, then the probability of being pivotal is also higher, and all the more so if the party is large.

It is difficult to measure the specific and fixed costs and benefits of taking part in a vote in the European Parliament directly. Nevertheless, we can use proxies for these measures. First, the closer the vote, the more likely each additional MEP will make the difference on one side or the other. Hence, the closeness of a vote is a good proxy of the probability that an MEP will be pivotal if he/she participates in a vote. Specifically, participation is likely to be higher when the parliament is split into evenly balanced left and right coalitions and it is likely to be lower when all the main political groups vote together.

Second, the likely policy impact of the decision in the parliament is a good approximation of the specific benefit of being on the winning side in a vote. For example, if a vote is on an issue where the European Parliament has the power to shape legislation, the policy impact of the outcome of the vote will be high. Hence, we should expect higher participation rates with more legislative powers of the parliament, across time and issue area. Specifically, participation in voting in the parliament should increase as the powers of the parliament have grown in the various reforms of the EU treaties in the 1980s and 1990s. In addition, participation should be higher under the co-decision, assent and budgetary procedures, where the parliament has equal legislative power with the Council, than under the consultation procedure, where the parliament only has a delay power, but should be higher under the consultation procedure than on non-binding 'own resolutions' of the parliament (Scully, 1997a).

Third, the clearest fixed cost of voting in the plenary sessions in Strasbourg is the day of the week on which the vote is held. Because MEPs have to travel to or from Brussels and Strasbourg, or their home country and Strasbourg, at the beginning and the end of each plenary session week, they are constrained by the times of train and flight connections on Monday and Friday – and Strasbourg is not the most well-connected city in Europe, to say the least! The leadership of the parliament understands this situation and hence tries to organise all the important votes in the middle of the week. This, of course, lowers the policy incentives for participating on Monday and Friday even further and also raises the opportunity costs of remaining in Strasbourg for these days. As a result, participation is likely to be higher in votes held on a Tuesday, Wednesday or Thursday than in votes held on a Monday or Friday (although the parliament abolished plenary sessions on Fridays in 2000).

Fourth, the main fixed benefits of voting depend on the political group the MEP belongs to. The three main political groups in the parliament are more likely to be pivotal in votes than the smaller groups. The Socialists and EPP are likely to be pivotal because they are the largest groups, and the Liberals are likely to be pivotal (in particular periods at least) because they hold the balance of power between the two big groups. As a result, these three political groups have strong incentives to encourage their members to participate by rewarding 'good behaviour', for example, via promotion within the group or the assignment of more interesting and influential committee positions. For example, as we show elsewhere in the book, only the three main political groups operate strict 'whipping' instructions and show high levels of party cohesion.

Hence, we should expect the MEPs in these political groups to participate more than the MEPs in the smaller political groups.

Another fixed benefit that operates at the level of the political group is whether a political group is likely to be on the winning side in a vote. Being on the winning side is proof to actors outside the parliament – such as interest groups and the governments in the Council and the Commission – that the political group is able to get what it wants in the parliament. If a political group repeatedly loses, it is less likely to be taken seriously in the Brussels policy community or in the EU legislative process. As a result, we should expect MEPs to be more likely to vote if their political group is going to be on the winning side in the vote, regardless of whether the Yes or No side wins and regardless of the size of the political group.

There are of course important external factors that influence MEP participation rates independently of these strategic considerations. For example, some MEPs, particularly from France and Italy, are members of their national parliament or they hold other local or regional offices as well as the European Parliament, and so have to divide their time between these 'dual mandates'. Also, MEPs are elected under different electoral systems, and each system encourages a different set of incentives for MEPs in terms of how they allocate their time for party work (in Brussels) or constituency work (back home). For example, MEPs elected in single-member districts, as was the case in the United Kingdom until 1999, are more likely to spend time in their constituencies than in Brussels or Strasbourg than MEPs elected on national party lists (Bowler and Farrell, 1993). Similarly, the further a member state is from Strasbourg, and the higher the costs of travelling from a member state to Strasbourg, the more costly it will be for MEPs to participate in votes. However, these external factors all vary across member states, and so should lead to variations between each national group of MEPs rather than variations over time, between the political groups, or across issue area.

In sum, if MEPs are strategic when deciding to participate in votes in the European Parliament, their behaviour should be explained by the closeness of the vote, the powers of the parliament at a particular time plus the power of the parliament under the specific legislative or non-legislative procedure of the vote, the day of the week of the vote, whether an MEP is in one of the three main political groups and which political groups are on the winning side of the vote. If participation in the parliament is either random or is primarily driven by external factors, such as which member state an MEP comes from, the size of these strategic effects should be minimal.

4.2   Variations in participation rates across time, political group and country

Before investigating the influences on MEP participation in detail we first look at some broad patterns in participation rates across time, political groups and member states. We measure the total 'participation rate' as the number of MEPs who registered either a Yes, No or Abstain preference in a roll-call vote divided by the total number of MEPs at that time. Figure 4.1 shows the average total participation rate in the European Parliament in each year between the start of the first directly elected parliament, in July 1979, until the end of the fifth parliament, in June 2004 – because each five-year term runs from July in the first year until June in the fifth year, we report the average participation rate in the first and last six-month periods of each parliament, in addition to the average participation rate in each intervening year.

The variations in participation in votes over time illustrate several clear patterns. First, there is a general positive trend over time. Second, there is a marked difference between the trends in the first three parliaments and in the last two parliaments. In the first three parliaments there was a novelty effect, with higher participation rates at the beginning of each parliament, and a gradual decline towards the end of each parliament. In contrast, in the fourth and fifth parliaments, participation gradually increased each year. Part of the step-change in participation in the mid-1990s is explained by a change in the rules governing the payment of the daily attendance allowance of MEPs, which meant that in addition to being present in Strasbourg for plenary sessions MEPs must participate in the votes to claim their expenses.

We measure the participation rate for each political group as the number of members of the group who took part in a vote divided by the total number of members of the group at that time. Figure 4.2 shows the patterns in participation rate over time for the three main political groups in the parliament and the average participation rate for the other, smaller, groups ('The Smalls'). These patterns demonstrate, first, a generally higher level of participation for the two largest political groups. There is a break in the pattern for the liberals. During the first three parliaments they behaved like the other smaller groups. Then, in the fourth and fifth parliaments, their participation rates followed the pattern of the two largest groups. This is not surprising, given that the liberals became the pivotal party between the two main groups in the fourth and fifth parliaments, as we show in Chapters 8 and 9. The smaller groups, meanwhile, had less incentive to participate, as they

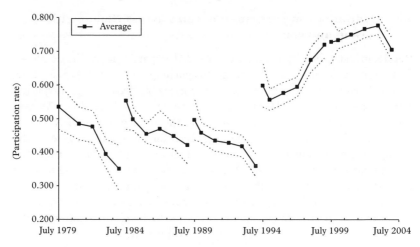

Figure 4.1. Average annual participation in the European Parliament, 1979–2004, with standard deviations shown.

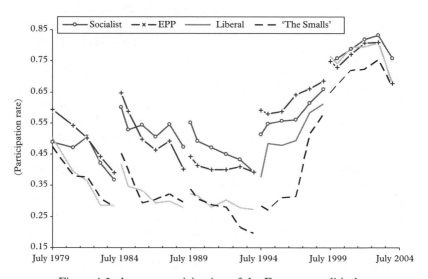

Figure 4.2. Average participation of the European political groups

have been relatively marginalised since 1979. Nevertheless, participation rates jumped in the fifth parliament for the smaller groups, as a result of the higher number of close left–right splits in this period (the average majority in the fifth parliament was 72 per cent, compared with 76 per cent in the fourth parliament).

Table 4.1. *Mean participation by member states*

Party	EP1	EP2	EP3	EP4	EP5
Luxembourg	0.42	0.54	0.44	0.67	0.85
Finland	—	—	—	0.90	0.84
Netherlands	0.58	0.57	0.57	0.77	0.84
Germany	0.54	0.59	0.50	0.73	0.81
Greece	0.46	0.46	0.41	0.58	0.81
Belgium	0.44	0.48	0.55	0.74	0.81
Sweden	—	—	—	0.49	0.80
Austria	—	—	—	0.65	0.78
Denmark	0.40	0.32	0.33	0.53	0.77
Spain	—	0.42	0.49	0.67	0.76
United Kingdom	0.58	0.53	0.55	0.70	0.75
France	0.33	0.32	0.34	0.47	0.74
Portugal	—	0.29	0.37	0.60	0.72
Ireland	0.42	0.51	0.51	0.60	0.69
Italy	0.34	0.30	0.26	0.40	0.56

Table 4.1 shows the average participation rate for each national delegation of MEPs in each of the five parliaments. Again, the general trend is upwards for all member states. One can see from Table 4.1 that there is considerable variance in participation rates between the different national groups of MEPs. However, when looking at the columns from left to right, one sees that this variance has declined over time, with no great differences between the member states in the fifth parliament. Italy is the only exception and has a much lower participation rate than the other countries in the fifth parliament. This is explained by the fact that Italy is the only member state that maintained a high number of MEPs with dual mandates in their national parliaments.

4.3   Explaining the patterns

To explain the variations in participation rate over time and by issue area it is not sufficient to look at the broad aggregate patterns. We therefore use regression analysis to investigate the main determinants of participation in the parliament. We take a two-sided approach. We explain the determinants of participation in the long run by analysing the determinants of average vote participation rates of the European political groups. We next analyse more short-term or high-frequency determinants of participation by focusing on characteristics of individual votes as the determinants of participation.

We first estimate changes in participation in the European Parliament over time with a simple linear regression model. The dependent variable in the model is the average participation of a political group (in terms of the proportion of MEPs from the group who voted Yes, No or Abstain) in all votes in a six-month period.

We include four sets of independent variables. First, we use three dummy variables that capture the increases in the parliament's powers in the three Treaty reforms since the mid-1980s: the Single European Act (*SEA*), which takes the value 0 for each period up to January–June 1987 and 1 thereafter; the Maastricht Treaty (*Maastricht*), which takes the value 0 for each period up to January–June 1993 and 1 thereafter; and the Amsterdam Treaty (*Amsterdam*), which takes the value 0 for each period up to January–June 1999 and 1 thereafter. Second, we include two control variables that capture the proportion of times a political group is on the winning side in a six-month period (*Winning*) as well as the size of the parliament as a whole in the period in question (*EP size*). Third, we include a series of dummy variables for each of the political groups. The Socialist group is excluded as the baseline category. Fourth, we include two types of measures to take account of time trends: a *Trend* variable, which takes the value 1 in the first period, 2 in the second period and so on; and dummy variables for each of the five European Parliaments (the first parliament is excluded as the reference category).

Table 4.2 presents the results. There are several noteworthy findings. First, the reforms of the Maastricht and Amsterdam Treaties, in 1993 and 1999, respectively, lead to higher participation in the European Parliament. Their combined effect in Model 1, without fixed effects for each of the parliaments, is roughly 40 per cent. In contrast, the SEA, which entered into force in 1987, did not increase participation in the parliament. It is associated with a decrease of nearly 7 per cent. This accords with the view that the parliament had considerably more influence in the EU policy process after the introduction of the codecision procedure (by the Maastricht Treaty) and its subsequent reform and extension (by the Amsterdam Treaty) than following the introduction of the co-operation procedure (by the SEA), which initially only applied to a limited number of policy areas. The significance of the Maastricht Treaty disappears in Models 2 and 3 once dummy variables for each parliament are introduced. This is because the introduction of the Maastricht Treaty coincided with the beginning of the fourth parliament, which is also when the new system of daily allowances was introduced, which provided greater financial incentives for MEPs to participate in votes. Hence, the increased participation in the fourth and fifth parliaments is only partly explained by the timing of the Maastricht Treaty.

Table 4.2. *Determinants of political group participation, semi-annually*

	Model 1		Model 2		Model 3	
	Coefficient	*t*-stat.	Coefficient	*t*-stat.	Coefficient	*t*-stat.
Constant	0.401***	(4.69)	0.855***	(8.29)	0.821***	(7.61)
SEA	−0.067***	(4.04)	0.000	(0.00)	0.005	(0.27)
Maastricht	0.103***	(5.38)	−0.002	(0.10)	0.005	(0.22)
Amsterdam	0.300***	(2.99)	0.150***	(5.08)	0.159***	(5.17)
Winner	0.158***	(2.92)	0.141***	(2.84)	0.141***	(2.85)
EP size	−0.000	(0.40)	−0.001***	(4.88)	−0.001***	(4.02)
EPP	0.005	(0.26)	0.005	(0.27)	0.005	(0.27)
Liberal	−0.098***	(5.18)	−0.099***	(5.84)	−0.099***	(5.84)
Gaullists	−0.143***	(6.79)	−0.146***	(7.73)	−0.146***	(7.72)
UK Cons	0.110***	(4.28)	0.107***	(4.58)	0.107***	(4.58)
Green	−0.065***	(2.85)	−0.065***	(3.16)	−0.065***	(3.15)
Regionalists	−0.204***	(7.70)	−0.198***	(8.32)	−0.198***	(8.32)
Radical-Left	−0.135***	(6.40)	−0.138***	(7.29)	−0.138***	(7.29)
Radical-Right	−0.113***	(3.47)	−0.098***	(3.30)	−0.098***	(3.30)
Anti-European	−0.088***	(3.26)	−0.091***	(3.78)	−0.091***	(3.77)
Independent	−0.152***	(4.59)	−0.157***	(5.17)	−0.157***	(5.18)
Non-attached	−0.186***	(8.07)	−0.190***	(9.16)	−0.190***	(9.16)
Time					−0.002	(1.06)
EP2			0.016	(0.87)	0.027	(1.26)
EP3			0.002	(0.09)	0.024	(0.74)
EP4			0.248***	(5.93)	0.273***	(5.69)
EP5			0.386***	(7.55)	0.422***	(6.90)
Observations	447		447		447	
Adjusted R-squared	0.758		0.807		0.807	

Note: Dependent variable: average semi-annual participation of a political group. Parameters of the models are estimated by linear regression with robust standard errors. *T*-statistics in parentheses. *Significant at 10%; **significant at 5% ***significant at 1%.

Second, we find that being on the winning side is positively related to participation across all specifications. It increases participation by 14 to 16 per cent. We also find that an increase in the number of MEPs in a given parliament (as a result of enlargement) reduces participation – although the substantive effect of this is small (less than 0.1 per cent) and is only significant in Model 3.

Third, the sign and size of the coefficients for the political group variables captures the pattern observed in Figure 4.2. Specifically, the socialists and EPP participate more than the smaller groups. The only exception is the comparatively small group of British conservatives and allies, which only existed in the first two parliaments.

Finally, the large size of the adjusted R-squared for all models demonstrates that the political considerations analysed in the regressions explain a large amount of the variance in participation rates over time.

Next we investigate the determinants of changes in participation rates between individual votes for all 15,000 votes between 1979 and 2004. Here we are interested in the short run or high-frequency determinants of participation and emphasise therefore the role played by the characteristics of individual votes. As before, we estimate participation in each vote using a linear regression model. The dependent variable in the model is the participation of a political group in a vote. We then use two types of independent variables. First, we include a set of variables that capture the political and institutional character of a vote: a continuous variable that captures how close the vote was, which hypothetically ranges for 0 if a vote is tied to 100 if all the MEPs voted the same way in a vote (*Closeness*); a dummy variable that captures the majority required for the vote to pass, which is coded 1 if an absolute majority (*AM*) of all MEPs was required for the issue to pass rather than simple majority; and five dummy variables for each of the main EU legislative procedures – the co-decision procedure (*COD*), the assent procedure (*AVC*), cooperation procedure (*SYN*), the consultation procedure (*CNS*) and the budgetary procedure (*BUD*). In other words, this model is similar to the models used for explaining time trends, but instead of focusing on the effect of the timing of treaty reforms, this specification allows us to focus on the effect of individual legislative and non-legislative procedures on participation rates at any given time. We estimated separate models for each political group. And because the results are highly similar across the political groups we also calculated an average model for all the political groups.

Table 4.3 presents the average results plus the results for the three main political groups. First, as we predicted, participation is higher in all the legislative procedures and the budgetary procedure than in non-legislative procedures, regardless of the period in question. Also, consistent with the results in Table 4.2, participation is higher under the co-decision procedure than under the cooperation procedure. The different sizes of the coefficients for the main legislative procedures also demonstrate that participation is higher under the co-decision, assent and budgetary procedures than under the consultation procedure, as we predicted.

Second, not surprisingly, the 'absolute majority' requirement (under which legislation can only be passed by a majority of all component MEPs rather than a simple majority of only those participating in a vote)

Table 4.3. *Determinants of political group participation, by individual vote*

	Average, over all political groups		Socialists		EPP		Liberals	
	Coefficient	t-stat.	Coefficient	t-stat.	Coefficient	t-stat.	Coefficient	t-stat.
Closeness	0.042***	(14.02)	0.040***	(11.96)	0.043***	(12.54)	0.032***	(9.33)
AM	0.034***	(8.94)	0.041***	(9.76)	0.041***	(9.40)	0.030***	(6.99)
COD	0.038***	(11.42)	0.042***	(11.40)	0.038***	(9.98)	0.024***	(6.42)
AVC	0.132***	(5.95)	0.117***	(4.76)	0.105***	(4.16)	0.152***	(6.05)
SYN	−0.004	(0.85)	0.040***	(7.83)	0.013*	(2.50)	−0.003	(0.64)
CNS	0.014***	(5.15)	0.019***	(6.11)	0.008***	(2.66)	0.001	(0.48)
BUD	0.145***	(3.42)	0.189***	(35.86)	0.194***	(35.76)	0.119***	(22.18)
EP2	−0.001	(0.17)	0.076***	(14.39)	0.015***	(2.83)	−0.040***	(7.35)
EP3	−0.099***	(21.05)	−0.006	(1.13)	−0.095***	(17.91)	−0.074***	(13.91)
EP4	0.082***	(17.84)	0.115***	(22.76)	0.122***	(23.43)	0.148***	(28.72)
EP5	0.304***	(67.70)	0.300***	(6.54)	0.233***	(45.70)	0.381***	(75.27)
Tuesday	0.154***	(17.97)	0.162***	(17.17)	0.214***	(21.99)	0.132***	(13.70)
Wednesday	0.191***	(22.98)	0.208***	(22.66)	0.258***	(27.42)	0.175***	(18.74)
Thursday	0.051***	(6.16)	0.072***	(7.90)	0.110***	(11.77)	0.048***	(5.20)
Friday	−0.136***	(15.33)	−0.185***	(18.82)	−0.131***	(12.96)	−0.134***	(13.36)
Saturday	−0.052	(1.55)	−0.086**	(2.34)	−0.027	(0.71)	−0.034	(0.91)
Constant	0.267***	(3.09)	0.322***	(32.84)	0.320***	(31.71)	0.262***	(26.18)
Observations	14642		14642		14642		14642	
Adjusted R-squared	0.73		0.65		0.64		0.73	

Note: Dependent variable: participation of a party group in each vote. Parameters of the models are estimated by linear regression with robust standard errors. *T*-statistics in parentheses. *Significant at 10% **significant at 5% ***significant at 1%. The results for the other party groups are not reported.

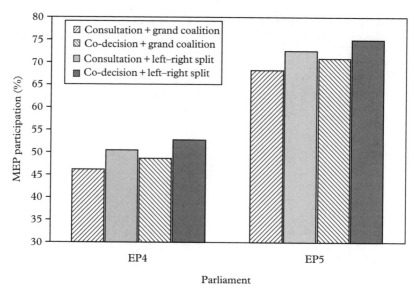

Figure 4.3. Key determinants of participation in the European Parliament

Note: Using the results for the average party group model in Table 4.3, the figure illustrates the absolute effect on participation rates in the fourth and fifth Parliaments of the legislative procedure and the closeness of the vote, holding all other variables at their mean value.

significantly increases participation. This is a result of two effects. One is technical, where the political groups who would like something to pass need to mobilise more members when an absolute-majority is required. The other effect is political, since an absolute-majority is mainly used in the second reading of the co-decision procedure, and hence the use of an absolute-majority in a vote is also capturing the policy-making importance of a vote.

Third, as predicted by the theory, the closeness of a vote is also significant, with a positive sign. This demonstrates that the higher the likelihood that an MEP or political group will be pivotal, the greater the incentive to participate in a vote.

Fourth, and also as expected, participation is lower on Monday, Friday and Saturday, and higher on Tuesday, Wednesday and Thursday.

Figure 4.3 summarises some of the key results. The figure displays two sets of participation rates for the fourth and the fifth parliament's, respectively. For each parliament, we look at the effect of the legislative procedure (consultation or co-decision) and at closeness or lopsidedness. On average, there was approximately a 20 per cent increase in participation between the fourth and fifth parliaments, which reflects an increase in the overall policy-making influence of the European Parliament between 1994 and 2004. Also, the policy-making significance of a vote had an effect within each parliament, as participation was approximately 5 per cent higher in both parliaments in votes where the parliament has co-equal legislative power with the Council (under the co-decision procedure) than in votes where the parliament only had a delay or consultation right (under the consultation procedure). Moreover, participation was higher when votes were split along left–right lines rather than a grand coalition between the two big party groups. In fact, the closeness of a vote is a more powerful influence on participation rates than the legislative power of the parliament and the procedure of the vote because in both parliaments there was higher participation on closely fought votes under the consultation procedure than very one-sided votes under the co-decision procedure.

4.4   Conclusion: politics determines participation

What we find, then, is that MEPs are serious and strategic politicians. Participation in roll-call votes in the European Parliament has risen over time, and by the 1999–2004 parliament was comparable with the level of participation on important legislative issues in most democratic parliaments. Also, the variance in participation rates across all the political groups, both large and small, and across all the member states declined significantly. By the fifth parliament, there was little difference between the MEPs in their propensity to vote.

We also find that strategic considerations by MEPs, as expressed by power of the parliament or closeness of the vote, are the main determinants of participation, both across time and between votes in any particular period. In the early years of the directly elected assembly, when the parliament had little legislative powers and the political group leaders had little possibility of mobilising their 'backbenchers' to turn up to vote, the opportunity cost of participating in votes as opposed to undertaking some other political activity was relatively high. As a result, the average rate of participation in this period was low for most MEPs and all political groups.

However, as the policy-making power of the parliament grew, most notably as a result of the Maastricht Treaty, and as the two largest political groups competed more vigorously to shape policy outcomes in their preferred direction, the incentives for participation increased. For the MEPs in the two main political groups, turning up to vote could be the difference between wining and losing, and staying away would antagonise the party whips and one's political group colleagues. But, even for the smaller political groups, the incentives for participation also grew. With more policy-making power for the parliament, and with votes increasingly split along left–right lines, the chances of being pivotal in determining which side won an important policy battle, increased for all the political groups in the parliament.

Overall, then, the European Parliament is like other democratic assemblies, in that calculations about the political consequences of voting determine individual- and political group-level participation rates. This goes hand in hand with what we demonstrate in the next few chapters, that political interest also shapes relations within and between the parliament's political groups.

5   Trends in party cohesion

If we follow the reasoning from Chapter 2, a strong party system requires that parties are cohesive, in other words that the elected members of the same party vote in a disciplined way, following the position reached by their party leaders in the parliament. A political party will attract support by making commitments to particular policies or goals that are distinct from the commitments of other parties. If a party is able to work as a highly organised team, it will be able to turn these promises into policy outcomes. If a party is not able to 'rally its troops', it will have little chance of shaping policy outcomes, and so will leave its supporters disappointed. Scholars of the EU have hence argued that for transnational parties to increase the democratic accountability of the EU they must be able to act cohesively to implement the policy platforms they announce (e.g. Attinà, 1992; Andeweg, 1995; Hix and Lord, 1997). If voting in the European Parliament breaks down along national lines rather than party lines, the transnational political groups cannot claim to be able to articulate the classic ideological viewpoints in the EU policy-making process with any real degree of effectiveness. Testing for the cohesiveness of parties is the first natural step towards understanding the effectiveness of parties. As in the previous chapter, where we looked at the long-run and short-run determinants of participation, we analyse in this chapter the long-run determinants of cohesion. In the next chapter, we look more closely at the short-run determinants of cohesion.

Previous studies of roll-call voting in the European Parliament suggests that the political groups in the European Parliament are relatively cohesive when compared with parties in the US Congress (e.g. Attinà, 1990; Quanjel and Wolters, 1993; Brzinski, 1995; Raunio, 1997). However, previous research was based on small samples of votes and thus could not establish how party cohesion has evolved in the twenty-five years since the first European Parliament elections in 1979. Moreover, previous research did not analyse which factors explain variations in the level of voting cohesion of a particular political group.

In this chapter we use our dataset of roll-call votes to analyse in detail how party cohesion has changed in the European Parliament and what explains these changes. The chapter is organised as follows. Section 5.1 discusses some theoretical explanations of party cohesion from the general political science literature and the existing research on the European Parliament. Section 5.2 then introduces how we measure voting cohesion in the European Parliament. Section 5.3 describes the main trends in party cohesion across the five directly elected parliaments. In Section 5.4 we then investigate the causes of these trends using a statistical analysis.

What we find is that voting in the European Parliament is primarily along party lines rather than national lines, and is increasingly so. We also find that as the powers of the European Parliament have increased, the political parties in the Parliament have become increasingly cohesive, despite growing ideological and national diversity amongst their members. However, national fragmentation of the political groups has a negative effect on cohesion. This suggests that the difficulty of overcoming the collective action problem, rather than ideological diversity *per se*, affects party cohesion. Overall, these results suggest an optimistic message for democratic politics in the EU, since more power for the Parliament would lead to more powerful transnational political parties.

5.1   Theories of party cohesion

The general political science literature on legislative institutions and behaviour predicts that the cohesion of parliamentary parties is explained by two types of institutions: (1) external institutions, namely the structure of relations between the parliament and the executive; and (2) internal institutions, namely the structure of incentives inside a parliament.

On the external side, legislative parties are more cohesive in parliamentary than in presidential systems (e.g. Huber, 1996a; Shugart and Carey, 1992; Bowler et al., 1999; Tsebelis, 2002, ch. 3). In parliamentary systems, where the executive is 'fused' to a parliamentary majority, survival of the executive depends constantly on majority support as a vote of confidence motion by a majority can cause a government to fall at any time. This creates strong incentives for cohesion because parties in government do not want to lose the precious rents associated with holding office (Huber, 1996b; Diermeier and Feddersen, 1998; Persson et al., 2000). Governments can reward loyal backbenchers with ministerial seats or punish disloyal representatives by refusing them future political jobs and even denying them future re-election. The re-election prospects of the parliamentarians from the governing parties are also closely associated with the performance of their party leaders in government (Cox, 1987).

In contrast, in 'separated-powers' systems, where the executive cannot be sacked by a parliamentary majority, parties in government are less able to enforce party discipline amongst their supporters in the parliament (Rohde, 1991; Krehbiel, 1998; Cameron, 2000). Even if the party controlling the executive has a majority in the legislature, loyalty to their party leaders in the executive is less important since lack of discipline does not threaten survival of the executive. Also, because the elections for the executive and the legislature are held separately, and usually at different times, the connection between the performance of a party in government and the re-election prospects of its legislative representatives is less direct than in parliamentary systems (Alesina and Rosenthal, 1995; Shugart and Carey, 1992).

Institutionally, as we discussed in Chapter 1, the EU has some characteristics of a separated-powers system, where the executive (the Commission) does not require the support of a majority in the European Parliament to govern once it has been elected. The Commission cannot introduce a vote-of-confidence motion in the European Parliament or dissolve the parliament, leading to new parliamentary elections. The Commission can only be censured by a 'double-majority': a two-thirds majority vote that must constitute an 'absolute majority' of all MEPs. This high voting threshold means that in practice the censure procedure in the European Parliament is more akin to the power of a parliament in a separated-powers system to 'impeach' the president than the ability of the majority in a parliamentary system to sack a government.

Nevertheless, even in separated-powers systems, the structure of incentives inside the legislature can lead to powerful legislative party organisations. As discussed in Chapter 2, legislators who expect to have similar preferences on a range of policy issues can reduce the transaction costs of coalition formation by establishing a party organisation (Kiewiet and McCubbins, 1991; Cox and McCubbins, 1993: 83–136). This party organisation constitutes a division-of-labour contract, where backbenchers provide labour and capital (such as information gathering and policy expertise) while leaders distribute committee and party offices, communicate party positions and enforce the terms of the party organisation contract. The party will benefit from reduced volatility of voting and higher predictability, a better reputation of reliability with voters and more efficiency in decision-making thanks to better specialisation and inclusive agendas.

The benefits associated with joining a party organisation also entail costs. Sometimes the party takes a position that may be unpopular with particular constituencies of a legislator. In this situation, a legislator may vote against her party to signal to supporters that the party's position is not radical enough. But, by doing so, she may contribute to the defeat of her party's position and give the majority to her political enemies. Recent theory shows indeed that there are two motives in voting: communication and decision (Piketty, 2000; Castanheira, 2003). In the former, a vote is used to communicate one's policy preferences; in the latter a vote is used to help obtain a majority. But, it is reasonable to assume that when there is more at stake in a vote, the decision motive is stronger than the communication motive.

Since the EU is not a parliamentary system with a governing majority and an opposition, the national and European parties that make up the Commission and the Council must build coalitions in the European Parliament on a case-by-case basis. Hence, we can expect the parties in the European Parliament to be significantly less cohesive than parties in parliamentary systems and have similar cohesion levels to parties in separated-powers systems. However, since the European Parliament has less power than many legislative chambers in separated-powers systems (such as the US Congress), we would expect the communication motive to be at least as important as the decision motive, and hence undermine cohesion in the European Parliament. But increased powers of the Parliament should lead to increased cohesion of party groups because with higher stakes the decision motive should outweigh the communication motive.

But the reverse may also be true. With more powers, national parties have more incentives to influence how 'their' MEPs vote if their policy preferences diverge from those of their European party group. For example, case studies of particular high-profile votes show that party cohesion can be undermined when important national interests are at stake, as we show in Chapters 10 and 11 (e.g. Hix and Lord, 1996; Gabel and Hix 2002a). Moreover, MEPs from national parties that are in government in the domestic arena might come under particular pressure, as these parties are represented in the other branch of the EU legislature (the Council) and so are likely to have high stakes in votes in the parliament.

These theoretical arguments give primacy to institutions as the main determinants of legislative behaviour. One could argue that this view undervalues the role of policy preferences or 'ideology' in driving how MEPs vote.[1] If ideology drives legislative voting, then increased

---

[1] In the US context, Poole and Rosenthal's (1997) work provides a more ideological view of Congressional voting.

homogeneity of policy preferences within a party should produce more party cohesion. The problem is that often ideology and interest produce observationally equivalent predictions (Krehbiel, 1993: 237). For example, if a high percentage of legislators of the same party vote the same way in a vote, the party organisation is assumed to have produced this cohesion. But if these legislators would have voted the same way because they share the same preferences, the effect of party organisation, independent of the legislators' preferences, could not be determined.

To summarise, political science theory suggests that there are incentives for Members of the European Parliament to form parties and act cohesively. However, the leaders of the parties in the European Parliament are unlikely to be able to enforce party discipline as effectively as the leaders of parties at the domestic level in Europe. Moreover, when seeking to explain variations in party cohesion, theory suggests that we need to look at measures of ideological closeness as well as the effectiveness of political group organisation and the changing powers of the European Parliament. The European Parliament is an especially interesting arena for studying voting cohesion because the institutions governing its functioning have changed in the twenty-five years since the first direct election of the European Parliament.

5.2   Measuring cohesion in the European Parliament

To measure party cohesion we use an 'Agreement Index' as follows:

$$AI_i = \frac{\max\{Y_i, N_i, A_i\} - \frac{1}{2}[(Y_i + N_i + A_i) - \max\{Y_i, N_i, A_i\}]}{(Y_i + N_i + A_i)}$$

where Y_i denotes the number of Yes votes expressed by group i on a given vote, N_i the number of No votes and A_i the number of Abstain votes. The Agreement Index consequently equals 1 when all the members of a party vote together and equals 0 when the members of a party are equally divided between all three of these voting options. For example, if a party casts 30 votes and all the party members vote Yes, the cohesion index is 1. But, if these deputies are completely divided, with 10 voting Yes, 10 voting No and 10 Abstaining, the cohesion index is 0.

This agreement index is similar but not identical to other measures of cohesion in parliaments. For example, Rice's 'index of voting likeness' is the absolute difference between the number of Yes and No votes of the members of a party, divided by the sum of the Yes and No votes (Rice,

1928).[2] However, the problem with the Rice index is that it cannot be used when parliamentarians have three voting options, as in the European Parliament (where MEPs can record a Yes, No or Abstain vote). Attinà (1990) consequently developed a cohesion measure specifically for the European Parliament, where the highest voting option minus the sum of the second and third options was divided by the sum of all three options. But the Attinà index can produce negative scores on individual votes, since if a party is split equally between all three voting options the Attinà index produces a cohesion score of −0.333.

Our Agreement Index is an alternative to the Rice and Attinà indices for measuring party cohesion in the European Parliament (or in any parliament that has three voting options) since it enables all three voting choices to be taken into account, and produces cohesion scores on a scale from 0 to 1. Nevertheless, the cohesion scores produced by our index can be compared with scores produced by these other two indices. Our results are perfectly correlated with the Attinà scores, as our index is simply a re-scaling of the scores from 0 to 1, and correlate at the 0.98 level with the Rice scores for the same data on the European Parliament. It is worth noting, however, that the Rice index and our index are quite different for parties that tend to Abstain as a block. For example, if a party is split between 10 Yes votes, 10 No votes and 100 Abstain votes, the Rice index would measure the party as completely divided (0.000) whereas our index would show the party as quite cohesive (0.750).

If there is not much variation in the overall majority size in a parliament in different periods, the cohesion of a party in one period can be easily compared with the cohesion of a party in another period. However, if there is considerable variation in the overall majority size, measuring the absolute level of cohesion of a party is deceptive, as parties will inherently be more cohesive if all the parties are voting the same way (in a 'lop-sided' vote) than if a vote is more evenly split. As Figure 5.1 shows, the majority size of the European Parliament as a whole varied considerably between 1979 and 2004. The cohesion of the whole parliament increased between 1979 and 1987 but declined afterwards. Put another way, the political groups were inherently more likely to be cohesive in the third parliament than in the first or fifth parliaments.

---

[2] To measure the difference between how committee members and other party members vote in the US Congress, Cox and McCubbins (1993) develop a variant of Rice's 'index of vote likeness', which they call the 'mean absolute difference' (MAD) index: whereby the absolute difference between the per cent of committee contingents from the same party voting Yes and the rest of the party voting Yes is averaged across a set of votes. In other words, this is Rice's index applied to the difference between committee contingents and parties rather than between parties.

Figure 5.1. Cohesion of the European Parliament as a whole

Note: This graph shows the average 'agreement index' of the European Parliament as a whole in all votes in a six-month period, calculated as a two-period moving average.

So, to be able to compare cohesion scores in different periods in the European Parliament we also calculate a 'relative cohesion' index. We do this by dividing the Agreement Index of each political group (or national group of MEPs) in a given period by the Agreement Index of the parliament as a whole in the same period. We then divide the resulting score by 2 so that the 'relative cohesion' index scores are predominantly between 0 and 1, and are hence comparable with the 'absolute cohesion' scores. This is a better measure of cohesion as it explains the cohesion of party groups relative to the cohesion of the parliament as a whole.

5.3 Main trends: growing party voting and declining national voting

Table 5.1 shows the average relative cohesion index of each of the six main political groups in all the roll-call votes in each of the five parliaments since 1979. Figure 5.2 then shows the average relative cohesion of the *political* groups in each parliament relative to the average relative cohesion of each *national* group of MEPs in each parliament. The dotted lines represent the standard deviations around these averages.

Table 5.1 and Figure 5.2 illustrate three clear trends. First, in general, political parties are more cohesive than national groups of MEPs. The

Table 5.1. *Average relative cohesion of the six main political groups*

	1979–1984	1984–1989	1989–1994	1994–1999	1999–2004
Socialists	0.754	0.781	0.770	0.831	0.931
EPP	0.888	0.850	0.764	0.833	0.897
Liberals	0.833	0.759	0.726	0.791	0.919
Gaullists	0.783	0.763	0.778	0.734	0.787
Radical Left	0.817	0.804	0.753	0.756	0.831
Greens	—	0.753	0.755	0.860	0.971

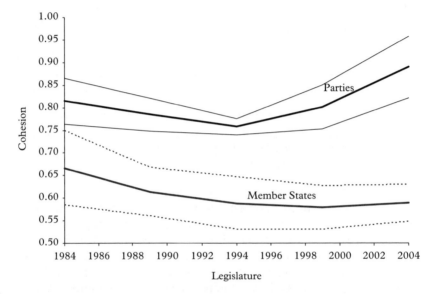

Figure 5.2. Average relative cohesion of the political groups and the member states

average relative cohesion score of the six main political groups in the European Parliament across the whole period from 1979 to 2004 was 0.809. In contrast, the average relative cohesion score of each national group of MEPs from all fifteen member states in the whole period was 0.603, which is significantly lower.

Second, whereas party cohesion has increased, the voting cohesion of national groups of MEPs has declined. The average relative cohesion of the six main political groups in the parliament rose from 0.814 in the first parliament to 0.889 in the fifth parliament. In contrast, the average relative cohesion of each national group of MEPs declined from 0.667 in the first parliament to 0.589 in the fifth parliament.

Third, as Table 5.1 shows, the two largest political groups, the socialists and EPP, have generally been more cohesive than the smaller parties. The average relative cohesion score of the two largest parties was 0.821 in the first parliament, which rose to 0.914 in the fifth parliament. Interestingly, though, in the fourth and fifth parliaments, the greens emerged as more cohesive than either of the two big groups.

Overall, party cohesion has thus risen while national cohesion has declined, and the big parties seem more cohesive than the smaller parties. However, we cannot tell from these aggregate data whether these trends are a result of the changing powers of the European Parliament or the changing internal make-up of the political groups, or both.

5.4   Determinants of party cohesion in the European Parliament

To investigate the determinants of the changing patterns of cohesion within each political party we undertake a statistical analysis. We first introduce the variables we use in this analysis before presenting the results.

5.4.1   Variables

We take as the dependent variable the average relative cohesion index of each of the six main political groups in each of the fifty six-month periods between July 1979 and June 2004. Five of the political groups were present in all five parliaments, while one of the political groups (the greens) was present in only four parliaments. This gives us a total of 290 observations (5 parties in 50 periods, plus 1 party in 40 periods).

We use three types of explanatory variables: (1) roll-call vote characteristics; (2) characteristics of political groups; and (3) a measure of the power of the European Parliament.

For the first type, we use the number of roll-call votes in a given period (*No. of RCVs*).[3] Including this variable enables us to investigate whether more roll-call votes reduce or increase party cohesion. A higher frequency of roll-call votes may indicate changes in the level of issue intensity, since if an issue is highly contentious, one could expect more amendments to be proposed and hence more votes to be held.

Turning to political group characteristics, we look at a number of variables that measure the impact of group size and internal national and ideological diversity on party cohesion. First, we include the size of the group as a percentage of all MEPs (*Political group size*). Larger parties

---

[3] This variable is divided by 1000; otherwise the estimated coefficients are very small.

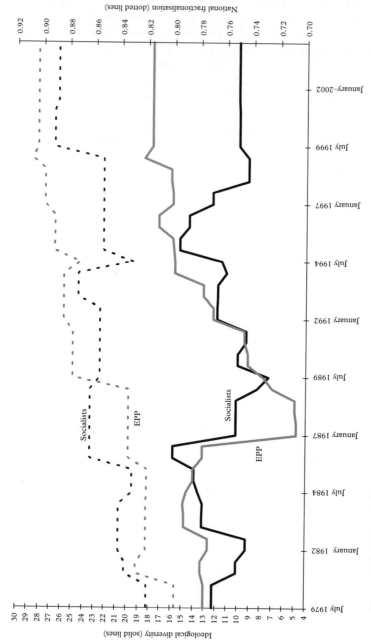

Figure 5.3. National fractionalisation and ideological diversity in the two main groups

are likely to be more often in the majority because of their sheer size. If that is the case, the incentives for cohesion might be stronger because a party that is more often in the majority has higher stakes in being cohesive. The relationship between size and cohesion is not necessarily a monotonic relationship as small centrist parties might be pivotal more often. In any case, size may potentially positively affect cohesion.

Second, to measure national diversity in a political group we use the level of 'fractionalisation' of the group between its national member parties (*National fractionalisation*). We use Rae's (1967) measure of the fractionalisation of a political body, where the fractionalisation of a political group is calculated as follows:

$$National \ fractionalisation_i = 1 - \sum_{j=1}^{n_i} s_{ji}^2$$

where s_{ji} is the share of national party j in political group i with n_i national parties. As Figure 5.3 shows, national fractionalisation has increased in the two main political groups. This is partly a result of successive EU enlargements to smaller countries than the EU average,[4] but is also due to the expansion of these groups to include several national parties that previously sat in one or other of the smaller groups. Fragmentation can be seen as a proxy for the difficulty of overcoming the internal collective action problem discussed in Chapter 2. Indeed, in a case of low fragmentation, for example, a party with a large delegation from one member state and smaller delegations from the others, an agreement will be more easily reached as the large national delegation will be less tempted to free-ride on the others. It will also be in a more hegemonic position and have strong agenda-setting powers. On the other hand, with high fragmentation, say with many small national delegations from all member states, there will be more free-riding and bargaining to reach an agreement will be tougher.

Third, to measure the ideological profile of a political group we use an established exogenous measure of national party policy positions: the Manifestos Research Group dataset (Budge et al., 2001). We start with the left–right position of each national party in a political group in each of the six-month periods between 1979 and 2001.[5] From these national party locations we calculated the mean left–right position of each political group by multiplying the position of each national party in the group by the

[4] This is a purely mechanical effect, as adding a political group with a smaller than average size increases measured fragmentation.
[5] We use the Budge et al. (2001) 'integrated' left–right measure, which includes party manifesto statements covering socio-economic and socio-political issues.

percentage of MEPs of that national party in the group. We then calculated two variables: (1) the distance between the mean left–right position of the political group and the mean left–right position of the European Parliament as a whole (*Political group ideology*) and (2) the internal ideological diversity of a political group (*Ideological diversity*). The internal ideological diversity of a political group was calculated as follows:

$$Ideological\ diversity_i = \sum_{j=1}^{n_i} |NP_j - MEAN_i| s_{ji}$$

where NP_j is the left–right location of national party j, $MEAN_i$ is the weighted mean location of political group i, and s_{ji} is the share of national party j in political group i. As Figure 5.3 shows, there has been substantial variation in ideological diversity within the two main political groups, and growing ideological diversity in the EPP since 1987. The variations in ideological diversity result from the changing membership of the groups as well as the changing ideological positions of the national member parties of the groups, as expressed in the manifestos of these parties when a national election is held. In particular, the growing ideological diversity in the EPP is explained by the enlargement of the EU, which has increased the heterogeneity of the membership of all the political groups, and expansion of the EPP to incorporate several of the smaller groups. For example, as a result of the merger of several of the smaller conservative groups into the EPP, the EPP is now a 'broad church' of more centrist Christian democrats and more right-wing conservative and nationalist parties.

Fourth, the last variable looking at internal characteristics of a political group is the percentage of MEPs in a political group who are from national parties that are in national government (*% of NPs in government*). Here we use the data on the partisan make-up of governments in Europe in Müller and Strøm (2000), which we updated in 2004 with our own research. This variable investigates whether MEPs from parties in government are more or less likely to vote with their party group. It is not clear *a priori* what the effect of this variable should be. One possibility might be that more MEPs from national parties in government might lower cohesion as it would force MEPs to vote with their country rather than with their European political group. However, one might also argue that a deal reached in the Council has a strong support among all parties in government and that the latter would put pressure on MEPs to support the deal in the European Parliament. This would be all the more the case if a European political group is strongly represented in the Council (cf. Hoyland, 2005).

In the third type of explanatory variable we include four variables that measure the power of the European Parliament. First, we include three dummy variables representing the increases in the Parliament's powers in the three Treaty reforms since the mid-1980s: the Single European Act (*SEA*), which takes the value 0 for each period up to January–June 1987 and 1 thereafter; the Maastricht Treaty (*Maastricht*), which takes the value 0 for each period up to January–June 1993 and 1 thereafter; and the Amsterdam Treaty (*Amsterdam*), which takes the value 0 for each period up to January–June 1999 and 1 thereafter. Second, we include a variable (*Trend*) representing the time trend from 1979 to 2004, which takes the value 1 for the first six-month period, (July–December 1979), 2 for the second period, and so on.

In addition to a constant, we include five dummy variables indicating the political groups (*EPP, Liberal, Gaullist, Left, Green*). These dummies capture the effect of party-specific factors that do not vary over time. The estimates associated with these dummies represent the difference between the level of cohesion of these political groups and the socialists, which is the reference group. Regressions including these dummies focus not on the variation between the political groups but rather on the patterns of variation *within* each of the political groups. This is important to bear in mind when interpreting the results of the econometric analysis.

Finally, we include dummy variables for the three enlargements of the EU in this period: *Enlargement1* for Greece in 1981 (which takes the value 0 for every period before to January 1981 and 1 thereafter); *Enlargement2* for Spain and Portugal in 1986; and *Enlargement3* for Austria, Sweden and Finland in 1995.[6]

5.4.2   *Results*

Table 5.2 shows the results of the estimations of relative party cohesion in the European Parliament between 1979 and 2004 with fixed effects for parties (relative to the socialists). Note first that the *National fractionalisation* and *Political group size* variables are highly correlated, so too are the variables indicating the power of the European Parliament (*SEA, Maastricht, Amsterdam*) and the *Trend* variable. We consequently check the sensitivity of our results to this problem by excluding one of the two correlated variables in separate models.[7]

---

[6] Our data go until 2004 and thus do not cover the enlargement of the European Parliament to 25 countries after the 2004 elections.

[7] We also checked for other potential problems. First, non-stationarity of our dependent variables may be a source of concern, given that we have 50 time periods. Performing tests of unit roots in panels, however, leads us to reject the null hypothesis of non-stationarity. Second, to check for heteroskedasticity, we use fixed effects and

Table 5.2. *Determinants of party cohesion*

	Model 1	Model 2	Model 3	Model 4
Constant	0.833**	0.674**	0.826**	0.838**
	(22.16)	(27.17)	(2.96)	(2.22)
No. of RCVs	−0.105*	−0.102*	−0.076	−0.035
	(2.16)	(2.05)	(1.48)	(0.69)
Political group size	0.033**	0.038**	0.027*	0.051**
	(3.13)	(3.31)	(2.56)	(4.19)
National fractionalisation	−0.207**		−0.192**	−0.202**
	(5.87)		(5.43)	(5.22)
Political group ideology	0.000	−0.001	0.000	0.000
	(0.64)	(1.57)	(0.09)	(0.98)
Ideological diversity	0.000	0.001	0.001	0.000
	(0.35)	(1.60)	(0.90)	(0.21)
% of NPs in government	0.044**	0.048**	0.042**	0.052**
	(3.31)	(3.62)	(3.08)	(3.60)
SEA	−0.065**	−0.066**	−0.037	
	(2.93)	(2.88)	(1.91)	
Maastricht	0.014	0.012	0.041*	
	(0.64)	(0.54)	(2.19)	
Amsterdam	0.054*	0.053*	0.085**	
	(2.55)	(2.43)	(4.53)	
Trend	0.004*	0.003*		0.004**
	(2.49)	(2.15)		(4.05)
EPP	0.033**	0.033**	0.032**	0.034**
	(5.32)	(5.05)	(5.17)	(5.30)
Liberal	0.047**	0.053**	0.038**	0.071**
	(3.11)	(3.30)	(2.58)	(4.12)
Left	−0.003	0.061**	−0.007	0.026
	(0.16)	(2.91)	(0.33)	(1.00)
Gaullist	−0.041	0.030	−0.048*	−0.007
	(1.72)	(1.29)	(2.07)	(0.24)
Green	0.062**	0.086**	0.065**	0.081**
	(3.03)	(3.89)	(3.27)	(3.33)
Enlargement1	0.012	0.012	0.031	−0.002
	(0.68)	(0.66)	(1.79)	(0.12)
Enlargement2	−0.029	−0.025	−0.007	−0.084**
	(1.71)	(1.44)	(0.38)	(4.91)
Enlargement3	0.004	−0.012	0.022	0.011
	(0.22)	(0.69)	(1.18)	(0.59)
Observations	290	290	290	290
R-squared	0.495	0.455	0.473	0.401

Note: Dependent variable: relative cohesion of a political group in a six-month period between 1979 and 2004. Parameters of the models are estimated by fixed effects with panel-corrected standard errors and correction for heteroskedasticity and correlations between parties. Robust *t*-statistics in parentheses, *significant at 10%; **significant at 5%; ***significant at 1%.

Several conclusions can be drawn from these results. First, an increase in the size of a political group will lead to higher cohesion. In fact, a 5 percentage point increase in the share of seats of a political group corresponds with a 0.19 per cent increase in the cohesion of the group, as measured by our Agreement Index.[8] This thus confirms the idea that an increase in size of a political group makes it more likely to influence policy outcomes and thus have bigger stakes in votes. This effect is of first-order importance to explain the increase in cohesion because the main political groups (socialists, EPP, liberals and greens) have tended to see their size increase over time, and quite clearly so since 1989, while the smaller political groups have become more fragmented and less cohesive.

Second, increased internal fractionalisation of a political group along national lines decreases party cohesion. A 10 per cent increase in the national fractionalisation of a political group leads to a 1.9 per cent decrease in the cohesion of the group. This confirms the hypothesis of the internal collective action problem between the national parties in the parliament.

Third, the ideological variables do not have a significant effect on party cohesion. When a political group moves further away or nearer to the mean of the European Parliament as a whole, the group's cohesion is not affected. Also, when a political group becomes more ideologically heterogeneous (when ideological diversity increases), the group's cohesion does not decline. In other words, the effect of internal *national* diversity is larger and more significant than the effect of internal *ideological* diversity.

These two results suggest a particular interpretation of the effectiveness of party discipline in the European Parliament. The fact that variation in ideological diversity has no effect on cohesion indicates that policy preferences of MEPs and national parties alone cannot explain variations in party cohesion. Policy preferences surely matter for policy and for coalition formation, as we will see in Chapter 8. However, they do not explain cohesion within political groups. In other words, if MEPs are more or less cohesive, it is not because they have closer or more distant policy preferences. If this were the case, then the econometric analysis would have detected an effect. What we find instead is that variations in ideological diversity are successfully buffered by the

panel-corrected standard errors. Thus, we controlled for both heteroskedasticity and correlation across political groups. Third, to check for serial auto-correlation (if the error term for a political group is correlated across time periods) we specified models that correct for first-order and second-order auto-correlations. This did not change the direction or significance of the reported results.

[8] The substantive elasticities are calculated at the means of the dependent and independent variables using the results in model 3.

discipline of the transnational party organisations. But the ability of European parties to discipline their members is limited by national fractionalisation. In other words, the national parties are able to partly overcome their collective action problems by agreeing to vote together on most issues. However, their ability to agree is limited by the degree of fractionalisation. It is thus the varying difficulty to reach an agreement, *independent of the issues to be agreed on*, that explains variation in cohesion.

These are interesting insights for political science. They show that a theory of cohesion based on preferences alone is rejected in the case of the European Parliament. On the other hand, they show that fractionalisation of a party is an impediment to overcoming the internal collective action problem.

Fourth, the percentage of MEPs from parties in government has a significant effect. But more MEPs from parties in government actually lead to higher, rather than lower, party cohesion. Pressure from parties in national government thus produces more cohesion rather than less. One must remember that the European Parliament generally does not initiate legislation. Legislation is initiated by the Commission that is usually most concerned about the prospect of a veto in the Council. If the Council then adopts a legislative proposal, one may expect parties from national governments to put pressure on their MEPs to ensure that this legislation passes the hurdle of the European Parliament. This is thus a new and interesting finding.

Fifth, our results confirm that the political groups have become more cohesive over time. In terms of specific Treaty reforms, the Amsterdam Treaty had a clear effect of increasing party cohesion, whereas the Maastricht Treaty did not, and party cohesion actually declined following the entry into force of the SEA, all other things being equal. The political groups were 11 per cent more cohesive after the introduction of the Amsterdam Treaty than before. This perhaps illustrates the importance of the Amsterdam Treaty in terms of the reform and extension of the European Parliament's powers in the EU legislative process, as discussed in Chapter 1. This also indicates that more power to the European Parliament has led to more rather than less party cohesion. Note too that the various enlargements of the EU have not had a significant effect on party cohesion, whereas one could have expected a negative effect – although the enlargement effect is partly picked up in the national fractionalisation measure.

Sixth, regarding the coefficients for the individual political groups, we see that the EPP, the liberals and the greens have tended to be more cohesive than the socialists, everything else being equal.

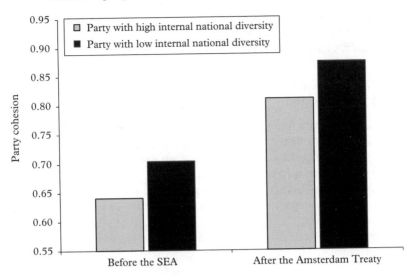

Figure 5.4. Key factors affecting party cohesion

Note: Using the results from Model 1 in Table 5.2, the figure illustrates the effect of a change of one standard deviation (either up or down from the mean) in the level of national fractionalisation on the level of relative cohesion of a political group in the first and fifth parliaments, holding all other variables at their mean value.

Figure 5.4 illustrates the relative effects of two of the key determinants of party cohesion in the European Parliament: (1) the level of internal national diversity, expressed by the fractionalisation of party groups and (2) the power of the institution. An increase in national fractionalisation, for example, if a political group expands to add new member parties, leads to a decrease in the level of cohesion of a political group. Also, the increase in the powers of the European Parliament through the Treaty reforms in the 1980s and 1990s has led to more well-organised and cohesive transnational parties. Moreover, the size of the effect of the increased powers of the parliament is larger than the effect of national diversity. A party that had a low level of national fractionalisation in the first parliament but was then more internally fractionalised by the fifth parliament (for example, as a result of an expanded membership) was still more cohesive in the fifth parliament than in the first parliament because of the increased incentives for acting cohesively with policy-making influence at stake. This is strong suggestive evidence that power to influence policy is a key determinant of cohesion in parliaments. The more power a parliament has, the more lower parties have an incentive to get together to form a cohesive bloc to compete with other blocs to secure their collective policy aims.

5.5   Conclusion: growing policy-making power leads to growing party cohesion

Our results indicate that the political parties in the European Parliament have become increasingly well organised. The cohesion of the political groups has increased over time as the main groups have gained in size and as the powers of the Parliament have increased. This increase in cohesion has occurred despite an increase in the internal national fractionalisation of the parties, which we have shown to have a significant negative effect on cohesion. This indicates that the transnational European parties are able to have a disciplining effect on their national member parties. Also, while cohesion of parties has grown, cohesion of the Parliament as a whole has decreased steadily since the late 1980s due to a decline in the number of votes that are highly consensual.

These results are remarkable given the specific institutional structure of the EU. The Commission is not based on a coalition of parties commanding a majority in the European Parliament. As a result, party leaders in the European Parliament cannot use the traditional threat of government collapse to enforce party discipline within their own ranks.

Our findings consequently suggest a particular explanation of political organisation and behaviour in the European Parliament. The relatively high and increasing levels of party cohesion, and the declining levels of national cohesion, suggest that the external and internal institutional context of the European Parliament provides considerable, and increasing, incentives for the establishment of binding division-of-labour contracts (party organisations) between MEPs who have similar party-political preferences rather than national preferences. This leads to party organisations based on transnational party families, and increasing cohesion within these organisations, despite growing internal ideological and national diversity within these parties.

These conclusions suggest that as the powers of the European Parliament have increased, the organisational power of the transnational parties has also increased. More power to the European Parliament has meant more cohesion of the European political groups in the long run.

6   Agenda-setting and cohesion

In the previous chapter we discussed long-term trends in party cohesion and found that increased powers to the European Parliament had led to increased cohesion of parties. Here we focus on the short-run determinants of cohesion and look at the characteristics of particular votes: how important they are, who sets the agenda and for what purpose, and so on.

As discussed in the previous chapter, there are several competing explanations of why parliamentary parties are cohesive. If the members of the party share the same preferences over policy, then on most issues these members will vote together naturally, without the need for any additional pressure or incentives from the party leadership. We found evidence that, despite increased ideological diversity (as a result of expansion of most of the groups to new parties from the existing member states and new member states), voting cohesion has increased and not decreased, suggesting that preferences alone cannot explain cohesion. We presented evidence that suggests that the explanation of cohesion based on the idea that the members of the political groups in the European Parliament have homogeneous *a priori* preferences does not hold. We showed, for example, that growing internal ideological diversity in the political groups had no negative effect on the cohesion of the groups.

Figure 6.1 illustrates the difference between policy preferences of MEPs and their voting behaviour. In a survey of the MEPs in the fifth European Parliament (1999–2004) by the European Parliament Research Group, the MEPs were asked, among other things, to locate themselves on a 10-point left–right scale, where 1 represented the furthest left position and 10 represented the furthest right position.[1] Figure 6.1a shows the distribution of the 61 socialist and 72 EPP MEPs

---

[1] See www.lse.ac.uk/collections/EPRG/survey.htm

(a) Left–right self-placement

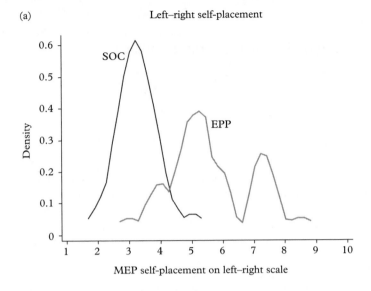

MEP self-placement on left–right scale

(b) NOMINATE location

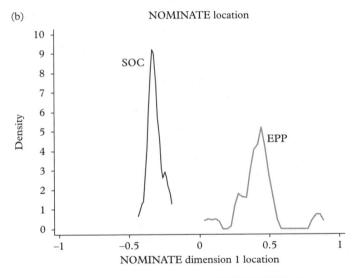

NOMINATE dimension 1 location

Figure 6.1. MEP Self-placement and NOMINATE locations in the fifth parliament

who responded to this question. In comparison, Figure 6.1b shows the distribution of the 'revealed' voting locations of these same 133 MEPs on the first dimension produced by applying the NOMINATE scaling method (Poole and Rosenthal, 1997) to the roll-call votes in the fifth parliament.[2] In terms of basic ideological preferences of MEPs, Figure 6.1a reveals a considerable overlap between the socialist and EPP members, with some members of the socialists (such as some of the British Labour MEPs) placing themselves in the middle of the ideological spectrum and some members of the EPP (such as the Belgian and Italian Christian democrats) placing themselves considerably to the left. Nevertheless, Figure 6.1b shows that, in their revealed voting behaviour, the centrist socialists voted more with their socialist colleagues to their left than with the ideologically closer EPP MEPs, while the centre-left EPP members voted more with their EPP colleagues to their right than with the ideologically closer socialist MEPs. Hence, despite internal ideological heterogeneity, the political groups in the European Parliament are capable of acting as independent and cohesive political organisations.

This pattern of behaviour could be the result of party members forcing their members to follow voting instructions. In most parliaments, party leaders can enforce party discipline with a variety of carrots and sticks, such as promises of promotion to key political offices in the parliament or the threat of expulsion from the party.

Alternatively, party leaders can use their control of the agenda to ensure party cohesion despite diverse policy preferences amongst their members (cf. Cox and McCubbins, 2005). The idea here is that there are high transaction costs associated with the use of 'carrots and sticks' to discipline elected representatives. A cheaper method is to use control of the legislative agenda to filter out proposals and bills that threaten to divide the party and to only put forward bills and proposals for which there is sufficient support among the rank and file legislators. This presupposes that the party leaders control the legislative agenda so that they can ensure that issues only arise on which their party members have similar policy preferences, and so will naturally vote together on these issues.

If cohesion cannot be explained by policy preferences alone, the question remains open of whether cohesion is a result of party pressure or party leadership agenda control. Do MEPs follow voting instructions because of incentives and threats from their leaders? Or do MEPs vote together because their party leaders only allow votes to take place on issues on which they are certain their members will back them? To answer these questions, one needs to look at agenda-setting in

---

[2] NOMINATE is a well-known scaling method used in political science to map the voting behavior of individual legislators in a multi-dimensional space. We discuss in Chapter 9 the application of NOMINATE to the European Parliament because it is a useful tool for identifying how many independent dimensions one detects in voting behavior and what the main lines of conflict in a parliament are.

the European Parliament. Our findings are instructive because the European Parliament is particularly interesting in terms of who holds agenda-setting powers. The Commission has the exclusive right of legislative initiative, which means that many votes in the European Parliament escape agenda control of the majority party leadership in the European Parliament. Moreover, agenda-setting powers are much more dispersed than in a normal parliamentary regime, and arguably more than in most existing presidential systems. It is thus possible to differentiate between votes where agenda control applies and votes where it does not.

The rest of this chapter is organised as follows. In the next section we discuss the general theory of agenda-setting and how the agenda is shaped in the European Parliament, and set out some propositions about what we should expect to observe in voting in the European Parliament if the leadership pressure or agenda-control explanations are correct. Section 6.2 then presents some descriptive evidence of agenda control, which suggests that different 'agenda cartels' existed in each European Parliament, but these cartels are relatively weak. Section 6.3 then tests the theories more directly, with a statistical analysis of the determinants of party cohesion in each individual roll-call vote since 1979.

We find that no single party (or coalition of parties) can restrict the agenda sufficiently to ensure that votes are only held on issues on which the party's (or parties') members have homogeneous preferences. This is because the policy agenda in the European Parliament is set externally to the parliament, by the European Commission, as well as internally, by the political groups. Also, agenda-setting offices inside the parliament are allocated to the political groups broadly in proportion to their size. Consequently, because of these institutional barriers to agenda control, growing party cohesion in the European Parliament cannot be explained by strategic agenda control by the political parties.

6.1   Agenda-setting and political parties

6.1.1   The agenda cartel theory of parties

The issues a parliament tackles are not chosen randomly. Decisions are made about when an issue is put to the floor, who makes the proposal and whether the proposal can be amended. As we discussed in Chapter 2, if a parliament operates according to an 'open' and competitive agenda-setting procedure, whereby any member of the chamber can make a proposal, then policies are likely to converge on the median member of the chamber. This is because any proposal or counter proposal made by the median member of the chamber will be supported by a majority of the chamber, either to the left or to the right of this member.

However, if one actor – such as the majority party – is the sovereign agenda-setter, then policy outcomes will be quite different (cf. Romer and Rosenthal, 1978; Tsebelis, 2002). First, the agenda-setter can choose the policy that is closest to his or her ideal policy amongst all the policies that the parliament will collectively prefer to the status quo. As a result, if agenda-setting powers are concentrated, not only will the agenda-setter never be worse off than the current policy, but he or she should also be able to move policies closer to his or her ideal policy. Second, if agenda-setting powers are restricted so that the parliament is likely to amend a proposal so that the agenda-setter prefers the status quo to the new policy, the latter will not make a proposal in the first place. Agenda control thus has an impact on what policies will be proposed and adopted.

Gary Cox and Mathew McCubbins (2005) propose a theory of political parties that builds on these basic agenda-setting ideas. In common with other theories of legislative parties (e.g. Cox and McCubbins, 1993), they assume that there are collective incentives for members of a legislature with broadly similar policy preferences to form a political party, which involves a division of labour between leaders (who set the broad policies of the party) and followers (who collect information for the leadership and implement these policies). They then add an additional assumption, that 'the key resource that ... parties delegate to their [leadership] is the power to set the legislative agenda' (Cox and McCubbins, 2005: 24). The result is what Cox and McCubbins call an 'agenda cartel', where the members of the party collude to monopolise the legislative agenda.

According to Cox and McCubbins, if parties are agenda cartels this has significant implications for policy outcomes. Policy outcomes will be different if agenda-setting is controlled by a single party (or coalition of parties) than if an agenda is freely set by the individual members of a parliament. If the agenda is controlled by a particular party, the party leadership will not allow bills to be submitted to the floor, which might move policy outcomes further from their own policy preferences than the current policy status quo. So, under an agenda cartel model, policy outcomes should only be moved towards the policy preferences of the particular party (or parties) that controls the agenda.

Although explaining party cohesion is not the primary purpose of their theory, Cox and McCubbins' approach implies that parties can use agenda-setting powers to enforce party discipline rather than use the usual carrots and sticks. If a party is likely to be split on a particular issue, the party leadership will keep this issue off the agenda. As they explain:

> If all the party is doing is blocking changes to status quo policies that its members either agree to preserve or cannot agree on how to change, then it does not need much in the way of arm-twisting, cajoling, or rational argumentation in the run-up to floor votes. The majority party keeps unwanted issues off the agenda mostly by the *inaction* of its officeholders
>
> (*ibid.*: 214).[3]

Furthermore, in deciding what issues the party proposes, there is a trade-off between proposal rights (who in the party can suggest an item to be put to the parliament) and veto rights (who within the party can block an item from being proposed). If proposal rights are increased – for example, if the number of party members needed to propose a bill is reduced – then the party will be able to make more proposals, but the voting cohesion of the party will decline. On the other hand, if veto rights are increased – for example, if the number of members required to block a bill is reduced – the party will be able to make less proposals, but the cohesion of the party will increase. As a result, Cox and McCubbins predict the following:

> The more *heterogeneous* the preferences within a given coalition [within a party], the more that coalition's partners will wish to limit the proposal rights of other partners, which necessarily entails strengthening their own and others' veto rights. ... The more *homogenous* the preferences within a given coalition, the more that coalition's partners will agree to expand each others' proposal rights, which necessarily entails weakening their own and others' veto rights
>
> (*ibid.*: 7).

This theory applies across both separation-of-powers systems and parliamentary systems. In the US House of Representatives, for example, parties have few powers to force their members to follow voting instructions. However, the majority party in the House has a monopoly on agenda-setting, controlling all the key committee positions and monopolising the floor agenda, and any numerical majority of this party can veto the placement of items on the floor of the chamber. As a result, the majority party is able to select the issues that are put to the floor, and hence rarely loses votes and is able to maintain a high level of party discipline despite highly heterogeneous preferences amongst the members of the party (Cox and McCubbins, 2002).

---

[3] Emphasis in the original.

In parliamentary systems, the party or coalition of parties that form the cabinet collectively monopolise agenda-setting. If each member party in a coalition government can veto a legislative proposal from the cabinet, then it can stop any item from being proposed, which would either move policy outcomes further from its preferences or undermine its legislative cohesion. This consequently provides an explanation of why parties in government in parliamentary systems are almost never defeated in the parliament (on Japan see Cox et al., 2000; on Germany see Chandler et al., 2005).

The theory also applies to 'mixed' systems of government, where agenda-setting powers are controlled both externally and internally in a parliament. For example, in Brazil, which is a separation-of-powers system but the president has considerable agenda-setting authority, the parliamentary parties who support the president are rarely defeated (Amorim Neto et al., 2003).

6.1.2 Agenda-setting in the European Parliament: external and internal 'cartels'

As we discussed in Chapter 1, the particular relationship between the European Parliament and the EU executive (the Commission) makes the EU a 'mixed' political system. On the one hand, like a parliamentary system, the Commission has a monopoly on legislative initiative, and is initially 'elected' by a majority in the European Parliament, and so it can be selective when making proposals to the parliament and can expect that a majority in the parliament will share its basic policy preferences. On the other hand, like a separation-of-powers system, the Commission has few powers to force the parties in the parliament to support its proposals or to prevent the parties in the parliament from amending its proposals significantly. Indeed, since the Commission can only be fired by a two-thirds majority, one lacks the traditional vote of confidence instrument in parliamentary government that can be used to force majority coalition members to vote cohesively.

Also, given the current allocation of powers within the EU, the existence and make-up of the Council means that the Commission is unlikely to be primarily concerned with making proposals that satisfy the wishes of the main parties in the European Parliament. For about half of all EU legislation, which is adopted under the consultation procedure, the Council is the dominant actor. For this legislation, the Commission will be less concerned with making proposals that satisfy a particular coalition in the European Parliament than making proposals that will pass through the Council. Also, even on legislation adopted under the co-decision procedure, which must pass through an oversized majority (a qualified-majority) in the Council as well as a simple majority in the European Parliament, the Commission will try to balance the interests of the governments in the Council and the parties in the Parliament. Also, the coalitions in the two institutions (Council and European Parliament) are likely to be different, as the coalition of governments in support of the legislation in the Council is likely to cut across the main political groups in the European Parliament – that have members from national parties that are in government (and so represented in the Council) and national parties that are in opposition.

Despite these factors, the parties in the European Parliament do exercise some independent agenda-setting powers. First, the European Parliament is free to adopt 'resolutions' or 'own initiative reports'. The former are statements by the European Parliament on any issue it feels obliged to address and the latter are specific calls for the Commission to initiate legislation in a particular area. Although these statements are not legally binding, they are important signals of the positions parties will take on future legislation in a particular area. Second, on EU legislation initiated by the Commission, the European Parliament is free to propose any amendments. Under the consultation procedure, the European Parliament has an incentive to propose amendments that are acceptable to the Commission, as these are then likely to be supported by the Commission and backed by the Council. Under the co-decision procedure, however, legislation cannot pass without the positive support of the parliament. As a result, once the Commission has made a proposal under the co-decision procedure, the European Parliament is completely free to amend legislation as it sees fit (by a simple majority at first reading and an absolute majority of all MEPs at second reading). In this sense, under the main legislative procedure of the EU, once legislation has been proposed, the European Parliament has significant independent agenda-setting power.

The process of agenda-setting inside the European Parliament on legislative issues is as follows. After the Commission has proposed a draft bill (in the form of a draft Directive or Regulation), the bill is forwarded to the Council and European Parliament at the same time. The Conference of Presidents of the parliament, which brings together the President of the parliament and the leaders of the parliament's political groups, decides to which standing committee the bill will be referred. This is usually a straightforward question, since the subject of the Commission's proposal usually clearly determines which committee in the parliament will scrutinise the legislation. For example, legislation on environmental standards in the single market will be referred to the European Parliament's Committee on Environment, Public Health and Food Safety.

Once a bill has been referred to a committee, the committee assigns a *'rapporteur'* for the bill from amongst the MEPs in the committee. This *rapporteur* is responsible for preparing the Parliament's response to the legislation, in the form of a 'report' that contains three elements: a set of amendments to the bill; a 'legislative resolution' setting out the Parliament's position on the legislation; and an 'explanatory statement' of the amendments and the resolution. Rapporteurships are assigned through an auction system, where each political group gets a quota of points in proportion to its total number of MEPs in the parliament. Each bill is discussed by the 'committee co-ordinators' of the political groups (the 'whips' of the political groups in the committees), who decide on the number of points each bill is worth and then make bids on behalf of the groups. Groups can raise their bid to the maximum level (five points) if the report is controversial. Groups sometimes raise bids to make their opponents 'pay' more for them. In general, though, this system means that the largest political groups are allocated rapporteurships on most of the key bills. Once a political group has won the right to act as the *rapporteur* on a particular report, most of the other groups will appoint a 'shadow *rapporteur*', who will monitor the work of the *rapporteur* and prepare the position of his/her political group on the bill under discussion. Once a *rapporteur* has been appointed he or she has a right to remain the *rapporteur* on the bill in all the readings of the bill in the Parliament.

In line with the logic of division of labour inside parties discussed in Chapter 2 and which is at the basis of Cox and McCubbins' approach, the *rapporteur* in the European Parliament is relatively autonomous to shape the position of his or her party on the issue of the bill. A *rapporteur* will of course liaise with the senior figures of the party in his or her committee, such as the committee chair or vice-chair and the party coordinator on the committee. However, once a *rapporteur* (or shadow *rapporteur* for that matter) has spent time focusing on the detailed issues involved in a piece of legislation, he or she usually has more specialist information about the issues in the particular bill, and so is best placed to work out what the position of his or her party should be on the bill. In return, the MEP will receive signals from his or her colleagues about the party's position on the issues on which he or she is not a specialist. As a result of this specialisation, it is not unreasonable to assume that the *rapporteur* and his or her party share the same position on the legislation in question.

Once the *rapporteur* has prepared the report, the committee then votes on and amends the report. The *rapporteur* is the agenda-setter in the committee, in the sense that he or she has the monopoly on the right of proposal. However, any other member of the committee is free to propose an amendment to the *rapporteur's* proposal, which is then accepted or rejected by a simple majority in the committee. Once a report has been passed by the committee, it is submitted to the full plenary of the European Parliament, and will appear on the agenda of the next plenary session. At this stage, the European Parliament operates an 'open rule', in that any political group can propose amendments to the report from the committee. The plenary votes first on the amendments to the proposal from the committee (these are changes to the European Parliament's proposed 'amendments' to the legislative bill), and then on the Commission's draft legislative bill as a whole (as now amended by the parliament). The position of the European Parliament is then communicated to the Commission and Council, in the form of a statement of whether the European Parliament has accepted, rejected or amended the draft legislation.

The process of adopting non-legislative resolutions and own initiative reports is very similar. Each committee is free to propose a non-legislative resolution or an own initiative report on any subject they wish. *Rapporteurs* are assigned in these cases in exactly the same way as they are assigned on legislative issues. Also, the committee then votes on these non-legislative reports and the plenary discusses and amends these reports in essentially the same way as they do with legislative reports.

As we explained in Chapter 1, not all decisions in the plenary are taken by roll-call vote. A political group or approximately five per cent of MEPs (32 of the 626 MEPs in the fifth parliament and 37 of the 732 MEPs in the sixth parliament) can request that an issue on the agenda of the plenary can be taken by a roll-call vote. These requests must be made by the evening before the vote. In practice, approximately one-third of votes are by roll-call, with the other two-thirds either by a show of hands or a (non-recorded) electronic vote. In other words, a political party in the European Parliament can decide which issues it would like to see held by a roll-call vote. But a party cannot prevent other parties calling roll-call votes on issues it would prefer to be decided by secret ballot, for example, because its members are divided on the issue.

In sum, no single party or coalition of parties can dominate agenda-setting in the European Parliament. On the one hand, the coalition in the Commission constitutes a quasi-agenda cartel external to the parliament, in that the Commission possesses a monopoly on the initiation of EU legislation. When initiating legislation, the Commission must take into account how its proposals will be received in the Council and in the European Parliament. Because the Commission is composed of politicians appointed by the national governments, and because national governments are composed of parties from a variety of political families, most Commissions are not dominated by a single political family and the median member of the Commission is usually relatively centrist. Hence, the main external agenda-setter is in general likely to spontaneously propose legislation that is relatively close to the median MEP.

On the other hand, agenda-setting offices inside the European Parliament (rapporteurships) are allocated broadly in proportion to the size of the political groups. So, the main political parties in the European Parliament control more agenda-setting power than the smaller groups. But the smaller groups will control some agendas and will be able to propose amendments to agendas set by the bigger parties. Also, because roll-call votes are not held on all issues, parties have some control over which issues actually get decided 'out in the open'. However, as just mentioned, a party that would like to keep a vote 'behind closed doors' cannot prevent another party forcing a roll-call vote on this issue.

6.1.3   *Propositions about agenda-setting and party cohesion in the European Parliament*

The general theory of agenda control by Cox and McCubbins recognises a trade-off between floor discipline and agenda control by party leaders, with effective use of the latter reducing the need for the former. This, together with our discussion of agenda-setting in the European Parliament, implies that parties should be less cohesive on issues on which they do not control the agenda and should be more cohesive on issues on which they do control the agenda.

First, the clearest example of a situation when a party is not in control of the issue on the floor is a 'hostile amendment' by another party to a bill on which a party's MEP is the *rapporteur*. Since the party holding the rapporteurship on a bill is the main agenda-setter, and since a report only reaches the plenary after it has been discussed and approved by a committee, then most amendments on the floor will not be supported by the party of the *rapporteur*. Nevertheless, a party may support amendments to its bill that it was not able to pass in the committee. Hence, truly 'hostile' amendments for a party are those amendments on which the majority of the party holding the rapporteurship votes against. But, hostile amendments are only likely to be proposed if they have a reasonable chance of passing. The MEPs in the party may be united against some of these hostile amendments. But there are likely to be some hostile amendments on which some members of the party are in favour and some members of the party are opposed (if all the members of the party are in favour, then by definition it is not a hostile amendment). Hence, according to the theory of agenda control, a party is likely to be less cohesive on hostile amendments than either on 'friendly amendments' (amendments which the party supports) or on amendments to bills on which MEPs from other parties are the *rapporteurs*.

Second, when the agenda is set externally (by the Commission), the parties in the parliament are less in control. On non-legislative resolutions and own initiative reports the parties in the parliament (via their MEPs in the committees who write the reports for these procedures) are free to decide which issues to address and when and how these issues should be put to the plenary. In this case, parties have agenda control. In contrast, once the Commission has proposed a piece of legislation, the parties in the parliament must respond, whether they support the legislation or not and whether they are divided on the issues involved or not. Hence, according to the theory of agenda control, parties are likely to be less cohesive in votes on pieces of legislation (or the budget) than in votes on non-legislative items.

Third, related to this issue of external agenda-setting, the particular agenda cartel in the Commission and Council is likely to have a greater impact on some parties in the European Parliament than others. Almost all the main national parties of government sit in the socialist, EPP or liberal groups. However, not all national parties who sit in the socialist, EPP and liberal groups are in government or have Commissioners. Hence, agendas set by the Commission and backed by the Council will not necessarily be the agendas of the national parties in the socialist, EPP and liberal groups that are in the opposition. As a result, according to agenda-control theory, the three centrist parties in the parliament are likely to be less cohesive on legislative issues than the smaller political groups.

Fourth, parties are likely to be more cohesive in votes where they requested a roll-call than in votes where other parties requested a roll-call. On the one hand, this proposition accords with the logic of the agenda-control theory. If a party leadership is unable to enforce party discipline, the party is unlikely to request a roll-call on an issue on which its members have heterogeneous preferences, as this might lead to a party split in the vote and so undermine the signal the party was hoping to send. Hence, a party should only request a roll-call vote on issues where the members of the party have relatively homogeneous preferences, and hence should be more cohesive in these votes than in other votes. On the other hand, this proposition also accords with the logic of a party discipline explanation. Presumably a party is more interested in enforcing discipline on issues that are more important to the party and its supporters. But, a party leadership can only monitor the behaviour of its members in these votes if a roll-call vote is held. Consequently, parties are more likely to request a roll-call vote on exactly those votes on which they have the most interest in enforcing party discipline.

In other words, if parties are more cohesive in roll-call votes that they request than in other votes, it shows either that parties can select issues on which their members are already homogeneous or that parties can enforce discipline on the issues they care about most, or both.

Finally, relating to the trade-off between the preference heterogeneity of party members and party agenda control, parties whose MEPs have more heterogeneous preferences are less likely to be able to use strategic agenda-setting to produce party cohesion in votes. If a party has a high level of heterogeneity of preferences amongst its members then it is likely to have a high threshold for the proposal of party positions and a low threshold for the veto of party positions. In other words, in order to keep unity of the party, the party will wish to limit the proposal rights of its members and it will wish to increase veto rights of its members. In this situation, the party is unlikely to be able to act collectively to secure rapporteurships and form alliances with other parties on issues it cares about. Conversely, if a party leadership can enforce party discipline irrespective of the level of preference heterogeneity of its members, the party is likely to be able to secure a large number of rapporteurships and be able to build alliances with other parties to ensure that these reports are passed by the committee and the full plenary.

Specifically, consider the ideological diversity of the six main political groups, as shown in Figure 6.2. Whereas the socialists, radical-left and

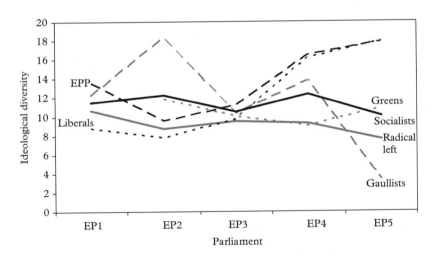

Figure 6.2. Average ideological diversity of the political groups in each parliament

Note: For the calculation of the ideological diversity of a political group, see Chapter 5.

Gaullists were more ideologically homogeneous in the fifth parliament than in the first parliament (relative to their group's size), the EPP, liberals and greens were more ideologically heterogeneous. So, the socialists should be more able to use strategic agenda-setting in the later parliaments than in the earlier parliaments, while the reverse should be true for the EPP.

6.2   Descriptive evidence of agenda-setting and policy influence

To test the agenda-control theory we first look at some descriptive evidence of the relationship between agenda-setting and policy influence in the European Parliament. Figure 6.3 shows the proportion of votes in which the majority of the MEPs in each party were on the winning side in each of the five directly elected parliaments. The political groups are ordered in each parliament from left to right, according to their location on the first dimension revealed by NOMINATE, as we show in Chapter 9.

Following the logic of the median-voter theory, if no agenda control is taking place, the median party in the parliament should be on the winning side most, and the parties on the extreme right and left should be on the winning side least, with the parties between the median and the extremes winning less than the median party but more than the extreme parties. If agenda control is taking place, however, the parties with the agenda-setting power should be on the winning side more than their ideological location should predict. To investigate these arguments, the figure indicates the location of the median party in the parliament (shaded in dark grey) and the political affiliation of the main external agenda-setter – the political group that contains the median member of the Commission (indicated by downward diagonal lines). In the first, second and fourth parliaments, the location of these two actors was the same: in the liberal group. However, in the third parliament, whereas the median member of the Commission was still a liberal, the median member of the Parliament was on the left (in the socialist group). And, the reverse was true in the fifth parliament, when the median MEP was in the liberal group and the median member of the Commission was a socialist.

The results suggest that extremist parties tend to do worse than centrist parties, which would tend to support the median voter theory relative to the theory of agenda control. This is clearest in the second parliament. Also, the party in the centre of most parliaments (the liberals) does better than its numerical share of seats would suggest. But it is impossible to tell whether this is because the median on the

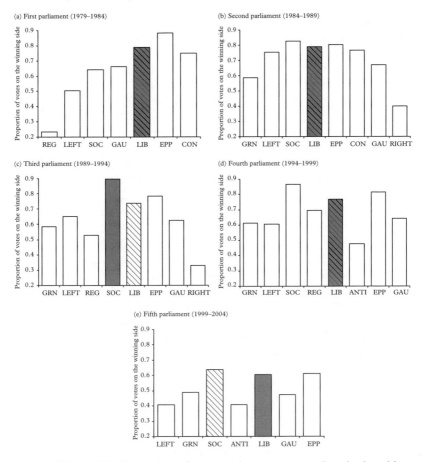

Figure 6.3. Proportion of times each party was on the winning side

Note: The political groups are ordered from left to right in each parliament according to their average location on the first dimension of NOMINATE. The political group that contains the median MEP is shaded. The political group that has the median member of the Commission is indicated by downward diagonal lines.

floor of the parliament can amend issues to its ideal point or because the median member of the external agenda-setter is already very centrist.

In support of the agenda-control theory, however, political group size seems to be a better predictor of the proportion of times a political group is on the winning side, than the ideological location of a group. This reflects the fact that agenda-setting powers (such as committee chairs and rapporteurships) are allocated in proportion to group size. Also, which groups tend to do better than their numerical size would seem to reflect the patterns of coalition formation, a subject to which we will return in Chapters 8 and 9. In the first parliament, when the EPP and liberals often voted together, they were more successful than the socialists, despite the fact that the socialists were the largest party at that time. Then, in the second, third and fourth parliaments, the 'grand coalition' of the socialists and EPP dominated, but with high levels of consensus amongst all the main political groups. Finally, in the fifth parliament, all the groups were less often on the winning side than in the previous few parliaments, which reflects the higher level of left–right conflict in this period. Moreover, this conflict in the fifth parliament reflects a battle between the external and internal agenda-setters: where the EPP (often supported by the liberals) were the main agenda-setters inside the parliament, but the socialists (who were no longer the largest party) dominated the Commission, and so could set the agenda externally.

These inferences are supported by the evidence in Figure 6.4, which shows the relationship between the control of rapporteurships and success. The larger the proportion of rapporteurships a party controlled in a particular parliament, the higher the proportion of times it was on the winning side relative to the other parties. However, it is difficult to identify this relationship independently of party size, as party size is clearly related both to the proportion of rapporteurships and the proportion of times a party is on the winning side – so the two largest political groups controlled the most rapporteurships and were on the winning side more often, while the smaller political groups controlled less rapporteurships and were on the winning side less often.

Nevertheless, independent of party size, controlling the agenda is a bigger predictor of success for some political groups than others. The liberals do particularly well, in that in each parliament they were on the winning side more than their proportion of rapporteurships would predict. At the other extreme, the greens were on the winning side less than their proportion of rapporteurships would predict.

In sum, these aggregate descriptive results suggest that there is some relationship between the agenda-setting resources of a party and policy outcomes from the European Parliament. Specifically, the larger political groups, who control most of the internal agenda-setting offices, get the policy outcomes they desire, independently of their distance from the median member of the parliament. Also, the party that was closest to the median member of the Commission – the main external agenda-setter – tended to do better than its size or ideological location would suggest.

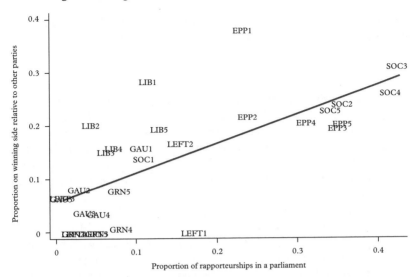

Figure 6.4. Relationship between agenda-setting and winning

Note: SOC1 is the socialist group in the first parliament, SOC2 is the socialist group in the second parliament, and so on. To control for variations in the level of consensus in each parliament (as shown in Figure 6.2), the predicted value in the figure is the difference between the proportion of times a political group is on the winning side in a parliament and the proportion of times the least successful of the six political groups is on the winning side in the same parliament. For example, in the fifth parliament, the least successful of the six political groups was the radical-left, who were on the winning side 40.8 per cent of the time, and the most successful group was the socialists, who were on the winning side 63.8 per cent of the time, which gives these two groups a relative score in the fifth parliament of 0 and 23.0, respectively.

Nevertheless, this evidence of a relationship between agenda-setting and policy outcomes does not necessarily mean that parties are able to use strategic agenda control as a way of ensuring party discipline in votes. To investigate this we need to look in detail at the relationship between agenda-setting and the cohesion of the political groups.

6.3   Statistical analysis

To formally test the importance of agenda-setting in the European Parliament we focus on the determinants of party cohesion in each individual vote. Our goal here is to test the trade-off between agenda control and floor discipline predicted by the theory. We first introduce the variables we use in the analysis and then present the results.

6.3.1   Variables

We define the dependent variable as the relative cohesion of a political group in a roll-call vote. We use the same measure of relative cohesion as in Chapter 5, namely the absolute cohesion of a political group divided by the cohesion of the parliament as a whole. Recall that this captures the effect of variance in the overall size of the majority in each vote, on the assumption that it is easier to be cohesive when all the MEPs are voting together than when the vote is highly contested. We also look at the six main political groups, as in Chapter 5: the socialists, EPP, liberals, Gaullists, radical-left and greens. However, this time we look at the voting behaviour of these groups in each individual vote since 1979 rather than the average behaviour of these groups in a six-month period. In the analysis of cohesion we consider each political group separately.

We have three main sets of variables to test the theoretical propositions. First, we include two variables that test the strategic use of amendments: *Hostile amendment*, which takes the value 1 if the vote is on an amendment to a (legislative or non-legislative) report where the party holds the rapporteurship and the majority of the party votes against the amendment, and a value of 0 otherwise; and *Whole report*, which takes the value 1 if the vote is on the report as whole, regardless of who is the *rapporteur*, and 0 otherwise. There are four possible categories of votes of interest here: (1) a vote on an amendment where the party holds the rapporteurship (a hostile amendment); (2) a vote on an amendment where the party does not hold the rapporteurship (other amendments); (3) a vote on a whole report where the party holds the rapporteurship; and (4) a vote on a whole report where the party does not hold the rapporteurship. If the theory of agenda control holds, a party is likely to be less cohesive on amendments on which it holds the *rapporteur* (hostile amendments) than on amendments on other bills. Hence, what we are interested in is a direct comparison between cohesion on hostile amendments and cohesion on all other amendments. We consequently include the *Whole reports* variable (which controls for the two categories of votes in which we are not interested), so that the baseline category is simply *other amendments*.

Second, to capture the effect of external agenda-setting we include four variables, one for each of the main legislative procedures of the EU: *Co-decision, Cooperation, Consultation* and *Budget* (for both the budgetary adoption and discharge procedures). Each of these variables takes the value 1 if the vote was on a bill or amendment under the relevant procedure, and 0 otherwise. A number of votes are under other procedures where the European Parliament has institutional power, such as the assent procedure, and the investiture or censure of the Commission. But, because these other votes constitute a very small number, the main comparison for the four legislative procedure variables is the voting behaviour of the parties on the non-legislative resolutions and own initiative reports, for which the agenda is set completely internally in the parliament.

Third, we include a variable that tests the strategic use of roll-call votes. The variable *Party-called RCV* takes the value 1 if the party in question requested a roll-call on the vote, and 0 otherwise. If parties strategically call roll-call votes, then they are likely to be more cohesive in votes on which they call a roll-call than in votes on which other parties call a roll-call.

We also include several control variables. First, *Participation* is the proportion of all MEPs who took part in a vote. We include this variable as a proxy for the importance of a vote, on the assumption that more MEPs will take part in a vote if the issue is highly salient.[4] Second, we include seven variables that control for the substantive issue of the vote: *Economic* (such as market regulation and competition policy), *Environment* (such as product packaging), *Social* (such as workers' rights and gender equality), *External* (including trade, aid, and foreign and defence policy), *Agriculture* (related to the Common Agricultural Policy), *Institutional* (such as reform of the EU) and *Internal EP* (such as organisation of the timetable of the parliament). These variables take the value 1 if a vote is on the relevant issue, and 0 otherwise. Each vote can be classified as relating to up to three issues. Third, we include two types of variables that control for the timing of a vote: four dummy variables for each European Parliament (the first parliament is excluded as the baseline); and five dummy variables for the day of the week (Saturday is excluded as the baseline).

6.3.2   Results

Table 6.1 shows the results of separate models of the cohesion of each of the six main political groups in all votes in all five European Parliaments.

---

[4] Note that the level of MEPs' participation in a vote is not fully exogenous to the level of relative cohesion of a party. However, in this context, we use this variable only as a control variable.

Table 6.1. *Testing agenda-setting: pooled results*

	Socialists	EPP	Liberals	Gaullists	Greens	Radical Left
Constant	2.175***	2.237***	2.051***	2.042***	1.967***	2.493***
	(6.01)	(6.83)	(7.78)	(6.40)	(5.99)	(5.21)
Hostile amendment	0.020	−0.011	0.077*	0.046	−0.371***	0.133
	(0.75)	(0.45)	(1.67)	(0.57)	(4.89)	(1.53)
Whole report	−0.172***	−0.197***	−0.135***	−0.176***	−0.200***	−0.169***
	(8.57)	(9.29)	(6.93)	(8.36)	(8.60)	(7.63)
Co-decision	−0.086***	−0.074***	−0.063***	0.077***	0.043	0.053**
	(3.61)	(2.97)	(2.73)	(2.98)	(1.64)	(2.01)
Cooperation	−0.000	−0.064*	−0.043	0.011	0.098***	0.066*
	(0.00)	(1.85)	(1.29)	(0.33)	(2.82)	(1.82)
Consultation	−0.080***	−0.102***	−0.048**	0.083***	−0.043*	−0.065***
	(4.05)	(5.01)	(2.51)	(3.86)	(1.92)	(3.02)
Budget	−0.141***	−0.159***	−0.155***	−0.042	−0.126***	−0.137***
	(4.61)	(5.39)	(5.39)	(1.36)	(3.48)	(4.20)
Party-called RCV	0.208***	0.160***	0.123***	−0.103***	0.090***	0.138***
	(9.72)	(8.79)	(3.89)	(3.98)	(3.39)	(4.48)
Participation	0.022	0.144**	0.051	0.058	−0.126*	−0.115*
	(0.37)	(2.39)	(0.87)	(0.91)	(1.80)	(1.80)
Economic	0.055**	0.039	0.033	0.052*	0.039	0.029
	(1.97)	(1.39)	(1.26)	(1.80)	(1.31)	(0.98)

Environment	−0.014	0.011	0.018	0.004	0.002	−0.005
	(0.58)	(0.45)	(0.77)	(0.17)	(0.06)	(0.19)
Social	−0.061*	0.005	−0.021	0.014	−0.008	0.006
	(1.95)	(0.16)	(0.67)	(0.40)	(0.22)	(0.18)
External	−0.100***	−0.111***	−0.061**	−0.024	−0.050	−0.008
	(3.33)	(3.60)	(2.02)	(0.73)	(1.46)	(0.25)
Agriculture	−0.004	−0.010	−0.014	0.020	−0.026	−0.009
	(0.16)	(0.34)	(0.51)	(0.65)	(0.87)	(0.31)
Institutional	0.025	−0.000	0.004	0.042	0.034	0.003
	(0.82)	(0.00)	(0.15)	(1.44)	(1.09)	(0.08)
Internal EP	−0.062*	−0.072*	−0.086**	−0.013	−0.088**	−0.054
	(1.57)	(1.87)	(2.22)	(0.33)	(1.97)	(1.27)
Observations	14653	14652	14623	14438	13662	14404
Adjusted R-squared	0.04	0.03	0.03	0.01	0.04	0.02

Note: Dependent variable: relative cohesion of a political group in a vote. Dummy variables for each parliament and each day of the week are included but not reported. Parameters of the models are estimated by linear regression. *T*-statistics in parentheses. *Significant at 10%, **significant at 5%, ***significant at 1%.

The main findings are as follows. First, in general, parties are *not* significantly less cohesive on hostile amendments than on other amendments. To reiterate, a hostile amendment for a party is an amendment on one of the party's reports that the party does not support. The fact that parties are as cohesive in votes on hostile amendments as in votes on friendly amendments suggests that parties in the European Parliament can enforce party discipline on the floor irrespective of who has placed the issue on the agenda. The only party for which this is not true is the greens, who are significantly less cohesive on hostile amendments than on friendly amendments. This demonstrates that when an MEP from the green group is a *rapporteur*, the other parties are able to propose amendments that are supported by part of the green MEPs.

It is also worth noting that parties are less cohesive in votes on whole reports than on amendments – whether hostile or friendly. However, this variable is included as a control, to isolate a direct comparison of the effect of a hostile amendment compared with a friendly amendment. We do not have any specific prediction about the expected relationship between voting on a whole report and voting on an amendment. But the finding that a party is generally less cohesive on whole bills than on amendments is probably explained by the fact that whereas original reports and amendments are usually close to a party's ideal point, many whole bills, once amended, are further from the preferences of some members of the party than the status quo. Put another way, a floor compromise will increase the overall level of support for a bill but is likely to reduce the level of support within the party groups.

The second main result related to our propositions is that the main parties are less cohesive on legislative and budgetary votes than on non-legislative resolutions or own initiative reports. In contrast to the finding about hostile amendments, which suggests that parties can enforce discipline, this finding suggests that parties are less able to enforce discipline when the agenda is set externally to the parliament (by the Commission) than when the agenda is set internally in the parliament. However, as we predicted, this result is mostly only true for the three political groups (the socialists, EPP and liberals) that are likely to be internally split when the agenda is set by the Commission and when the parliament has to negotiate with the parties in government in the Council. The three groups to the right and left of these main groups, who generally do not have members from parties in government in the Council or who have Commissioners, are more cohesive in votes under at least one of the legislative procedures than on non-legislative issues.

Third, a party is generally more cohesive in votes when it requested the roll-call than in votes when the roll-call was requested by another party or was required by the rules of the parliament. This observation is generally consistent with both an agenda-control explanation and a party-discipline explanation. However, one party, the Gaullists, behaves less cohesively than the other parties on their own roll-call votes. Because the Gaullists have equal access to agenda-setting as the other parties (in proportion to its size), the fact that they are less cohesive in their own roll-call votes than in other votes suggests that the Gaullists are less able than the other parties to enforce voting discipline, as we found in Chapter 5.

Fourth, the coefficients on the issues of the votes reveal some interesting patterns. In general, the substantive subject of the vote does not seem to affect the level of cohesion of the parties. Nevertheless, parties are generally less cohesive on external relations issues (such as trade, aid, security and defence policies) and internal parliamentary issues (such as the organisation of the parliament's timetable). This is not surprising. Some external relations issues probably split MEPs on national lines as well as along party lines. Also, parties are not likely to issue voting instructions on many internal organisational issues, which allow the MEPs a 'free vote'.

Fifth, looking broadly at the results between the parties suggests that some parties are better than others at using the agenda powers and enforcing party discipline. On one side, the socialists and EPP are more cohesive when the agenda is set internally in the parliament (in other words, when they dominate agenda-setting) and can control their MEPs on hostile amendments and in their own roll-call votes. On the other side, the greens are not able to control their troops on hostile amendments, and the Gaullists cannot enforce party discipline in their own roll-call votes. Also, the Gaullists, greens and radical-left are just as cohesive on legislative as on non-legislative issues, suggesting that they are marginalised whether the agenda is set externally to or internally within the European Parliament. It is hard to compare the effect of preference heterogeneity on agenda control between groups of different sizes, as larger parties have significantly more agenda-setting power than the smaller parties. However, amongst the smaller groups, the radical-left group is more homogeneous than the greens and Gaullists, and there is some evidence that this group is more able to act cohesively when it controls the agenda than these other two groups.

Table 6.2 shows the same models as in Table 6.1 but estimated for each parliament separately. These results confirm the findings in the pooled analysis. First, hostile amendments only undermined the

Table 6.2. *Testing agenda-setting in each Parliament*

		Socialists	EPP	Liberals	Gaullists	Greens	Radical-Left
EP1	Hostile Amendment	0.209	−0.231***	0.230	0.083		0.071
		(1.23)	(2.71)	(1.24)	(0.61)		(0.19)
	Co-decision						
	Party-called RCV	0.350***	0.067	0.097	0.284		0.160
		(4.96)	(0.93)	(0.79)	(1.44)		(1.42)
	Observations	885	885	876	868		861
	Adjusted R-squared	0.06	0.11	0.10	0.09		0.05
EP2	Hostile Amendment	−0.093	0.050	0.039	0.939***	−0.251	−0.171*
		(1.64)	(0.69)	(0.32)	(14.01)	(1.28)	(1.83)
	Co-decision						
	Party-called RCV	0.311***	0.060	0.336***	0.215**	0.101	0.574***
		(5.93)	(1.37)	(2.70)	(2.55)	(1.45)	(3.80)
	Observations	2134	2133	2127	2102	2067	2103
	Adjusted R-squared	0.06	0.04	0.02	0.04	0.05	0.05
EP3	Hostile Amendment	0.030	−0.121**	−0.088	0.311	−0.586***	0.861***
		(0.64)	(2.26)	(1.00)	(1.24)	(7.95)	(2.61)
	Co-decision	0.075	−0.028	−0.048	0.265*	0.232*	0.010
		(0.77)	(0.24)	(0.56)	(1.79)	(1.72)	(0.07)
	Party-called RCV	0.081**	0.267***	0.346***	−0.067	0.000	0.248**
		(2.12)	(6.68)	(4.85)	(0.58)	(0.00)	(2.50)
	Observations	2732	2732	2720	2634	2723	2553
	Adjusted R-squared	0.02	0.04	0.03	0.02	0.02	0.03

		(1)	(2)	(3)	(4)	(5)	(6)
EP4	Hostile Amendment	−0.002	0.012	−0.024	0.277	0.000	0.728**
		(0.05)	(0.25)	(0.16)	(1.62)	(0.00)	(2.44)
	Co-decision	−0.107***	−0.081**	−0.038	0.079*	0.061	0.013
		(2.68)	(2.01)	(0.97)	(1.85)	(1.39)	(0.30)
	Party-called RCV	0.275***	0.275***	0.074	−0.236***	0.220**	−0.056
		(6.53)	(7.08)	(1.23)	(7.66)	(2.24)	(1.14)
	Observations	3739	3739	3737	3728	3709	3724
	Adjusted R-squared	0.03	0.04	0.02	0.03	0.02	0.02
EP5	Hostile Amendment	0.089*	0.030	0.108	−0.154	0.000	−0.025
		(1.65)	(0.68)	(1.63)	(1.27)	(0.00)	(0.15)
	Co-decision	−0.100***	−0.104***	−0.090***	0.042	−0.007	0.056
		(3.00)	(2.96)	(2.81)	(1.20)	(0.19)	(1.57)
	Party-called RCV	0.149***	0.116***	0.021	0.029	0.063*	0.161***
		(3.15)	(3.76)	(0.42)	(0.50)	(1.90)	(3.58)
	Observations	5163	5163	5163	5106	5163	5163
	Adjusted R-squared	0.02	0.02	0.01	0.01	0.01	0.02

Note: Dependent variable: relative cohesion of a political group in a vote. Each model is specified as in Table 6.1 but the estimated coefficients of the other variables are not reported. Parameters of the models are estimated by linear regression. *T*-statistics in parentheses. *Significant at 10%, **significant at 5%, ***significant at 1%.

cohesion of the EPP in the first parliament and the EPP and greens in the fourth parliament. Second, once the parliament gained significant legislative powers – in the fourth and fifth parliaments – the three main parties were less cohesive in votes under the co-decision procedure than in votes on non-legislative resolutions and own initiative reports (the variables for the other legislative procedures are included in the models, but not reported). Third, most parties were significantly more cohesive in their own roll-call votes in most parliaments. The only time a party was less cohesive in its own roll-call votes than in other votes was the Gaullists in the fourth parliament.

6.4   Conclusion: agenda control alone cannot explain party discipline

If a party can control which issues get to the floor of a parliament and how these issues are proposed it should not need to pressure its members to follow voting instructions, as the party should be able to limit votes to issues on which its members have similar preferences. The problem for parties in the European Parliament is that no single party or coalition of parties controls the agenda. First, the agenda on legislative issues is set externally by the Commission, and on these issues political bargaining inside the parliament is also influenced by the coalition that emerges in the other chamber of the EU's legislative process: the Council. Second, even when the parliament itself possesses independent agenda-setting power – for example, on non-legislative resolutions or when proposing amendments to legislation initiated by the Commission – agenda-setting offices (rapporteurships) are allocated on a broadly proportional basis between the political groups. So the leaderships of the parties in the European Parliament have only a limited opportunity to use their agenda-setting powers to control the voting behaviour of their backbench members.

Nevertheless, where the party leaders do control the agenda we found some evidence that they can use this power to enforce party discipline. In particular, the main political groups are more cohesive on non-legislative issues, when the agenda is set internally by the MEPs from these parties, than on legislative issues, when these parties are forced to respond to initiatives from the Commission. We thus find some support for the agenda-control hypothesis. In general, though, enforcing party discipline through agenda control only affects the level of party cohesion at the margins.

Against the agenda-control thesis we found that parties can enforce discipline in the most extreme circumstances – when the party is forced to vote on an amendment to one of its own bills that is proposed by another party and that it does not support. The fact that parties are as cohesive in these 'hostile amendments' as on other amendments suggests that party leaderships are able to force their members to follow party voting instructions even when they prefer the amendment to the text on the table. Also, as the legislative power of the parliament has grown, the parties in the parliament have been increasingly forced to respond to agendas that have been set externally to the parliament. Hence, the fact that we observe growing party cohesion despite growing legislative powers is further support for the view that the party leaders in the parliament are able to use mechanisms other than agenda control to enforce party discipline.

We thus conclude that though we find some support for the agenda-control hypothesis, we also find evidence of enforcement of party discipline that is independent of agenda control.

7   Who controls the MEPs?

We have so far excluded two possible explanations of growing party cohesion in the European Parliament. First, we found in Chapter 5 that parties have not become more cohesive and more competitive as a result of growing internal ideological homogeneity. Second, we found in Chapter 6 that growing party cohesion cannot be explained only by strategic control of the legislative agenda inside the European Parliament. There is genuine enforcement of party discipline.

However, there are at least two other possible explanations as to why disciplined party politics has emerged in the European Parliament. One is that the *European* political groups are able to force their MEPs to vote together, irrespective of the MEPs' personal preferences or the preferences of the MEPs' national parties. Another is that the *national* political parties that make up the European parties strategically choose to vote together and impose discipline on their MEPs even when their preferences diverge. At face value, these explanations might seem similar, in that in both cases national delegations of MEPs appear to be voting against their expressed preferences under pressure from the European political groups. However, they are in fact different. The first explanation assumes that the national political parties are acting involuntarily, while the second assumes that national political parties are acting voluntarily upon some strategic objective, such as a long-term collective policy goal rather than the immediate outcome of a particular vote. The first explanation is top-down while the second one is bottom-up.

In this chapter we try to disentangle these two explanations by focusing on who controls the MEPs. If MEPs are controlled by their European political groups, then growing partisan politics in the European Parliament is a result of powerful transnational party organisations, comparable with the parliamentary parties in domestic politics in Europe. However, if MEPs are controlled by their national parties, then growing party politics in the European Parliament is a result of the strategic behaviour of national political parties.

The rest of this chapter is organised as follows. In Section 7.1 we discuss the powers of the MEPs' two party 'principals': the European and national parties. Section 7.2 then maps how far the MEPs have voted with or against these principals in the five directly elected parliaments. In Section 7.3 we use a statistical analysis to investigate what factors explain variations in MEPs' propensity to vote against their European political groups and their national parties in the fifth parliament (1999–2004). Section 7.4 analyses the relative importance of European parties and national parties in determining the voting behaviour of MEPs in all five parliaments.

Our main finding is that MEPs are ultimately controlled by their national parties rather than their European political groups. If an MEP is torn between her national party and her European party in a particular vote, the MEP is likely to vote with her national party and against her European party. However, this does not mean that European parties are inherently weak. What is surprising is how rare these conflicts between European and national parties are. This consequently suggests that in most cases of a potential conflict between a national party and its European political group, the national party will voluntarily decide not to vote against the European party.

7.1 MEPs: agents with two principals

A commonly used analytical tool in the social sciences is 'principal–agent' analysis (e.g. Jensen and Meckling, 1976; Bolton and Dewatripont, 2005) which is also used in political science (e.g. McCubbins and Schwartz, 1984; Epstein and O'Halloran, 1999). The central problem analysed in principal–agent theory is that one actor (the principal) needs to delegate tasks and resources to another actor (the agent) who will take action on behalf of the principal but who has interests and objectives of his or her own. Since the actions of the agent cannot be observed by the principal and only the outcomes of his or her actions can be observed, this creates a serious incentive problem that needs to be solved in order to minimise what is called 'moral hazard'. In the system of representative government, citizens are the principals who delegate decision-making authority to their elected representatives, the agents, to make laws on the citizens' behalf. Owing to the conflict of interest between voters and politicians, an elected politician might personally wish to increase public spending while the voter in his or her district might wish to cut taxes. When such a conflict occurs, the rules and procedures that govern the relationship between the two actors determine how far the agent is controlled by the principal. These forms of control relate to how easy it is for the principal to replace the agent or how the actions of the agent are communicated to the principal.

Applying the principal–agent framework to the European Parliament, each MEP is in effect the agent of two principals: his or her national party, and his or her European political group (cf. Hix, 2002b). On the one hand, national parties are more important than the European parties in influencing whether MEPs are returned to the European Parliament in the next election. National parties control the selection of candidates in European elections. This is a very powerful tool in disciplining politicians. Also, European elections tend to be fought on national issues rather than European issues, as we explained in Chapter 1. This means that the performance of the European political groups is less important than the general popularity of national parties in determining which MEPs are re-elected.

National parties also control MEPs' access to future office and policy goals in the national arena. MEPs may seek to win elections to their national parliaments, to influence national policies, or to be promoted to national governmental office. For example, previous research has shown that although an increasing number of MEPs choose to stay in the European Parliament or to obtain a position in another EU institution or somewhere in the Brussels policy community, many MEPs do return or intend to return to domestic political careers (Scarrow, 1997). And, it is the national party leaderships that are the most influential in determining which party members are elected to parliament or government in the domestic arena. The national parties have at their disposal all the tools of parliamentary politics to discipline MEPs from their national party.

In contrast, the European political groups are more influential than the national parties in influencing the ability of MEPs to secure policy and office goals inside the European Parliament. This is because the European party leaderships control the allocation of committee assignments and rapporteurships (reports on legislative dossiers), the parliamentary agenda, access to political group leadership positions and other offices in the parliament, as well as speaking time in the plenary sessions. The European political groups have also set up two offices to control their members. First, the group 'whips' monitor the behaviour of the group members. The whips hand out voting instructions to each MEP at the start of each voting session, monitor how each MEP has voted in roll-call votes and inform the party leadership of major breaches of party voting instructions. Second, the 'group coordinators' are the most senior members of the groups in each committee, and are the eyes, ears and mouths of the group leaderships. The coordinators are the spokespersons for the groups in the committees, monitor the work of the groups' *rapporteurs* and other committee members and communicate the views of the group leaderships to the committee members.

However, the power of the European political groups to directly control their members is weak compared with most parliamentary parties in democratic systems. This is partly because the leaderships of the European parties do not have the ability to decide whether an MEP can stand for re-election or even to use the threat that failing to follow party instructions will undermine the electoral chances of the party at the next election. The European political groups are also relatively weak because the process of assigning offices and positions in the parliament is coordinated between the European party leaderships and the national party delegations in each group. For example, once a European political group has won a particular committee assignment, such as a committee chair, the leadership of the group awards this office to a particular national party delegation, which in turn chooses who among its MEPs will be given the position. Once a national party delegation has been assigned a particular position they are normally protective of this resource. If the European party is unhappy with a particular committee chair or *rapporteur*, the national party will try to hold on to this position, and so will try to appoint to this position another member from among its ranks or will demand that it be compensated for losing this position by being awarded another position.

Nevertheless, European political groups do possess the ultimate sanction of expelling an individual MEP or national party delegation from the group. National parties that are not members of one or other of the political groups, who sit as 'non-attached members', are marginalised in the internal workings of the parliament, with less access to the legislative agenda and less resources. Expulsion from the political groups is extremely rare, as it has to be supported by a majority of all MEPs in the group and is only credible if expelling the party would not weaken the political group compared with its opponents in the parliament. For example, in the fifth European Parliament, there was a lot of discussion about the possibility that the British conservatives would be expelled from the EPP because most British Conservative MEPs voted against the majority of the EPP in approximately one-third of all roll-call votes. However, most members of the EPP decided against such an action, as expelling such a large national delegation would significantly weaken the EPP compared with the socialists. It would, for example, result in the EPP securing less-important committee chairs in the next round of committee assignments (which are reassigned half-way through the five-year term of the parliament). But in June 2005 the EPP group expelled one of the British conservative MEPs, Roger Helmer, for failing to follow EPP instructions to vote against a Commission censure motion proposed by a group of anti-European MEPs and for openly criticising the EPP group leader, Hans-Gert Poettering, for having put pressure on the EPP MEPs to support the Commission. Expulsion is rarely observed, however, because if the group leadership is overwhelmingly supported by its members, the threat of expulsion is usually enough to ensure that a particular MEP or national party abides by the wishes of the majority of the group on a key issue.

In sum, MEPs are like elected parliamentarians in many other democratic political systems, in that they have two competing principals (see, for example, the discussion in Figueiredo and Limongi, 2000). Perhaps unique, though, are the levels and the specific resources that the two party principals in the European Parliament possess to shape the behaviour of 'their' MEPs. While national parties can use their control of candidate re-selection and their control of the process of European elections to influence whether an MEP is elected to the parliament in the first place, European parties can use their control of resources and power inside the parliament to influence whether an MEP is able to secure his or her policy and career goals once elected. A key question, then, is what happens when an MEPs' two principals are in conflict, for example, in a particular vote in the European Parliament. Does the MEP side with her European party or her national party? If she sides with the former, then growing transnational party competition and cohesion has evolved as a direct result of the power of the European party organisations. If she sides with the latter, however, then democratic party politics in the European Parliament is more the product of the strategic behaviour of national parties than the power of European parties.

7.2   Voting with and against the European and national parties

To look at whether MEPs are controlled by their European parties or their national parties we look first at the patterns of MEP voting *vis-à-vis* these two sets of principals. Table 7.1 shows the proportion of times each MEP voted with and against his or her national and European parties in all roll-call votes in the fifth parliament. To calculate these figures we excluded all MEPs who were not members of a political group (the non-attached MEPs) and also excluded MEPs whose national parties had less than three MEPs. For the remaining MEPs, for every vote we determined whether the MEP voted with or against the plurality of his or her European political group and with or against the

National party

	% of votes with the party	% of votes against the party	*Total*
European party % of votes with the party	88.92	1.78	90.70
% of votes against the party	6.56	2.74	9.30
Total	95.48	4.52	100.00

Table 7.1. Voting with/against national and European parties in the fifth parliament

Note: The table shows every vote by every MEP in the fifth European Parliament (excluding MEPs that were not attached to a political group or whose national party had less than three MEPs). Each MEP 'vote decision' was categorised as a vote either (1) with or against the majority of the MEP's national party delegation and (2) with or against the majority of the MEP's European political group.

plurality of his or her national party.[1] With approximately 600 MEPs included in the analysis and 5567 votes, the table summarises the results of looking at over 3 million individual MEP vote decisions.

The first result to highlight is the remarkably high level of consensus between the European political groups and national parties. In almost 90 per cent of all MEP vote decisions in the fifth parliament, MEPs did not find themselves torn between the positions of their European and national parties, and so were free to vote with both parties' majorities. Second, though, the results suggest that MEPs are more beholden to their national parties than their European parties. MEPs voted against their national parties less than 5 per cent of the time, while MEPs voted against their European parties more than 9 per cent of the time. Third, the difference between national and European parties is even clearer when the two principals were in conflict, with MEPs voting with the

[1] We included all votes to Abstain. So, if the majority of an MEP's national (European) party voted Yes, and the MEP voted to Abstain, then we treated this as a vote against the national (European) party. With such a small number of votes to Abstain, however, including or excluding these votes does not change the overall results.

Table 7.2. *Defection rates in each Parliament*

European Parliament	% of MEP Vote Decisions				
	With NP & EPG	With NP & against EPG	Against NP & with EPG	Against NP & EPG	Total
1st (1979–1984)	85.66	8.14	1.43	4.77	100.00
2nd (1984–1989)	90.09	4.87	1.24	3.80	100.00
3rd (1989–1994)	88.38	5.56	1.87	2.67	100.00
4th (1994–1999)	88.76	5.65	2.16	3.47	100.00
5th (1999–2004)	88.92	6.56	1.78	2.74	100.00

Note: NP = national party, EPG = European political group.

national party and against their European party over 6 per cent of the time yet against their national party and with their European party less than 2 per cent of the time.

Table 7.2 shows the same analysis for roll-call votes in each of the five parliaments. What is striking is the remarkable level of stability in these figures. In an overwhelming majority of votes in all parliaments, national parties and European parties vote the same way. But when there was conflict between these two principals, MEPs were more likely to vote with their national party than with their European party.

The fact that we observe a stable pattern of MEP defection from these two sets of principals might suggest that the general level of conflict between the European parties and national parties has remained stable. However, we cannot directly observe conflict between national parties and European parties in roll-call votes. If the majority of a national party votes against the majority of a European party, then the conflict is obvious. However, a national party might have a different position to its European party in a particular vote, yet decide not to instruct its MEPs to vote against the European party. This could be because the national party expects some reward from the European party for behaving, such as a particular committee assignment, or because the party has a long-term policy goal that it can only maintain if party cohesion is maintained. In this situation, the expected conflict between the national and European party on the issue would not be observed in the vote.

Furthermore, we know from our findings in the previous chapters that the *a priori* probability of conflicts between national parties and European parties is likely to have increased. First, the parliament has become increasingly competitive, with lower majorities and growing (left-right) competition between the European parties. Second, as measured by national party manifestos, the divergence of policy preferences between the national parties has increased in the main political groups as a result of EU enlargement and political group expansion. We also know that European parties cannot keep issues off the agenda on which they expect their member parties to have divergent opinions. Put together, a national party is more likely to find itself with a different position to its European party in a vote in a later parliament than in an earlier parliament.

Hence, these figures seem to confirm that national parties are more able than European parties to control their MEPs. Nevertheless, the stability of convergent voting between the national and European parties, despite growing inter-party conflict and intra-party diversity, suggests that national parties have increasingly compromised their views to support their European political groups.

7.3   Analysis of MEP voting defection in the Fifth Parliament

To investigate what factors determine whether an MEP will vote with or against his or her European party and national party we estimate a series of models of MEP 'voting defection', and test these models on the voting behaviour of MEPs in the fifth parliament. We first introduce the variables before presenting the results.

7.3.1   Variables

We look at two dependent variables: (1) the proportion of times an MEP voted against his or her European political group and (2) the proportion of times an MEP voted against his or her national party. We excluded the twenty MEPs who changed their national party or European political group affiliation during the fifth parliament.

Our main explanatory variables capture the expected policy distances between the three actors in question: the MEP, the MEP's European political group, and the MEP's national party. To measure these distances we use exogenous measures of MEPs' and national parties' policy positions on the two main dimensions of politics in the European Parliament: the left–right dimension, and the pro-/anti-EU integration dimension. To estimate the position of the MEPs on these two dimensions we use the results from a survey of the members of the fifth parliament by the European Parliament Research Group (cf. Hix, 2004).[2] In the survey, the MEPs were asked *inter alia* to locate themselves on two ten-point scales: one relating to the left–right, and the other to EU integration. The survey

---

[2] See www.lse.ac.uk/collections/EPRG/survey.htm

was completed by 195 MEPs (31 per cent of the 626 members), and these returns constitute a good sample of the total population of MEPs in the fifth parliament, whether measured by political group, nationality, gender or number of years as an MEP (see Hix, 2002b). To estimate the positions of the national parties and European political groups on these two dimensions we use Marks and Steenbergen's (2004) dataset of expert judgements of national party positions. The position of each European political group on the two policy scales was then calculated as the sum of each national member party's position weighted by the proportion of MEPs in the group held by the national party.

We then estimated the likely conflict between the three actors as follows. We first standardised all the scales, from 0 to 1. We then calculated two proxy measures for conflict between each MEP's two-party principals: the distances between the locations of the MEP's European political group and her national party on the left–right scale (*NP-EPG left–right distance*) and on the pro-/anti-EU integration scale (*NP-EPG EU integration distance*). We also calculated two proxy measures for conflict between each MEP and her European political group: the distances between the MEP's self-placement and her European political group's location on the left–right scale (*MEP-EPG left–right distance*) and on the pro-/anti-EU integration scale (*MEP-EPG EU integration distance*). Finally, we calculated two proxy measures for conflict between each MEP and her national party: the distances between the MEP's self-placement and the experts' placement of the MEP's national party on the left–right scale (*MEP-NP left-right distance*) and on the pro-/anti-EU integration scale (*MEP-NP EU integration distance*).

If MEPs are primarily controlled by their national parties and are fully disciplined by the latter, then as the distance between the national party and the European political group increases, the MEP's propensity to vote against the European political group should also increase, but this should not affect the MEP's propensity to vote against the national party. Conversely, if MEPs are primarily controlled by their European political groups and are fully disciplined by the latter, then as the distance between the national party and European political group increases, the MEP's propensity to vote against the national party should increase, but this should not affect the MEP's propensity to vote against the European political group. However, if MEPs are free agents, and driven by their personal policy preferences rather than by loyalty to their parties, the distance between an MEP's two principals should not be significant, but as the distance between the MEP and her national (European) party increases, the propensity of the MEP to vote against the national (European) party should also increase.

To these explanatory variables we add three sets of control variables. In the first set we include two dummy variables that control for particular institutional interests of national parties: (1) if an MEP's national party was in government in a member state during the fifth parliament (*In government*), which was coded 1 if the national party was in government and 0 otherwise and (2) if a fellow member of the MEP's national party was the leader of the MEP's European political group (*NP has EPG leader*), which was coded 1 if the national party had the group leader and 0 otherwise. On the first of these variables, if the national party of an MEP is in government, the party is represented in the other main legislative institution in the EU (the Council), and so may have more at stake in legislative votes in the European Parliament. For example, we found in Chapter 5 that the number of national party delegations in a European political group was positively related to the cohesion of the group, which suggests that MEPs from governing parties may be more likely to vote with their European political groups. On the second of these variables, a national party that holds the Presidency of a European political group is likely to have a significant influence in shaping the policies of the group, and so MEPs from these parties are less likely to be forced to choose between the policies of their national party and their European party.

In the second set of control variables we include two variables that take account of the size of the MEPs' two principals: (1) the number of members in the MEP's European political group (*EPG size*); and (2) the number of members in the MEP's national party delegation (*NP size*). We found in Chapter 5 that in the fifth parliament the larger European political groups were more cohesive than the smaller groups. Also, the larger a national party delegation the more influence it is likely to have in shaping the policies of its European political group, and so the less likely its MEPs will be to vote against their group.

In the third group of control variables we include two variables that account for personal characteristics of MEPs that might influence their behaviour independently of their personal preferences or their parties' policies: (1) the age of each MEP at the start of the fifth parliament (*MEP age*); and (2) the total number of years each MEP would have been in the European Parliament had the MEP stayed until the end of the parliamentary term in July 2004 (*Years as MEP*). We obtained these data from the records on each MEP held by the General Secretariat of the European Parliament. Presumably, the older a politician and the longer the politician has been in the European Parliament, the more likely he or she will hold a senior position in the national party delegation and the European political group, and so will be freer to determine their own voting behaviour.

Table 7.3. *Determinants of MEP defection*

	(1) Voting against European political group		(2) Voting against national party	
	Coef.	*t*-stat.	Coef.	*t*-stat.
Constant	0.034	(1.26)	0.040*	(1.88)
NP-EPG left–right distance	0.220***	(2.74)	−0.034	(0.54)
NP-EPG EU integration distance	0.030***	(4.41)	−0.003	(0.57)
MEP-EPG left–right distance	0.149**	(2.42)	−0.041	(0.92)
MEP-EPG EU integration distance	0.047	(1.65)	−0.004	(0.19)
MEP-NP left–right distance	−0.069	(1.23)	0.009	(0.22)
MEP-NP EU integration distance	−0.098***	(3.26)	−0.021	(0.94)
In government	−0.019*	(1.65)	−0.001	(0.13)
NP has EPG leader	−0.060***	(3.79)	0.009	(0.74)
EPG size	−0.000	(0.41)	0.000	(1.19)
NP size	0.001	(1.38)	−0.001	(1.55)
MEP age	0.000	(0.27)	−0.000	(0.26)
Years as MEP	0.001	(1.26)	0.002***	(3.31)
No. of observations	184		174	
Adjusted *R*-squared	0.40		0.03	

Note: Dependent variables: Proportion of times each MEP voted differently from the majority of her European political group (model 1) and national party (model 2) in all roll-call votes in the fifth European Parliament. Parameters of the models are estimated by linear regression with robust standard errors. *T*-statistics in parentheses. *Significant at 10%; **significant at 5%; ***significant at 1%.

7.3.2   Results

Table 7.3 presents the results of linear regression models for the two dependent variables. Starting with the propensity of MEPs to vote against their European political groups (in model 1), the main findings are as follows. First, in general, the *a priori* policy distance between an MEP and his or her two party principals, and between the MEP's two principals, are significant predictors of how often an MEP will vote against his or her European political group. The greater the policy distance between a national party and a European political group, the more likely the MEPs from this national party will vote against their European political group. This holds for distances on the left–right dimension as well as distances on the EU integration dimension, although distances between national parties and their European political groups on the left–right dimension explain over 30 per cent of the total variance in MEP defection from their European political groups.

Personal preferences of MEPs also make a difference. Specifically, the greater the distance between an MEP's personal ideological position on the left–right dimension and the average left–right location of the MEP's European political group, the more likely the MEP will vote against his or her European political group, independent of the position of his or her national party. Interestingly, though, the greater the distance between an MEP and his or her national party on the EU integration dimension, the less likely the MEP will defect from his or her European political group. This suggests that the more pro-European MEPs in a national party delegation are more likely to support the policies of their European political group.

Regarding the control variables, we find that if an MEP's national party has the leadership of the European political group, the MEP is significantly less likely to vote against the European political group. Also, MEPs from national parties in government are less likely to vote against their European political groups, which accords with our findings in Chapter 5.

Turning to the propensity of MEPs to vote against their national parties (in model 2), we find that very few variables are significant. This is not surprising given that MEPs rarely vote against their national parties, as the results in Tables 7.1 and 7.2 showed. Nevertheless, the policy distance between an MEP's European and national parties, or the distance between an MEP's personal preferences and the preferences of their two principals, do not have a significant effect on the propensity of MEPs to vote against their national parties. The only variable with any significance is the number of years that an MEP has been in the European Parliament. This suggests that the longer an MEP has been in the parliament, the more independent they will be from their national party. However, the results in model 1 suggest that longer-serving MEPs are neither more nor less likely to vote against their European political group.

Overall, these results reinforce the inferences from the previous section. MEPs are more likely to vote against their European political groups than their national parties. Moreover, the main reason for MEPs to vote against their European political groups is a policy conflict between their national party and their European political group. When this happens, an MEP is likely to vote with his or her national party and against his or her European political group.

7.4   Relative importance of European and national parties in all five parliaments

An alternative way of assessing whether MEPs primarily respond to instructions from European parties or national parties is to look at

Table 7.4. *Average influence of European and national parties on MEP voting*

European Parliament	European political group		National party		Obs.	R-squared
	Coef.	t-stat.	Coef.	t-stat.		
1st (1979–1984)	0.32***	(2.86)	0.68***	(10.46)	191	0.718
2nd (1984–1989)	0.35***	(3.66)	0.64***	(10.23)	217	0.725
3rd (1989–1994)	0.42***	(6.06)	0.58***	(10.04)	205	0.697
4th (1994–1999)	0.43***	(8.54)	0.58***	(12.95)	344	0.735
5th (1999–2004)	0.32***	(7.29)	0.69***	(19.07)	405	0.779

Note: Dependent variable: MEP vote decision (Yes/No) in a given vote. The coefficients are average effects in a given parliament. Parameters of the models are estimated by linear regression with robust standard errors. T-statistics in parentheses. *Significant at 10%; **significant at 5%; ***significant at 1%.

whether MEP voting behaviour is predicted more by European political group affiliation or national party affiliation. In this analysis, the dependent variable is the decision of an MEP in a vote (Yes or No) and the two independent variables are, first, the voting position of the MEP's European political group (measured as the proportion of the political group that voted the same way as the MEP) and, second, the voting position of the MEP's national party (measured as the proportion of the national party that voted the same way as the MEP) (cf. Noury and Roland, 2002). The small number of Abstain votes were deleted, and the non-attached MEPs and the MEPs from national parties with less than three MEPs were also not included in the analysis.

The model was then estimated for each vote, using a linear probability model with the constant dropped. This makes the coefficients on the two independent variables easy to interpret. Essentially, the size of the coefficients can be interpreted as the proportion of the total variation in MEP voting behaviour that is independently explained by European parties and by national parties (for a similar analysis of voting in the US Senate see Levitt, 1996).

A single model was estimated for every roll-call vote between June 1979 and July 2004. Table 7.4 shows the average results from these models for the roll-call votes in each directly elected parliament. For example, the number of observations in each parliament is the average number of MEPs (who were not non-attached or from national parties with less than three MEPs) who voted Yes or No in a roll-call vote in that parliament.

The results suggest that national parties are, on average, about twice as influential in determining which way MEPs vote than European parties. Also, the proportional influence of the two parties was more or less stable across all five parliaments. In other words, these results reinforce the results in Table 7.2, where we found that MEPs are about twice as likely to vote against their European political group as they are to vote against their national party.

7.5   Conclusion: European parties from national party actions

Our analysis suggests that national parties are the main aggregate actors in the European Parliament. This is not surprising if one considers that by controlling the candidate-selection and re-election process, most national parties are able to decide which of their MEPs will be returned to the European Parliament. Also, national party leaderships have a dominant influence on the future career prospects of MEPs, both within and beyond the European Parliament. National parties decide which of their MEPs they will support for key committee positions and offices inside the parliament and also whether MEPs will be chosen as candidates for national legislative or executive office. As a result, MEPs are beholden to their national parties to get elected and for their future prospects once they have been elected.

In contrast, European political groups have a less direct influence on the MEPs. European parties issue voting instructions to their members, employ party whips and party coordinators to communicate party positions and to monitor the behaviour of their members, and possess the ultimate threat of expelling a member from the group. However, if an MEP finds herself torn between the position of her national party and her European party, we find that she will usually follow the position of her national party. What is striking, however, is that revealed conflicts between national parties and European parties in roll-call votes are extremely rare.

Adding these findings to our results in Chapter 5, where we found that European political groups have become increasingly cohesive despite growing internal ideological diversity amongst the national member parties of the groups, suggests a particular explanation of the development of democratic politics in the European Parliament. Growing transnational party conflict and cohesion is a product of the strategic behaviour of national political parties. National parties are increasingly likely to find themselves in conflict with the majority of the European political group to which they belong. However, they clearly only issue instructions to their MEPs to vote against the European political group position if the issue is extremely salient and will not severely damage the future relationship between the national party and the European party.

A recent example illustrates this idea. In May 2005, the European Parliament debated and voted on a draft directive on the organisation of working time. A key provision of the draft legislation was the abolition of the 'opt-out' clause in the existing EU working time legislation, which allowed employees to voluntarily agree with their employers to work more than the maximum 48 hours per week. The United Kingdom and several other member states opposed abolishing this opt-out, and the British Labour government put pressure on the nineteen British Labour MEPs to vote against the directive in the European Parliament. The British Labour MEPs agreed with the position of their party leaders in London. However, in the final vote on the directive they voted with the other members of the Party of European Socialists (PES) in support of the directive and against the position of the British government in the EU Council.

The British Labour delegation did not defect from the PES for two main reasons. First, there was a large majority in the parliament in favour of the legislation (the vote passed by 378 to 262), so nineteen Labour MEPs voting against the bill would not have produced a policy outcome favoured by the British government and would hence have been purely symbolic. Second, voting against the PES on such an important piece of legislation for the European party would have threatened the future influence of the British Labour MEPs in the PES and in the parliament, as the PES leadership would in the future be reluctant to allocate key rapporteurships to Labour MEPs or to promote Labour MEPs to committee chairmanships or to senior positions in the PES or the parliament.

In other words, national parties control the MEPs and have the power to fully discipline the latter. However, the national parties tend to collectively come to agreements on the policy of their European party group. The national parties have delegated significant organisational and policy leadership powers to the European party and use their own power to discipline the MEPs to follow the European party line. In a way, talking about two principals can sound misleading. In reality, there is a strong congruence between the European party group and the national parties, as the latter operate to make the European party act cohesively in the European Parliament.

8   Competition and coalition formation

Competition between political parties is often considered to be central to modern democracy (e.g. Schumpeter, 1943). Competition provides citizens with a mechanism for choosing leaders and policies and for punishing elected officials for failing to hold to their promises or for being corrupt. Competition provides incentives for elites to develop rival policy ideas and propose rival candidates for office. Democratic contestation can also have a formative effect. In both America and in European countries, the operation of competitive party systems played a central role in the replacement of local identities by national identities (e.g. Key, 1961; Rokkan, 1999).

Political parties, however, are not inherently competitive. For example, in the 1950s Schattschneider (1960), among others, criticised American parties for being 'unresponsive' to voters concerns and for failing to 'mobilise' around different policy agendas. Similarly, Katz and Mair (1995) famously observed that in many democracies, instead of competing, the main parties now form a 'cartel' to secure government office and state funding of their activities.

Similarly, a widely held view of the European Parliament is that the two main political parties, the socialists and the EPP, tend to collude rather than compete for influence and compete over policy outcomes (cf. Kreppel, 2000, 2002b; Hix et al., 2003). These two parties share similar policy preferences on many issues on the EU agenda, such as the social-market model of European regulatory capitalism and further European integration (e.g. Marks and Wilson, 2000). Also, the two main political groups are forced to coalesce because of the EU legislative procedures, where an 'absolute majority' of all the MEPs is often required to amend legislation – for example in the second reading of the co-decision procedure (Corbett et al., 2005). The socialists and EPP also collude to promote their own power against the smaller groups in the internal workings of the parliament, for example by rotating the Presidency of the parliament between the two largest groups and in the system of allocating committee chairs (e.g. Westlake, 1994: 187–8).[1]

Existing research, using samples of votes, suggests that the political groups may compete more than what this received wisdom suggests (e.g. Bardi, 1994; Hix and Lord, 1997; Raunio, 1997; Kreppel and Tsebelis, 1999; Hix, 2001; Kreppel, 2002b; Noury, 2002). Building on this research, what we do in this chapter is to use our dataset of all roll-call votes in the parliament to investigate how and why party competition and coalition formation has evolved over the last twenty-five years. We start, in Section 8.1, by discussing some of the general political science literature on competition and coalition behaviour. In Section 8.2 we then identify some of the main trends in coalition behaviour since 1979, and in Section 8.3 we undertake a statistical analysis to determine which factors explain the patterns we observe.

We find that party competition and coalition formation in the European Parliament occur along the classical left–right dimension, and that the two main political groups vote together less than they used to. We also find that the main determinants of coalition behaviour in the European Parliament are the policy preferences of the parties rather than the desire to be a powerbroker.

8.1   Theories of party competition and coalition formation

In political science literature there are two main explanations of party competition and coalition formation. The first approach sees coalitions as primarily driven by the desire to be powerful. The second approach sees coalitions form on the basis of policy preferences.

In the first approach, any actor can coalesce with any other actor, regardless of the distance between their policy positions. Fewer coalition partners means fewer interests to appease in the distribution of benefits. Hence, Riker (1962) argued that coalitions are likely to be 'minimum-winning' – meaning that there should be no surplus members of a coalition than are needed to secure a majority. Looking at the particular context of legislative voting, where coalitions form on a case-by-case basis, Baron and Ferejohn (1989) model legislative bargaining in a similar vain, and derive the prediction that an agenda-setter should choose as coalition partners those who are the cheapest to buy. An empirical prediction of 'minimum-winning coalition' and 'cheaper to buy' coalition partner selection is that smaller parties should be more

---

[1] Committee chairs and vice-chairs are allocated by the d'Hondt system of proportional representation which, although broadly proportional, favours larger parties.

often in a coalition than larger parties, to the extent that the former are cheaper to buy than the latter. In other words, as the size of a party increases, *ceteris paribus*, its probability of being in a coalition with a given partner will decrease.

Related to these ideas, if a party is lucky enough to be in a position to be decisive in turning a losing coalition into a winning coalition it can demand a high price for participating in a coalition. Hence, the more likely a party is to be pivotal, the more power it will have in coalition bargaining, irrespective of its policy preferences. This insight consequently underpins the various 'power index' methods for measuring the power of actors with differential voting weights (e.g. Shapley and Shubik, 1954; Banzhaf, 1965).

In the context of the European Parliament, this first approach to competition and coalition formation predicts that relative size of the political groups rather than the policy preferences of the groups is the main determinant of coalition formation. Indeed, when power indices are applied to the political groups in the European Parliament, researchers find that the likelihood that a political group will be pivotal is highly correlated to the number of seats it has relative to the other political groups (e.g. Lane et al., 1995; Hosli, 1997; Nurmi, 1997). Similarly, one of the main reasons people assume that the socialists and EPP form an alliance is because this enables them to dominate the policy agenda and the internal workings of the parliament.

In opposition to this view, the second approach assumes that policy preferences drive coalition formation. In this view, a party is more likely to coalesce with, or a legislator is more likely to vote with, someone with closer preferences than with someone who is further away. Against Riker's policy-blind view, Axelrod argued that 'minimum-connected-coalitions' are more likely – between parties that are next to each other on the main dimension of political competition. Nevertheless, a policy-driven coalition need not be minimum-winning. For example, if there is a choice between an existing policy status quo that is highly undesirable and a moderate alternative policy proposal, then an 'oversized' coalition can result from purely policy-driven behaviour because most parties will prefer the new policy to the status quo (Grosclose and Snyder, 1996; Krehbiel, 1998).

As explained in Chapter 3, socio-economic interests and values tend to be paramount for political parties, since attitudes on these issues distinguish party families from each other. Party formation in the European Parliament, like in other normal democracies, is on a left–right basis. This reasoning should extend to coalition formation. Parties will tend to form coalitions with the parties that have the closest positions to theirs on the left–right dimension. In contrast, policies on European integration tend to divide actors in the EU policy process along national lines rather than party lines (Hix and Lord, 1997; cf. Hooghe and Marks, 1999). If parties try to compete against each other on the question of more or less European integration, they risk undermining their own internal party cohesion (Hix, 1999). Parties will thus try to use the limited agenda control they have to filter out divisive issues on European integration. If political behaviour is policy-driven rather than power-driven then policy-based coalitions should be primarily 'connected' along the left–right dimension.

In sum, variations in the patterns of party competition and coalition formation in the European Parliament may be determined by the changing relative power of the political groups, the changing policy preferences of the parties or some combination of the two.

8.2   Patterns of coalitions in the European Parliament

Table 8.1 shows the proportion of times the majority in one political group voted the same way as the majority in another political group in all the roll-call votes in the fifth European Parliament (1999–2004). The political groups in the table are ordered from left to right, except for the two 'protest' forces that do not fit easily into this dimension: the anti-European Group for a Europe of Democracies and Diversities (EDD), and the non-attached MEPs (NA). The coalition patterns suggest that coalitions in the European Parliament do follow the left–right dimension. Specifically, the closer two political groups are to each other on this dimension the more often they voted together in 1999–2004. For example, the EPP-ED, which was the largest group on the fifth parliament, voted with the ELDR more than with the PES, with the PES more than with the G/EFA, and with the G/EFA more than with the EUL/NGL. This follows the pattern observed in previous parliaments (e.g. Hix and Lord, 1997: 158–166; Raunio, 1997: 101–106).

These numbers also illustrate a relatively high level of political competition between the two main groups. Surprisingly, given the conventional wisdom, the EPP-ED and PES voted less often with each other than either did with the ELDR. The EPP-ED and PES also voted less often with each other than either of them did with the political group to their immediate extremes – the UEN for the EPP-ED and the G/EFA for the PES.

However, the EPP and socialists have not always been so competitive. Figure 8.1 shows the proportion of times the two major groups voted together in each two-year period, calculated as a rolling average in each successive six-month period. The peak of the socialist–EPP coalition was

Table 8.1. *Coalition patterns in the 1999–2004 Parliament*

Political group (Left to Right)	EUL/ NGL	G/ EFA	PSE	ELDR	EPP- ED	UEN	EDD	NA
Radical-Left (EUL/NGL)		0.793	0.691	0.554	0.424	0.459	0.592	0.524
Greens (G/EFA)	0.793		0.720	0.623	0.471	0.452	0.555	0.510
Socialists (PES)	0.691	0.720		0.729	0.645	0.526	0.526	0.568
Liberals (ELDR)	0.554	0.623	0.729		0.679	0.550	0.523	0.600
European People's Party (EPP-ED)	0.424	0.471	0.645	0.679		0.712	0.520	0.682
Gaullists (UEN)	0.459	0.452	0.526	0.550	0.712		0.626	0.738
Anti-Europeans (EDD)	0.592	0.555	0.526	0.523	0.520	0.626		0.638
Non-attached MEPs	0.524	0.510	0.568	0.600	0.682	0.738	0.638	

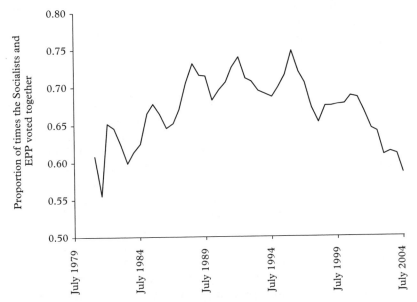

Figure 8.1. Frequency of the Socialist–EPP 'grand coalition'

Note: This graph shows the proportion of times the majorities of the socialist and EPP groups voted the same way in a given two-year period, calculated as a moving average. The vertical axis scale does not start at zero.

in the third parliament (1989–1994), when these two parties voted together more than 70 per cent of the time for most of this period. In the first, fourth and fifth parliaments, in contrast, the two largest political groups were more competitive. In fact, in the first parliament, the socialists were more likely to vote with the liberals, the greens and the radical-left than with the EPP (Hix et al., 2005). And in the fourth and fifth parliaments, the socialists voted with the liberals more than with the EPP, and for the first time the liberals voted with the socialists more than with the EPP.

So, why did the socialists and EPP vote together so often in the late 1980s and early 1990s? Why did the grand coalition decline in the late 1990s? And why did the liberals start to vote as often with the socialists as with the EPP? To answer these questions, and others, we need to delve deeper into the data.

8.3   Determinants of coalition formation

To analyse the determinants of the changing pattern of competition and coalition formation we undertake a statistical analysis. We first introduce the variables we use and then present the results.

8.3.1   Variables

We take as the dependent variable the proportion of times the majorities of any two of the six main political groups voted the same way in each six-month period between July 1979 and June 2004. Five of the political groups were present throughout this period, while one of the political groups, the greens, was not present in the first parliament (the first 10 periods). We hence have a total of 700 observations (10 pairs of coalitions between 4 political groups in the first 10 periods, plus 15 pairs of coalitions between 5 political groups in the last 40 periods).

We use four types of explanatory variables: (1) variables related to the political groups in the parliament, which aim to test one or other of the theories of party competition; (2) variables related to the powers of the European Parliament, which capture the impact of growing power of the parliament on coalition patterns; (3) variables that control for factors that might interfere with coalition patterns; and (4) 'fixed effect' variables for each pair of coalitions, so that the magnitudes for the other variables relate to changes in the occurrence of each particular coalition rather than to changes in the overall structure of party competition.

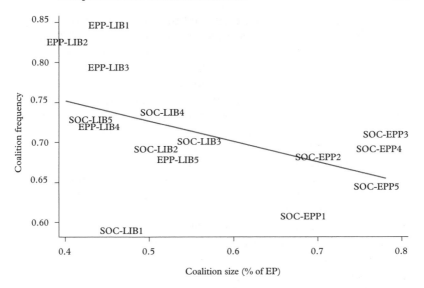

Figure 8.2. Coalition size and frequency

Note: EPP-LIB1 is the frequency of the EPP–liberal coalition in the 1979–1984 parliament, EPP-LIB2 is the frequency of the EPP–liberal coalition in the 1984–1989 parliament, and so on. Coalition size is the combined size of the two political groups in the coalition, in terms of the share of seats in the European Parliament. The vertical axis scale does not start at zero.

In the first type of variable, we include the size of a coalition (*Coalition size*), measured as the combined percentage of seats in the European Parliament held by the two political groups that make up the coalition. This variable hence investigates the effect of the 'power' of a coalition between two parties on coalition frequency. We compute coalition sizes for all pairs of parties independently of how close or far apart they are on the left–right axis.

As an illustration, Figure 8.2 plots the size of the two-party coalitions between the three largest political groups against their frequency in each of the five directly elected parliaments. The line in the figure is the result of a bivariate regression between these two variables. Thus for example, the point SOC-LIB1 close to the horizontal axis on the left refers to coalitions between the socialists and the liberals. This coalition's combined size is between 40 and 50 per cent and its frequency is somewhat below 60 per cent. The fact that the coalitions are spread from the top left to the bottom right of the figure suggests that the likely power of a potential coalition partner is at least partly relevant. For example, the two largest groups are more likely to form a coalition with the liberals than with each other because they need to give less away to a smaller coalition partner. Also, the decline of the frequency of the EPP–liberal coalition between the fourth and fifth parliaments went hand in hand with an increase in the combined size of these two parties. However, looking only at the socialist–EPP coalitions, it appears that the larger the combined size of these two political groups the more likely they were to vote together. But these results may not hold in a multivariate analysis and at a lower level of aggregation (looking at six-month periods rather than five-year periods), and also with the addition of all the other possible coalition combinations between the six main political groups.

To test the alternative, policy-driven, theory of coalition formation we use a variable that measures the distance on the left–right dimension between the two political groups in a particular coalition in a given period (*Ideological distance*). As in Chapter 5, we use the Manifestos Research Group dataset on national party positions on the left–right dimension to calculate this variable (Budge et al., 2001). From the left–right position of each national party in a political group in each of the six-month periods we calculated the mean left–right position of each political group by multiplying the position of each national party in the group by the percentage of MEPs of that national party in the group. The 'ideological distance' of a coalition is then measured as the distance between the mean left–right location of the two political groups in the coalition in the particular period.

As an illustration, Figure 8.3 plots the left–right ideological distance in the two-party coalitions between the three largest political groups against their frequency in each of the five directly elected parliaments, and the line represents the result of a bivariate regression between these two variables. The location of the coalitions in the figure and the steepness of the slope of the line suggest a strong relationship: if two political groups move further apart on the left–right dimension they vote together less. For example, the socialists and EPP voted together less in the fifth parliament than in the fourth because they moved further apart on the left–right dimension. Meanwhile, as the ideological distance between the socialists and liberals decreased, these two political groups voted together more often. Again, though, this result may not hold up in multivariate analysis at a lower level of aggregation and with the inclusion of all the coalition combinations of the six main political groups.

In the second type of explanatory variables we include the same four variables that we use in Chapter 5 to measure the power of the European Parliament. The first three variables are dummy variables representing the increases in the parliament's powers in the three Treaty reforms since the mid-1980s: the Single European Act (*SEA*), which takes the

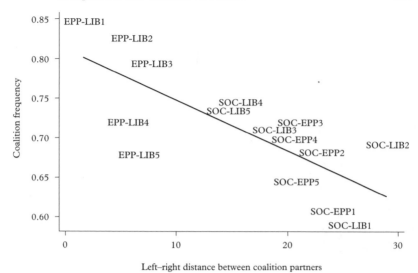

Figure 8.3. Ideological distance between parties and coalition frequency

Note: EPP-LIB1 is the frequency of the EPP–liberal coalition in the 1979–1984 parliament, EPP-LIB2 is the frequency of the EPP–liberal coalition in the 1984–1989 parliament, and so on. The left–right distance between each pair of coalition partners is the distance between the ideological position of each political group, which is calculated as the average left–right location of each national party (as measured by the party manifestos dataset) weighted by the number of MEPs each national party has in the political group. The vertical axis scale does not start at zero.

value 0 for each period up to January–June 1987 and 1 thereafter; the Maastricht Treaty (*Maastricht*), which takes the value 0 for each period up to January–June 1993 and 1 thereafter; and the Amsterdam Treaty (*Amsterdam*), which takes the value 0 for each period up to January–June 1999 and 1 thereafter. The other variable (*Trend*) represents the time trend from 1979 to 2004, which takes the value 1 for the first six-month period in the sample (July–December 1979), 2 for the second period, and so on. As in Chapter 5, in order to check for robustness of our results to the problem of the correlation between the *Trend* variable and the *SEA*, *Maastricht* and *Amsterdam* dummy variables, we exclude these variables in separate models.

In the third type of variable, we include two control variables. First, we include the number of roll-call votes in a given period (*No. of RCVs*).[2]

---

[2] Recall that this variable is divided by 1000; otherwise the estimated coefficients appear too small.

Table 8.2. *Determinants of changes in coalition frequencies*

	(1)	(2)	(3)	(4)
Constant	0.293*** (4.74)	0.291*** (5.39)	0.297*** (4.89)	0.378*** (7.24)
Coalition size	-0.002 (0.04)		-0.002 (0.04)	-0.001 (0.01)
Ideological distance	-0.002*** (4.61)	-0.002*** (4.67)	-0.002*** (4.61)	-0.002*** (4.57)
SEA	-0.032** (2.42)	-0.032** (2.42)	-0.029*** (3.28)	
Maastricht	-0.009 (0.78)	-0.009 (0.78)	-0.007 (0.79)	
Amsterdam	0.008 (0.67)	0.008 (0.67)	0.010 (0.86)	
Trend	0.000 (0.29)	0.000 (0.29)	0.023 (0.94)	-0.001*** (2.99)
No. of RCVs	0.019 (0.71)	0.019 (0.71)		0.049* (1.85)
Cohesion of all EP	0.668*** (8.07)	0.668*** (8.06)	0.664*** (8.18)	0.536*** (8.90)
Socialist–Liberal	0.020 (1.32)	0.021** (2.23)	0.020 (1.31)	0.021 (1.34)
Socialist–Left	0.048*** (2.68)	0.048*** (3.83)	0.048*** (2.68)	0.048*** (2.71)
Socialist–Gaullist	-0.101*** (6.02)	-0.100*** (11.58)	-0.101*** (6.02)	-0.100*** (5.99)
Socialist–Green	-0.005 (0.25)	-0.005 (0.29)	-0.005 (0.24)	-0.004 (0.20)
EPP–Liberal	0.078*** (4.39)	0.079*** (6.70)	0.078*** (4.39)	0.079*** (4.41)
EPP–Left	-0.109*** (5.80)	-0.108*** (10.49)	-0.109*** (5.81)	-0.108*** (5.78)
EPP–Gaullist	0.050** (2.41)	0.050*** (3.78)	0.050** (2.40)	0.050** (2.43)
EPP–Green	-0.154*** (8.33)	-0.154*** (18.47)	-0.154*** (8.35)	-0.153*** (8.28)
Liberal–Left	-0.064** (2.16)	-0.063*** (6.45)	-0.064** (2.16)	-0.063*** (2.14)
Liberal–Gaullist	-0.013 (0.41)	-0.012 (0.76)	-0.013 (0.41)	-0.012 (0.38)
Liberal–Green	-0.081** (2.44)	-0.080*** (5.89)	-0.081** (2.44)	-0.080** (2.40)
Left–Gaullist	-0.109*** (3.41)	-0.108*** (9.98)	-0.109*** (3.41)	-0.108*** (3.39)
Left–Green	0.066* (1.93)	0.067*** (4.29)	0.066* (1.94)	0.068** (1.98)
Gaullist–Green	-0.193*** (5.63)	-0.192*** (13.71)	-0.193*** (5.63)	-0.192*** (5.59)
Observations	700	700	700	700
R-squared	0.622	0.622	0.621	0.610

Note: Dependent variable: proportion of times the majorities of two particular party groups voted together in a six-month period between 1979 and 2004. The Socialist–EPP pair is excluded as the reference value. Parameters of the models are estimated by fixed effects with panel-corrected standard errors and correction for heteroskedasticity and correlations between parties. Robust *t*-statistics in parentheses, *significant at 10% **significant at 5% ***significant at 1%.

This enables us to investigate whether more roll-call votes reduces or increases the propensity of a coalition to form. Second, we include the Agreement Index of the European Parliament as a whole (*Cohesion of all EP*). This variable controls for the effect of the degree of consensus in a given period on the propensity of the political groups to vote together.

Finally, we include fourteen party-pair dummy variables (*Socialist–Liberal, Socialist–Left, Socialist–Gaullist, Socialist–Green, EPP–Liberal, EPP–Left, EPP–Gaullist, EPP–Green, Liberal–Left, Liberal–Gaullist, Liberal–Green, Left–Gaullist, Left–Green, Gaullist–Green*). The reference category is the socialist–EPP coalition. To reiterate, by adding these variables, our focus is not on the comparison between two party-pairs, but rather on the effect of the explanatory variables on within party-pair variation.

8.3.2   Results

Table 8.2 reports the results of four regression models of coalition patterns between 1979 and 2004. The main findings are as follows.[3] First, the policy preferences of the parties are more important than the likely power of the coalition for determining coalition patterns. Whereas the ideological distance variable is significant in all model specifications, the size ('power') of a two-party coalition is not significant in any specification. Indeed, dropping this variable, as in model 2, does not change any of the other results. In contrast, an increase (or decrease) in the ideological distance between two parties on the left–right dimension is a strong predictor of how often these two parties will vote together. In substantive terms, a one standard deviation change in the ideological distance between two parties implies a 16 per cent standard deviation change in the frequency that these parties will vote the same way. This result gives us a strong indication of the crucial importance of left–right politics in the European Parliament.

Second, this left–right result is reinforced by comparisons of the frequency of pairs of coalitions to the frequency of the socialist–EPP coalition. Here, we find all the expected signs. The socialists vote more

---

[3] We also checked for other potential problems. First, non-stationarity of our dependent variables may be a source of concern, given that we have 50 time periods. Performing tests of unit roots in panels, however, leads us to reject the null hypothesis of non-stationarity. Second, to check for heteroskedasticity, we use fixed-effects and panel-corrected standard errors. Thus, we controlled for both heteroskedasticity and correlation across political groups. Third, to check for serial auto-correlation (if the error term for a political group is correlated across time periods) we specified models that correct for first-order and second-order auto-correlations. This did not change the direction or significance of the reported results.

with the radical-left and less with the Gaullists, the EPP vote more with liberals, less with the radical-left, the greens and the Gaullists, and the greens vote more with the radical-left and less with the EPP.

Third, in contrast to the results we found in Chapter 5, changes in the powers of the European Parliament in the Maastricht and Amsterdam Treaties do not have an effect on coalition patterns. The SEA, meanwhile, had a negative effect reducing coalition frequency, meaning that on average the parties behaved more competitively after the introduction of this Treaty than before. Similarly, the *Trend* variable is not significant when the other variables that measure the increasing powers of the European Parliament are included. However, when this variable is included and the other three variables are excluded, as in model 4, the result is a small but significant decline in the frequency of these fifteen coalitions as the powers of the European Parliament have increased. In other words, as the European Parliament gained power, the political groups become more competitive.

Finally, regarding the two control variables, as one would expect, the size of the overall coalition in the European Parliament is a strong predictor of the propensity of any two parties to vote together. However, the number of roll-calls in a given period is only significant in one specification, and the magnitude of this effect is very small.

8.4   Conclusion: an increasingly competitive party system

Overall, we find that the political groups in the European Parliament are increasingly competitive in their voting behaviour. We also find that the main factor that explains this trend is the changing ideological location of the political groups relative to each other. For example, as the policy positions of the two main parties in the European Parliament diverged, they voted together less. Similarly, as the distance between the socialists and the liberals declined, while the distance between the EPP and the liberals increased, the liberals started to vote more with the socialists and less with the EPP.

In contrast, the size of the parties, which is generally assumed to be a main determinant of coalition behaviour, does not appear to play a major role in coalition formation in the European Parliament. Put another way, the fact that coalition behaviour is determined by left–right policy distances between the parties, rather than by the relative sizes of the political groups, suggests that policy preferences on socio-economic issues are more important for MEPs and national parties than simply being on the winning side.

So, the socialists and EPP did not form a 'grand coalition' in the late 1980s and early 1990s because this enabled them to command a stable majority and so dominate the policy agenda and the internal offices of the parliament. Rather, these two groups voted together frequently in this period because they had similar policy preferences on the key issues on the agenda of the European Parliament, such as the level of environmental and social protection in the European single market. The EPP then became more conservative and economically liberal in the late 1990s, partly as a result of more right-wing parties joining the EPP (such as the British, Spanish and Italian conservatives) but also because some of the key parties in the EPP became more economically liberal (such as the German Christian democrats). As a result, the EPP started having quite different views to the socialists on many of the market and regulation issues passing through the European Parliament.

Related to this, the liberals started to vote less with the EPP and more with the socialists in the fifth parliament for both policy preferences and strategic reasons. As the policy distance between the EPP and socialists increased, and these two parties started to vote together less, the liberals found themselves in a pivotal position for the first time. In policy terms, the liberals were still closer to the EPP than they were to the socialists in this period, as Figure 8.3 shows. But the liberals chose to vote more with the socialists than their policy preferences would otherwise predict, as they were in a good position to extract concessions from both the socialists and the EPP.

In other words, the transnational political parties in the European Parliament are not only cohesive organisations, as we find in the previous chapters, but they are also competitive. We found in Chapter 5 that internal ideological diversity of a political group does not undermine party cohesion in the long run, whereas in this chapter we found that socio-economic policy preferences are the main determinants of inter-party competition. This may seem contradictory. However, it is not. National parties sort themselves into European parties according to their preferences, but accept the discipline of the European party once they have joined because they know that this discipline is essential for competing successfully. Given the importance of socio-economic policy preferences in party formation, it is not surprising that this should also be paramount in coalition formation. Moreover, the two dynamics of party discipline and competition go hand in hand. The political groups are able to maintain internal cohesion precisely because inter-party competition and coalition behaviour is driven by partisan policy preferences. With increased party competition, if a national party is faced with a choice between the position of its European party, which might not be at exactly the same position as its ideal policy, and the position of another political group, the national party will usually prefer its European political group's position to the position of the rival political group. Growing power of the European Parliament leads to growing incentives for the parties in the parliament to try to shape EU policy outcomes in a particular ideological direction. With more at stake, increased European party cohesion and European party competition go hand in hand.

9   Dimensions of politics

One of the main ways of understanding politics inside legislative institutions is to investigate the shape of the policy space. The number of policy dimensions and the location of actors on these dimensions determine, among other things, which actors are pivotal and the possibility and direction of policy change (e.g. Tsebelis, 2002). Not surprisingly, a fast growing area of political science research in recent years has been the estimation of actors' ideal points. This has taken a variety of forms and methods, such as scaling of roll-call voting data (e.g. Poole and Rosenthal, 1997), hand coding of party manifestos (Budge et al., 2001), surveys of experts' opinions of parties' positions (e.g. Laver and Hunt, 1992), or computer coding of political statements (e.g. Laver et al., 2003).

The European Parliament is an especially interesting object for spatial analysis of the dimensionality of politics because of its unique features. There is considerable heterogeneity between the cultures, histories, economic conditions and national institutions of the EU member states. Therefore, politics in the European Parliament is likely to be more complex than politics in many national parliaments. MEPs are also members of national parties as well as European political groups. A legislature with such characteristics is potentially one with high dimensionality.

In this chapter we describe the policy space inside the European Parliament by applying an established scaling method to the roll-call votes between 1979 and 2004. The method we use provides not only a measure of the dimensionality of the policy space, but also ideal point estimates on each policy dimension for every MEP since 1979. We then use a statistical analysis to interpret the substantive meaning of the 'revealed' dimensions. Usually, scaling methods, like all factor analysis, suffer from the major weakness that the dimensions identified by the statistical technique are difficult to interpret rigorously. Interpretations of these dimensions are usually subjective and lack scientific content. They are, therefore, not necessarily convincing. In the particular case of the European Parliament, we are lucky to be able to use regression analysis to rigorously identify the determinants of the dimensions of politics in this institution, using information on actors' preferences, which is exogenous to voting behaviour in the European Parliament. This is not the case, for example, for the US Congress. We are thus better able to identify the dimensions of politics in the European Parliament than in most other legislatures.

We find one main dimension of politics in the European Parliament. This dimension is the classic left–right dimension of democratic politics. A second dimension is also present, although to a lesser extent. This dimension can be interpreted at first sight as the pro-/anti-Europe dimension. But regression analysis reveals that the second dimension also captures inter-institutional conflicts between the political groups and national parties in the parliament and the parties in 'government' in the EU Council and Commission.

The rest of this chapter is organised as follows. Section 9.1 briefly reviews some of the existing research on the dimensions of conflict in EU politics. Section 9.2 introduces the spatial models and the scaling method we use, known as NOMINATE. Section 9.3 presents the spatial 'maps' of MEPs' ideal points produced by the method. Section 9.4 then presents the substantive interpretation of the dimensions.

9.1   Dimensions of conflict in EU politics

Traditionally, politics between and inside the EU institutions has been understood as a battle between those in favour of further and faster European integration and those opposed (Marks and Steenbergen, 2002). In Treaty negotiations, for example, countries like Belgium, the Netherlands and Italy have tended to support delegating more powers to the EU institutions while countries like the United Kingdom and Denmark have tended to support preserving the powers of national governments (cf. Moravcsik, 1998). Also, because the Commission, the European Parliament and the European Court of Justice are likely to be the beneficiaries of more power at the European level, these 'supranational institutions' have traditionally been regarded as being on the integrationist side of the main dimension of EU politics with most of the member states' governments in the Council towards the opposite end of the dimension (e.g. Tsebelis and Garrett, 2001).

However, it has recently been argued that as the EU increasingly makes policies in the traditional areas of domestic politics we should expect the classic 'left–right' dimension to emerge in EU politics. At the domestic level in Europe, the left–right dimension captures parties' and citizens' preferences on two underlying sets of issues: intervention-free market issues, such as welfare policies, unemployment and inflation; and liberty–authority issues, such as environmentalism and minority rights (cf. Flanagan, 1987; Laver and Hunt, 1992). Parties on the left tend to take "interventionist/libertarian" positions, whereas parties on the right tend to take "free market/authority" positions. This does not preclude intermediate positions: intervention/authority (the traditional stance of Christian Democrats), and *laissez-faire*/liberty (such as some European liberal parties). However, these positions are less common than 'left-libertarianism' (such as greens and social democrats) and 'right-authoritarianism' (such as conservatives and contemporary Christian Democrats) (cf. Finer, 1987; Kitschelt, 1994).

Ministers in the EU Council, MEPs and Commissioners are all career party politicians, whose previous success and future prospects depend on supporting the policy positions of their national political parties (Hix and Lord, 1997). Consequently, in battles over the regulation of the single market, the level of social and environmental protection, constraints on national macro-economic policies, gender equality, the rights of minorities, and on many other issues, political actors in the EU institutions are likely to take positions that reflect their parties' left–right policy positions. If a left–right dimension exists in EU politics, we should consequently expect politicians on the left to favour economic intervention, such as EU social regulation and tax harmonisation, and liberal socio-political issues, such as environmental protection, gender equality and minority rights. Conversely, we should expect politicians on the right to favour a liberal and deregulated single market and authoritarian socio-political policies, such as restrictive immigration and cooperation to tackle drugs and crime.

Nevertheless, the pro-/anti-Europe dimension and the left–right dimension may not necessarily cut across each other. They may even be highly correlated. For example, in the 1960s and 1970s, when European integration primarily related to the liberalisation of trade between the member states, parties on the left tended to be anti-European whereas parties on the right tended to be pro-European. Then, the relationship reversed in the 1990s. Once the single market was created, the left became more supportive of further political centralisation than the right, in order to enable the state to regain control of the market (Hooghe and Marks, 1999; Tsebelis and Garrett, 2000; Hooghe et al., 2002). This combination of left/centralisation and right/decentralisation positions exists in many other multi-level polities, such as the United States, where the left generally supports economic intervention by the central government while the right defends 'states' rights'.

Against this view, even if some parties on the left are now in favour of European integration and some parties on the right are more opposed, a pro-/anti-Europe cleavage is likely to cut through all the main European 'party families' (Hix, 1994, 1999). As in other territorially divided polities, the costs and benefits of economic policies are likely to be distributed territorially as well as functionally. Put another way, any policy that benefits one transnational social group (such as business interests) at the expense of another (such as organised labour) is also likely to benefit the citizens of one member state more than another. Hence, political parties from the same ideological family but from different member states are likely to find themselves on the same side on some issues but opposed to each other on other issues. If this is the case, the left–right and pro-/anti-Europe dimensions will not collapse into a single dimension.

A third dimension, based on institutional interests rather than policy positions, might also combine with or cut across one or other of these policy dimensions. The main dimension of conflict within legislatures in parliamentary systems is the government-opposition battle. Despite policy differences between governing coalition partners or within governing parties, parties in government can usually force their members of parliament to vote together by threatening to resign or call new elections (Huber, 1996b; Diermeier and Feddersen, 1998). As we discussed in Chapter 1, the EU is not a parliamentary system of government, in that the Commission cannot dissolve the European Parliament and can only be censured by a 'double majority' (a majority of all MEPs and two-thirds of votes cast). Nevertheless, the Commission has the exclusive right of legislative initiative and is 'elected' by a simple majority of the European Parliament (after being proposed by the European Council). Hence, the national parties who have Commissioners and those transnational political parties who voted for the Commission in the investiture vote are likely to find themselves facing a choice between supporting 'their' Commission or opposing it. Similarly, the other chamber of the EU's legislative process is the EU Council, which is composed of ministers from national parties in government. On many legislative issues, the national parties whose ministers' voted for a piece of legislation in the Council are likely to put pressure on their MEPs to support the legislation in the parliament (cf. Hoyland, 2005). As unanimity or a high qualified-majority is used in the Council to pass a piece of legislation, the pressure on MEPs from parties who are in national governments is thus likely to be quite broad. Despite the fact that the EU is closer to a separation-of-powers system than to a classic model of parliamentary government, government-opposition conflicts may emerge in EU politics but in a different form than in a classic parliamentary system.

Existing empirical research suggests some independence of the two main policy dimensions. Separate EU integration and left–right dimensions have been found in the positions national parties take on Europe (Aspinwall, 2002; Marks et al., 2002), in the European party federations' election manifestos (Gabel and Hix, 2002b), and in mass attitudes towards the EU (Gabel and Anderson, 2002). These two dimensions have also been observed in initial research on the policy space inside the European Parliament (Kreppel and Tsebelis, 1999; Hix, 2001; Noury, 2002) and in the EU Council (Mattila and Lane, 2001; Mattila, 2004). However, existing research on the European Parliament has not investigated the full history of voting in the parliament since the first direct elections in 1979 and has not investigated how inter-institutional conflicts impact on MEP voting behaviour.

9.2   Estimating MEPs' ideal points from roll-call votes

To analyse voting in the European Parliament, we use a well-known model in the social sciences, called 'the spatial model of voting'. This model, originally proposed by Hotelling (1929) and further developed by Enelow and Hinich (1984), is the workhorse theory of modern legislative studies. The spatial model assumes that each MEP has a preferred point, or ideal position, in a given policy space. In addition, it assumes that each political choice – the policy consequences of voting Yes or No – is located in the same policy space. In other words, there is a spatial representation of both the MEPs and their choices. An MEP will thus vote for the choice that is closer to his or her ideal position. For example, a left-wing MEP will vote for workers' protection and a right-wing MEP will vote against it. In addition to left–right, the policy space may have additional dimensions such as attitudes towards European integration. On this dimension, pro-European members will vote for further transfer of competencies to the EU whereas anti-European members will vote against it.

There are a large number of methods, based on the spatial model, for extracting 'ideal point estimates' from parliamentary voting records (Poole, 2005). The method we apply is known as NOMINATE, which was originally developed by Keith Poole and Howard Rosenthal for the analysis of voting in the United States Congress (Poole and Rosenthal, 1997: 233–51). The method has since emerged as the main way of estimating actors' locations from voting records in other parliaments (e.g. Schonhardt–Bailey, 2003; Rosenthal and Voeten, 2004) as well as in international assemblies, such as the United Nations General Assembly (Voeten, 2000). In contrast to much of the literature, we are less interested in the estimation of the ideal points of individual MEPs than in the number of dimensions of politics. Indeed, the party cohesion we have studied in the previous chapters implies that MEPs will vote according to the position taken by their national party. It thus makes little sense to try to recover the individual preferences of MEPs from their voting behaviour. However, in Chapter 2, we argued that parties reduce the dimensionality of politics. NOMINATE is well suited for verifying how many independent dimensions of politics can be found in the European Parliament.

NOMINATE tries to collapse all the vote-splits into a small number of dimensions. The result is a set of Cartesian coordinates for each parliamentarian in a multi-dimensional policy space. The distance between any two sets of coordinates is an estimate of the ideological closeness of any two parliamentarians in a particular parliament. For example, if two members of a parliament voted exactly the same way in all the votes they would be estimated to be in exactly the same point. On the other hand, if they voted on opposite sides in every vote they would be estimated to be at opposite ends of all the revealed dimensions. The distribution of parliamentarians allows one to interpret the dimensions of the policy space.

Following the standard practice in the scaling of roll-call votes, we discarded MEPs who voted in fewer than twenty votes in a given parliament and dropped votes where more than 97 per cent of MEPs voted together. The number of MEPs discarded using this method was actually rather small (ranging from 9 per cent of the 548 MEPs who were present at one time or another in the first parliament to less than 1 per cent of the MEPs in the fourth parliament) and these discarded MEPs did not belong to any particular member state or political group. Table 9.1 lists the number of scaleable roll-call votes and legislators we were able to estimate in each European Parliament.

Table 9.1 also compares two goodness-of-fit measures of applying NOMINATE to the European Parliament with other assemblies. The first measure is the percentage of roll-call vote decisions correctly predicted by the set of legislator locations on the first and second dimensions. The second measure is the aggregate proportional reduction in error, which indicates how much the spatial model improves on a naïve benchmark model, such as everybody voting the same way in each vote. These measures reveal how well voting in the European Parliament is captured by one dimension or two dimensions, relative to other assemblies.

Table 9.1. *Dimensionality in the European Parliament and Other Assemblies*

	Number of scaleable roll-calls	Number of scaleable legislators	Percentage of roll-call vote decisions predicted correctly			Aggregate proportional reduction of error (APRE)		
			Dimension 1	Dimension 2	Dimension 2–Dimension 1	Dimension 1	Dimension 2	Dimension 2–Dimension 1
European Parliament 1 (1979–1984)	787	500	86.0	91.5	5.5	46.9	67.6	20.7
European Parliament 2 (1984–1989)	1690	612	88.6	92.4	3.8	52.9	68.6	15.7
European Parliament 3 (1989–1994)	2269	586	89.9	91.8	1.9	54.8	63.5	8.7
European Parliament 4 (1994–1999)	3360	716	87.8	90.0	2.2	48.5	58.0	9.5
European Parliament 5 (1999–2004)	5190	687	87.8	90.0	2.2	55.7	63.2	8.5
US House of Representatives (1997–1998)	946	443	88.2	89.2	1.0	64.4	67.4	3.0
US Senate (1997–1998)	486	101	88.0	88.5	0.5	64.2	66.0	1.8
French National Assembly (1951–1956)	341	645	93.3	96.0	2.7	81.8	89.2	7.4
United Nations General Assembly (1991–1996)	344	186	91.8	93.0	1.2	62.1	67.7	5.6

Note: US House and Senate data from Poole and Rosenthal (1997), UN General Assembly data from Voeten (2000), French National Assembly data from Rosenthal and Voeten (2004).

The first noteworthy finding is that this method produces one main dimension of voting, a finding that is common to all known studies of legislative behaviour. Nevertheless, we find that voting in the European Parliament is more multi-dimensional than in other parliaments. This can be seen from the magnitude of the goodness-of-fit statistics for the second dimension in the European Parliament compared with the other parliaments. We can see this most clearly in the last column of Table 9.1. The Aggregate Proportional Reduction in Error from adding the second dimension to the first dimension is higher in the European Parliament compared with United States. Even though it has been declining from 20.7 per cent in the first parliament to 8.5 per cent in the fifth parliament, the Aggregate Proportional Reduction in Error for the US House and Senate in 1997–1998 was lower than that in the fifth parliament, respectively 3.0 and 1.8 per cent. Nevertheless, the fact that the size of the statistics for the second dimension has gradually declined reveals that voting in the European Parliament has become increasingly one-dimensional.

9.3   Spatial maps of the five elected European Parliaments

What are the first and second dimensions estimated by this scaling method? One weakness of this and similar inductive scaling methods is that they cannot provide any substantive meaning of the dimensions. The method simply 'reveals' the main dimensions of voting and the locations of the actors on these dimensions. The identification of the policy content of the dimensions is usually based on subjective heuristic interpretation. This interpretation is sometimes obvious but is not rigorous and may be misleading.

First, we look at the spatial 'maps' produced by NOMINATE. The relative location of the actors in the political groups in these maps should tell us something about what the dimensions represent. However, we go beyond 'eye-balling' and subjective interpretation. We use a statistical analysis to compare the estimated ideal points with exogenous measures of actors' policy positions and their representation in the other EU institutions.

Figures 9.1a to 9.1e show the maps of each of the five directly elected European Parliaments, where each dot represents the estimated location of each MEP on the first two dimensions.[1] The location of the political groups in these figures suggests that the two dimensions of politics in the European Parliament are in fact the left–right and pro-/anti-Europe dimensions. On the first dimension, in all five parliaments the parties are

---

[1] We ignored higher dimensions because the goodness-of-fit statistics associated with these dimensions were very low.

(a)

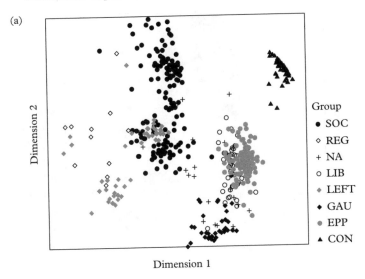

Figure 9.1a. Location of MEPs in the 1979–1984 Parliament

(b)

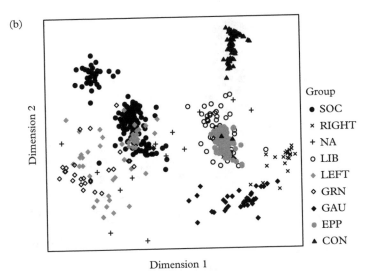

Figure 9.1b. Location of MEPs in the 1984–1989 Parliament

ordered from left to right exactly as one would expect with only a cursory knowledge of party politics in Europe: with the radical-left and greens on the furthest left, then the socialists on the centre-left, the liberals in the centre, the EPP on the centre-right, the British conservatives and allies

(c)

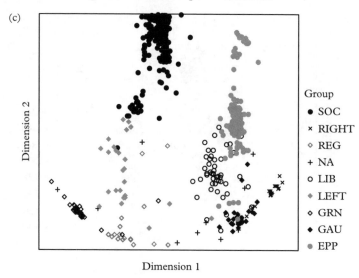

Figure 9.1c. Location of MEPs in the 1989–1994 Parliament

(d)

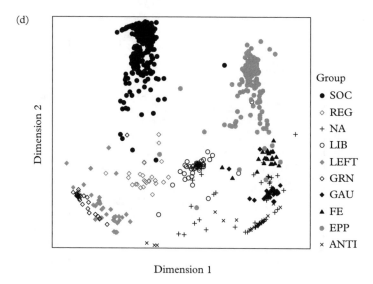

Figure 9.1d. Location of MEPs in the 1994–1999 Parliament

and French Gaullists and allies to the right of the EPP, the extreme right on the furthest right and the anti-Europeans divided between some MEPs on the extreme left and some on the extreme right.

(e)

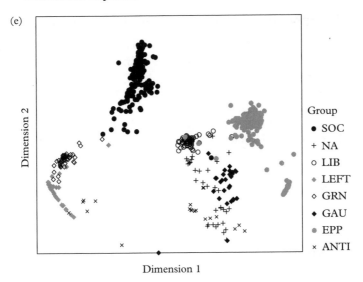

Figure 9.1e. Location of MEPs in the 1999–2004 Parliament

Also, on the second dimension, the main pro-European parties – the socialists, liberals and EPP – are at the top of the figures while the main anti-European parties – the radical-left, greens, Gaullists, extreme right and anti-Europeans – are at the bottom. Interestingly, the British conservatives, who changed position dramatically on the question of Europe, move from the top of the second dimension in the first and second parliaments to near the bottom of this dimension in the fifth parliament – as the outlying group of MEPs in the EPP in the bottom right hand corner of Figure 9.1e.

These maps also confirm the two main trends in voting behaviour in the European Parliament that we found in the previous chapters. First, all the political groups have become more cohesive, as illustrated by the declining dispersion of the positions of the MEPs in each political group across the five parliaments. Second, in terms of the structure of the party system, there is a clear difference between the first three parliaments and the fourth and fifth parliaments. In the first three parliaments, the party system was split into two blocs: a left bloc (of socialists, radical-left and greens), against a right bloc (of the EPP, liberals, French Gaullists and allies, and British conservatives and allies). However, the fourth and fifth parliaments reveal a different party system. In this new system, the liberals occupy a position between the socialists and EPP.

9.4   Interpretation of the meaning of the dimensions

The visual examination of the NOMINATE results gives us a reasonable interpretation of the dimensions of politics in the European Parliament but it is not rigorous. To interpret the substantive content of the dimensions we use a series of statistical models to explain the location of MEPs as a function of exogenous variables related to national party policy positions and the interests of political parties represented in the Council and Commission. We first introduce the variables and then present the results.

9.4.1   Variables

We define the dependent variables as the mean position of each national party's group of MEPs on each dimension in each parliament as estimated by NOMINATE. We thus treat each national party's delegation of MEPs in each parliament (as opposed to individual MEPs) as a separate observation. We use national parties as the unit of analysis for two reasons. First, exogenous measures of policy positions of actors in the European Parliament only exist for national parties. No comparable measure of the policy preferences of individual MEPs exists for all five parliaments. Second, consistent with our findings in the previous chapter, national parties are the main aggregate actors in the European Parliament below the level of the transnational political groups, and have a powerful influence on the behaviour of their MEPs. Hence, although we do not use exogenous measures of the preferences of the units that have been scaled (the MEPs), we do use exogenous measures of the central tendencies of these units. There were 57 national parties in the first parliament, 73 in the second, 85 in the third, 103 in the fourth and 119 in the fifth. We consequently have 437 observations when the scores for each national party in each parliament are pooled in a single dataset. However, we lose a number of observations in the statistical results because of missing data on the policy positions of some national parties.

We have three types of independent variables. First, as policy variables, we use exogenous measures of national party positions on the left–right axis and on the pro-/anti-Europe axis, testing the expectation that the policy space in the European Parliament combines these two underlying policy dimensions. We use one of the most widely applied exogenous measures of national party positions, from 'expert judgments' of party locations. This measure is fully exogenous to voting behaviour in the European Parliament and therefore leads us to an independent interpretation of the policy dimensions rather than a purely subjective interpretation. These data are taken from Marks and Steen-bergen's (2004) dataset of national party positions in 1984, 1988, 1992, 1996 and 1999. These five time-points correspond broadly with each of the five directly elected European Parliaments, and so allow us to have parliament by parliament external measures of national party positions. We call these variables *Left–right position* and *EU integration position*.

We expect these two policy conflicts to have independent effects on voting in the European Parliament, with left–right policy positions explaining national parties' positions on the first dimension and EU integration policy positions explaining national parties' positions on the second dimension. However, if these two underlying policy conflicts are beginning to merge into a single dimension in EU politics, then one would expect both these policy positions to explain positions on the first dimension of voting in the European Parliament, and maybe also to partially explain positions on the second dimension.

Second, to capture the effect of government-opposition dynamics at the national and European levels, we use two measures: (1) whether a national party was in government during the relevant parliament, which takes the value 1 if the national party was in government for a majority of the period and 0 otherwise (*In government*); and (2) whether a national party had a European Commissioner during the relevant parliament, which takes the value 1 if the national party had a Commissioner for the whole period of the parliament, 0.5 if the national party had a Commissioner for approximately half of the period of the parliament, and 0 otherwise (*Commissioner*).

The two biggest political groups contain almost all the main parties of government in the domestic arena and have dominated the Commission. However, as Figure 9.2 shows, there has been a dramatic change in the proportion of national parties from the socialists and the EPP who were in government or had a Commissioner in a given parliament. In the 1980s, most members of the EPP were in government and many members had a Commissioner, while most members of the socialists were in opposition and did not have a Commissioner. This situation was reversed in the late 1990s, with the socialists now the dominant force in the Council and the Commission. Meanwhile, most national parties in all the other political groups have been in opposition at home and have not been represented in the Commission, and hence have only been represented in the EU institutions via their MEPs. Hence, if the second dimension of voting in the European Parliament is related to govern-ment-opposition interests in the EU, the socialists should move to the top of the dimension over time, while the EPP should be moving to the bottom, and the governing parties within these political groups should

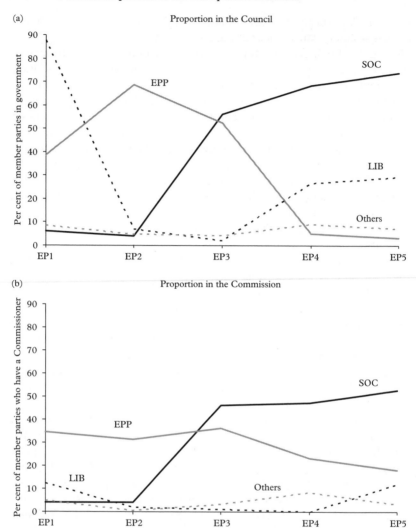

Figure 9.2. Proportion of each political group in the Council and Commission

be towards the top of their groups' cluster, while the opposition parties should be towards the bottom of their cluster.

Third, to examine whether policy positions and government-opposition dynamics explain differences in voting not only between but also within the political groups, we estimate separate models with dummy variables for each political group. Likewise, we introduce dummy variables for each EU member state, to analyse whether member state affiliation influences voting in the European Parliament.

9.4.2. *Results*

Table 9.2 shows the results of the analysis. Starting with the first dimension, five findings are worth emphasising. First, as observed in the maps of the parliaments, MEP locations on the first dimension are strongly explained by left–right policy positions. To evaluate the substantive effect of left–right policies on this dimension, it is useful to calculate standardised beta coefficients. The results show that a one standard deviation change along the left–right dimension (as measured by expert judgments) corresponds with a 78 per cent standard deviation change on the first dimension.[2]

Second, the left–right variable remains highly significant after the inclusion of political group dummy variables. This indicates that left–right policy positions also explain variations in MEP positions within the European political groups. In other words, a national party that has a policy position to the left of the average member of a European political group will be revealed to vote slightly to the left of the average member of this group. Whereas differences between the political groups can be observed from eye-balling the spatial maps, these internal differences cannot be observed in the spatial maps but are clearly shown in the statistical results.

Third, party policies on European integration and having a Commissioner are only significant without political group dummies. This means that once one controls for European party positions these variables are not relevant explanatory factors on the first dimension. Being in government, meanwhile, has no effect on MEPs' positions on this dimension.

Fourth, the magnitude of the coefficients on the political group variables confirms the intuition from the spatial figures: with the most left-wing parties having the lowest coefficients and the most right-wing parties having the highest coefficients – these coefficients relate to political group positions relative to the EPP (which is the baseline group).

Fifth, member state dummies are not significant on the first dimension. This consequently confirms our results from Chapters 5 and 8 that voting in the European Parliament is not driven by national interests.

---

[2] Using the results in model 1.

Table 9.2. *Interpreting the dimensions: pooled analysis*

	Dimension 1			Dimension 2		
	(1)	(2)	(3)	(1)	(2)	(3)
Constant	−0.925***	0.073	0.028	−0.675***	−0.066	−0.049
	(14.73)	(0.72)	(0.28)	(6.51)	(0.47)	(0.32)
Left-right position	1.686***	0.826***	0.861***	−0.206**	−0.257**	−0.189
	(31.73)	(7.85)	(9.61)	(2.41)	(2.22)	(1.60)
EU integration position	0.032***	−0.006	−0.001	0.100***	0.029*	0.023
	(3.53)	(0.57)	(0.11)	(8.16)	(1.86)	(1.38)
In government	0.052	0.019	−0.010	0.129***	0.036	0.047
	(1.52)	(1.03)	(0.51)	(2.61)	(1.05)	(1.28)
Commissioner	0.064*	−0.006	0.008	0.253***	0.017	0.007
	(1.81)	(0.28)	(0.34)	(4.34)	(0.41)	(0.15)
Greens		−0.954***	−0.952***		−0.577***	−0.568***
		(15.96)	(17.27)		(9.01)	(8.67)
Regionalists		−0.762***	−0.784***		−0.509***	−0.519***
		(13.64)	(15.09)		(4.89)	(4.62)
Radical-left		−0.743***	−0.697***		−0.512***	−0.469***
		(8.94)	(8.86)		(5.61)	(4.76)
Socialists		−0.474***	−0.467***		0.279***	0.296***
		(12.67)	(13.86)		(4.88)	(5.14)
Left Socialists		−0.453***	−0.555***		0.036	0.062
		(7.32)	(10.75)		(0.51)	(0.77)
Anti-Europeans		−0.444***	−0.463***		−0.655***	−0.661***
		(4.72)	(5.38)		(8.09)	(7.11)
Non-attached		−0.385***	−0.413***		−0.420***	−0.457***
		(6.10)	(6.93)		(4.93)	(5.26)
Liberals		−0.248***	−0.253***		−0.279***	−0.295***
		(8.73)	(8.94)		(6.72)	(6.82)
Gaullists		−0.091*	−0.097*		−0.588***	−0.562***
		(1.78)	(1.87)		(10.34)	(9.42)
Conservatives		−0.030	−0.006		0.597***	0.556***
		(0.66)	(0.13)		(4.37)	(4.01)
Radical-right		−0.009	−0.061		−0.206	−0.195
		(0.11)	(0.83)		(1.58)	(1.35)
Member-state fixed effects	No	No	Yes	No	No	Yes
Observations	352	352	352	352	352	352
Adjusted R-squared	0.70	0.89	0.90	0.29	0.63	0.63

Note: Parameters of the models are estimated by linear regression with robust standard errors. Robust *t*-statistics in parentheses. *Significant at 10%, **significant at 5%, ***significant at 1%. Dummy variables for the second, third, fourth and fifth European Parliaments are included but not reported.

Turning to the second dimension, the results are less clear-cut. The main result is that the policy content of the second dimension appears to be a combination of EU policy positions and left–right positions. However, the relationship between EU policy positions and location on the second dimension is stronger than the relationship between left–right positions and location on this dimension. More precisely, a one standard deviation change along the EU integration dimension (as measured by expert's judgements) corresponds with a 37 per cent standard deviation change on the second dimension, whereas a one standard deviation change on the left–right dimension only corresponds with a 10 per cent standard deviation change on this dimension.[3]

Also, MEPs from national parties in government and who have Commissioners are located towards the 'top' of the second dimension, while MEPs from parties in opposition are located towards the bottom. For example, as the spatial maps show, the socialists and EPP, who contain most of the main national parties of government and have most of the EU Commissioners, are towards the top of the figure. However, these institutional interests are not significant once party dummies are introduced, which reveals that these interests do not produce voting conflicts within the political groups.

Third, as with the first dimension, a large proportion of the variance is explained by the location of the political groups. The magnitude of these coefficients explains their location on the second dimension: with the most pro-European political groups having the most positive coefficients, and the most anti-European political groups having the most negative coefficients. One exception is the liberal group, which has historically been very pro-European, yet has a negative coefficient because this group has had lower scores on this dimension than the socialists and EPP. Nevertheless, the liberals are closer to the two largest parties on this dimension than are the other small parties, except the British conservatives and allies. The British conservatives, however, have a positive coefficient because they were relatively pro-European in the first and second parliaments when they were a separate political group.

Fourth, member-state variables (not shown) are not significant on the second dimension. In other words, there are no clear and consistent patterns of voting along national lines on the second dimension. This confirms previous findings that voting is along party lines, not national lines.

These results also hold when we look at the parliament by parliament results, as Table 9.3 shows. The first dimension is explained by

---

[3] Using the results in model 4.

Table 9.3. *Interpreting the dimensions: Parliament by Parliament results*

Dependent Variable	Dimension 1-EP1		Dimension 1-EP2		Dimension 1-EP3		Dimension 1-EP4		Dimension 1-EP5	
	(1)	(2)	(3)	(4)	(5)	(6)	(7)	(8)	(9)	(10)
Constant	-0.837*** (12.75)	-0.007 (0.03)	-0.887*** (8.74)	-0.296 (1.24)	-0.863*** (5.80)	-0.200 (0.91)	-1.082*** (9.61)	0.379** (2.60)	-1.219*** (10.31)	0.054 (0.29)
Left–right position	1.176*** (8.54)	0.485** (2.36)	1.621*** (14.07)	0.975*** (4.17)	1.523*** (14.63)	0.930*** (3.91)	1.789*** (17.74)	0.387** (2.39)	1.894*** (13.76)	0.807*** (3.76)
EU integration position	0.061*** (3.10)	0.028 (1.13)	0.004 (0.26)	0.003 (0.08)	0.026 (1.29)	0.010 (0.51)	0.025 (1.55)	-0.017* (1.69)	0.041** (1.98)	-0.005 (0.34)
In government	0.052 (0.72)	0.037 (0.86)	0.165** (2.36)	0.066 (1.31)	0.098 (1.29)	0.049 (1.56)	0.082 (1.46)	-0.016 (0.62)	-0.027 (0.30)	-0.010 (0.27)
Commissioner	0.088 (1.47)	-0.014 (0.35)	-0.066 (1.16)	-0.019 (0.40)	0.072 (1.03)	-0.002 (0.06)	0.094 (1.35)	-0.019 (0.71)	0.103 (1.18)	0.039 (1.19)
Political group fixed effects	No	Yes***	No	Yes***	No	Yes***	No	Yes***	No	Yes***
Observations	44	44	55	55	62	62	83	83	108	108
Adjusted R-squared	0.70	0.90	0.80	0.91	0.72	0.93	0.76	0.96	0.61	0.89

Dependent variable	Dimension 2-EP1		Dimension 2-EP2		Dimension 2-EP3		Dimension 2-EP4		Dimension 2-EP5	
	(11)	(12)	(13)	(14)	(15)	(16)	(17)	(18)	(19)	(20)
Constant	0.200	−0.092	−0.178	0.042	−0.433*	0.763	−1.091***	0.476	−0.761***	−0.115
	(0.82)	(0.38)	(1.46)	(0.23)	(1.70)	(1.38)	(10.77)	(1.43)	(14.10)	(1.39)
Left-right position	−0.909***	−0.676***	0.241	0.394**	−0.424*	−0.275	−0.036	−0.400	−0.083	−0.207**
	(3.36)	(3.08)	(1.63)	(2.53)	(1.80)	(0.89)	(0.20)	(0.96)	(1.05)	(2.44)
EU integration position	0.012	0.023	−0.004	−0.053*	0.085**	−0.070	0.171***	0.034**	0.130***	0.051***
	(0.27)	(0.69)	(0.16)	(1.85)	(2.32)	(1.05)	(7.06)	(2.39)	(12.00)	(4.64)
In government	0.112	−0.008	0.023	−0.042	0.207	0.015	0.294***	0.012	0.043	−0.003
	(1.02)	(0.08)	(0.23)	(0.68)	(1.09)	(0.22)	(3.00)	(0.25)	(0.84)	(0.13)
Commissioner	0.132	0.160	0.327***	0.121*	0.260	−0.053	0.355***	0.000	0.185***	0.003
	(1.00)	(1.46)	(2.76)	(1.78)	(1.25)	(0.54)	(2.95)	(0.01)	(2.83)	(0.07)
Political group fixed effects	No	Yes***	No	Yes***	No	Yes***	No	Yes***	No	Yes***
Observations	44	44	55	55	62	62	83	83	108	108
Adjusted R-squared	0.23	0.53	0.21	0.78	0.17	0.84	0.49	0.88	0.64	0.90

Note: Parameters of the models are estimated by linear regression with robust standard errors. Robust *t*-statistics in parentheses. * Significant at 10%, ** significant at 5%, *** significant at 1%. We indicate the level of significance of the coefficients of political group fixed effects if a majority of these variables are significant at the relevant level.

left–right policy positions in all parliaments both with and without political group dummy variables. Regarding the second dimension, the parliament by parliament results reveal that this dimension is less consistently related to a single set of policy preferences or institutional interests. The government participation variable is only significant in the fourth parliament on this dimension. This is in part due to the small number of observations in the parliament by parliament analysis compared with the larger sample size in the pooled analysis, as can be seen from the higher standard errors in the parliament by parliament results.

Regarding changes over time, and whether the left–right and EU integration dimensions have become more independent or merged, the results suggest that while the first dimension has become increasingly clearly associated with the left–right, the second dimension has become increasingly associated with pro-/anti-Europe positions. In the first parliament, for example, the first dimension of voting in the European Parliament was captured by both left–right and EU policy positions, while the second dimension also seemed to be related to the left–right. This is not surprising given the fact that in that period, left–right and EU policy positions of parties were relatively highly correlated (with a coefficient of 0.350). In no other parliament were these two sets of policy preferences correlated. Since the fourth parliament, government participation and EU policy positions are more clearly associated with voting patterns on the second dimension. In fact, EU policy positions are significant in the fourth and fifth parliaments both when party dummy variables are excluded and when they are included. Hence, in the late 1990s, EU policy positions explain variations between the European political groups as well as within the European political groups on the second dimension.

Put together with the results in Table 9.1, which show that the first dimension captures an increasing proportion of voting, the parliament by parliament results suggest that the second dimension may have declined in significance but has become more clearly associated with a set of institutional interests (being in government) and policy positions on EU integration that are independent of left–right preferences.

9.5   Conclusion: normal politics in a territorially divided polity

Politics in the European Parliament is surprisingly like in other democratic parliaments. The main dimension of voting behaviour both within and between the European political parties is the classic left–right dimension of democratic politics. Left–right politics explains an overwhelming proportion of voting in the European Parliament. In contrast, national interests, independent of national party positions, have very little systematic influence on voting in the European Parliament. This finding is surprising from the perspective of some of the 'state-interest' based theories of EU politics (e.g. Moravcsik, 1998).

There is a second, but considerably less salient and less stable, dimension of politics in the European Parliament. This dimension partly reflects pro- and anti-European integration positions of political parties. This dimension also captures government-opposition dynamics at the European level, with parties represented in the Council and Commission voting one way and parties not represented voting the other way. The main political families – the EPP, the socialists and the liberals – are all strongly pro-European and also dominate the seats in the Council and the Commission. As a result, on this dimension, conflict between these main political groups and the smaller political groups is explained by party policies towards European integration as well as party representation in the other EU institutions.

These results provide a new perspective on understanding the dimensions of EU politics. The dominance of the left–right conflict in the European Parliament supports the view that the dominant ideological positions in domestic politics shape actors' positions in the EU policy process more strongly and more consistently than more general preferences about the speed and nature of European integration. Nevertheless, the existence of a second dimension around pro-/anti-Europe positions, albeit to a lesser extent, suggests that the question of the allocation of powers to the centre or the states cannot easily be subsumed into the left–right dimension. In this regard, the EU is similar to most other territorially divided polities.

Finally, our results suggest an optimistic conclusion about the accountability and stability of EU governance. Politics in the European Parliament is very much like politics in other democratic parliaments, dominated by left–right positions and driven by the traditional party families of domestic European politics. From that point of view, transnational party politics in the European Parliament neatly counterbalances national-interest-based politics in the EU Council.

10   Investiture and censure of the Santer Commission

Following the reform of the Commission investiture procedure by the Maastricht Treaty, as described in Chapter 1, on 21 July 1994 the European Parliament voted for the first time on the choice of a Commission President, and backed Jacques Santer by a narrow margin. Many MEPs, mostly on the left, were reluctant to support Santer. This was partly because they disagreed with his policy agenda (as a Christian democrat politician) and partly because they were unhappy with the way the nomination process had been conducted by the European Council. So, when the Commission was later accused of gross mismanagement, many MEPs who had originally opposed Santer now found the ideal opportunity to challenge his legitimacy. The Commission survived two censure votes before resigning *en masse* in March 1999, just before a likely loss in the third censure vote.

The story of the Santer Commission is a revealing case of how the European Parliament exercises its executive-control powers. This case also enables us to test whether our argument, which holds for a large number of votes across a long time period, also explains MEP behaviour when there are high political stakes. If democratic politics exists in the European Parliament, then the positions of the European parties should make a difference, and the left–right dimension should structure MEP behaviour, regardless of whether the parliament is voting on a minor non-legislative resolution or on a Commission censure motion.

So, what we do in this chapter is test our argument about the emergence of democratic politics in the European Parliament by looking in detail at MEP behaviour in the four votes on the investiture and censure of the Santer Commission in the 1994–1999 parliament. In Section 10.1 we briefly discuss the general politics of the formation and termination of governments and how this applies in the EU context. Section 10.2 then provides some background on the history of the relationship between the parliament and the Commission in this period. Section 10.3 applies a statistical analysis to investigate the determinants of MEP voting on the Santer Commission, and Section 10.4 contains a brief conclusion.

What we find is that, contrary to popular wisdom, the battles in the European Parliament in the investiture and censure of the Santer Commission were between the European political groups and were about left–right policy preferences. National party interests, in terms of whether a national party was represented in government in a member state or had a Commissioner, did matter. Also, national interests played a role. Nonetheless, we find that the process of executive formation and termination in the European Parliament is primarily driven by ideological and European party politics.

10.1   Formation and termination of governments and the case of the EU

The election and removal of the EU Commission is a particular case of 'government' formation and termination. On the formation side, as we discussed in Chapter 1, since the Maastricht Treaty the Commission is proposed by the governments of the EU member states in the European Council (by unanimity until the Nice Treaty and by a qualified-majority thereafter) and is then approved by a simple majority in the European Parliament. The term of office of the Commission is five years. But the Commission can be removed by censure vote in the European Parliament. If the parliament sacks the Commission, a new Commission is chosen by the standard investiture procedure.

At face value, it might seem that the relationship between the Commission and the European Parliament is similar to the relationship between a cabinet and a legislative majority in a parliamentary system, in that the Commission must be supported by a majority in the European Parliament and can also be removed by the European Parliament. However, this is not in fact the case (cf. Magnette, 2001). First, the way the Commission is appointed guarantees that it is inevitably an 'over-sized coalition' rather than a minimum-winning coalition. For example, as Table 10.1 shows, the Santer Commission included members from all the main political groups in the European Parliament, stretched across a broad range from left to right, and the median member of the Commission was extremely centrist. Second, the Commission cannot be removed by a simple majority, as a censure motion in the parliament requires a 'double majority': a two-thirds majority in the vote, which must constitute an 'absolute majority' of MEPs (314 of the 626 MEPs in the fourth parliament). In practice, this means a large coalition must

Table 10.1. *The Santer Commission*

Commissioner	Member state	National party	Political group	Left–right location of national party
Monika Wulf-Mathies	Germany	SPD	PES	0.31
Manuel Marin	Spain	PSOE	PES	0.33
Edith Cresson	France	PS	PES	0.34
Anita Gradin	Sweden	SAP	PES	0.34
Karel Van Miert	Belgium	SP	PES	0.36
Ritt Bjerregaard	Denmark	SD	PES	0.36
Erkki Liikanen	Finland	SDP	PES	0.38
Neil Kinnock	United Kingdom	Lab	PES	0.38
Christos Papoutsis	Greece	PASOK	PES	0.40
Emma Bonino	Italy	Rad	ERA	0.46
Martin Bangemann	Germany	FDP	ELDR	0.51
Padraig Flynn	Ireland	FF	EDA/UFE	0.53
Jacques Santer	**Luxembourg**	**PCS**	**EPP**	**0.56**
Hans van den Broek	Netherlands	CDA	EPP	0.59
João de Deus Pinhiero	Portugal	PSD	EPP	0.60
Franz Fischler	Austria	OVP	EPP	0.61
Mario Monti	Italy	FI	FE/UFE	0.68
Marcelino Oreja	Spain	PP	EPP	0.72
Leon Brittan	United Kingdom	Con	EPP	0.74
Yves-Thibault de Silguy	France	RPR	EDA/UFE	0.77

Note: The table is sorted by the left–right location of the party of the Commissioners. These locations are taken from expert judgements of party positions in 1996 on a 0–1 scale, where 0 represents the furthest left position and 1 represents the furthest right position (Marks and Steenbergen, 2004). For the PCS, we use the score for the Belgian CVP, which is the most similar political party. PES = Party of European Socialists, ERA = European Radical Alliance, ELDR = European Liberal, Democrat and Reform Party, EDA = European Democratic Alliance, UFE = Union for Europe, EPP = European People's Party and FE = Forza Europa.

be in favour of sacking the Commission, and since the Commission is an oversized coalition in the first place, putting together a two-thirds coalition to remove the Commission is very difficult.

Nevertheless, because the European Parliament plays a role in the investiture and censure of the Commission, the general theories of government formation and termination in parliamentary systems may apply to the relationship between the Commission and the European Parliament (Laver and Schofield, 1990; cf. Laver, 1998, 2002). We discussed some of these theories in Chapter 8, when we looked at legislation coalitions in the European Parliament. We can also use these theories to help guide our empirical analysis here.

First, from an office-seeking perspective, an MEP is more likely to support the Commission (voting for investiture and against censure) if a colleague from the MEP's national party is a member of the Commission. Similarly, the members of a European political group are more likely to support the Commission if the Commission contains politicians from the national member parties of the political group. In the case of the Santer Commission, only three political groups were not represented in the Commission, the greens (G), the radical-left (EUL) and the anti-Europeans (EN). Hence, the Commission could expect broad support in the European Parliament throughout its term of office.

Second, from a policy-seeking perspective, the closer an MEP is to the policy position of a proposed Commission President or to the median member of a proposed Commission, the more likely the MEP will vote in favour of the candidate or team of Commissioners. Similarly, the closer the median member of European political group is to a proposed Commission President or to the median member of a proposed Commission, the more likely the members of the political group will vote in favour of the candidate or team of Commissioners.

Third, Lupia and Strøm (1995) argue that a government will collapse if one of the coalition partners expects to be in a more powerful bargaining position in the formation of a new coalition. In the EU context, MEPs are consequently likely to consider the potential make-up of the new Commission when deciding whether to vote in favour of removing the current Commission. Since the member-state governments are responsible for nominating a new Commission President and choosing the other members of a new Commission, the political make-up of the national governments at the time of a censure vote should influence MEPs' decisions. If a new Commission is likely to be closer to the policy preferences of an MEP or political group, the MEP or group will be more likely to vote in favour of censuring the Commission.

Fourth, Diermeier and Stevenson (1999, 2000) argue that the closer a government is to the end of its term the lower the costs of terminating the coalition. Similarly, the closer it is to the end of the Commission's term, the more likely the parliament will censure the Commission. The damage inflicted on the governance of the EU will decline the closer a censure vote is to the automatic selection of a new Commission.

In sum, our theory of democratic politics in the European Parliament is consistent with the general theories of government formation and termination and how these theories are likely to apply in the EU context. European political groups' interests, in terms of their desire to protect or increase their representation in the EU executive, should shape how they behave *vis-à-vis* the Commission. Also, the policy preferences of the MEPs and European political groups should determine which political groups and MEPs are likely to support the Commission and which are likely to oppose it.

10.2   The Santer Commission: from nomination to resignation

The Santer Commission experienced two historic firsts. This was the first Commission to be invested by the European Parliament. It was also the first Commission to be removed by the European Parliament (even if a censure vote was not actually passed). As Table 10.2 shows, there were four key votes in the European Parliament on the Santer Commission: two investiture votes (one on the nomination of Santer for Commission President and the other on the nomination of the Commission as a whole) and two censure votes. A third censure vote would have been held, but the Santer Commission resigned before this vote could take place.

The story began with the Maastricht Treaty, which introduced a new Commission investiture procedure. Under the new procedure, the European Parliament would have to be 'consulted' in the process of selecting a Commission President and would also be able to vote on the proposed college of Commissioners. As we discussed in Chapter 1, when drafting its new rules of procedure after the introduction of the new Treaty, the European Parliament interpreted this right to be consulted as a formal power of veto of the governments' nominee for Commission President and this interpretation was accepted by the governments. Hence, in practice, the Maastricht Treaty gave the European Parliament a right to veto the Commission President, an addition to the right to veto the Commission as a whole (Hix, 2002a).

Table 10.2. *Key votes on the Santer Commission*

	Vote 1	Vote 2	Vote 3	Vote 4
Date	21 July 1994	18 January 1995	20 February 1997	14 January 1999
Subject	Investiture of Santer	Investiture of Commission	Censure (BSE)	Censure (mismanagement)
Yes	260	417	118	232
No	238	103	326	293
Abstain	23	60	15	27
Total	521	580	459	552

Following the June 1994 European Parliament elections, the heads of state and government of the EU member states met in the European Council to decide on who should succeed Jacques Delors as the Commission President. Under the informal convention that the head of the Commission should rotate between the left and the right, there was a general understanding that since Delors was from the left, the next Commission President should come from the right. The two early favourites were two Christian democrat prime ministers, Ruud Lubbers from the Netherlands and Jean-Luc Dehaene from Belgium. However, John Major, the British conservative prime minister, threatened to veto Dehaene or Lubbers because of their apparent 'federalist' views. He proposed Sir Leon Brittan, a British conservative member of the Delors' Commission, but this idea garnered little support. In this discussion, the argument developed that the Commission president had to have been a prime minister. Eventually, Jacques Santer, the Christian democrat prime minister from Luxemburg, was accepted by all the government leaders as a harmless consensus candidate.

Santer was proposed to the first plenary session of the newly elected parliament in July 1994. On 20 July, Santer was 'interviewed' separately by the two largest political groups. He received a rapturous welcome by the MEPs in the EPP, who were eager to see one of their own elected as Commission President after ten years of a socialist at the helm of the Commission. Wilfried Martens, the President of the EPP group even went as far as threatening to expel any member of the EPP who voted against Santer (Hix and Lord, 1996: 66). The socialists (PES), meanwhile, were less impressed. They were angry that the deal in the European Council had been done 'behind closed' doors, especially since the new investiture procedure was meant to increase the democratic accountability of the Commission. They also saw Santer as a political lightweight, who would be pushed around by the right-wing EU governments, and so undermine the social democratic agenda that had been promoted by Delors. The rest of the parliament also looked set to split along left–right lines. The other political groups on the right, the Gaullists (EDA) and the Italian conservatives (FE) were expected to back Santer. On the other side, the three other groups on the left, the radicals (ERA), greens (G) and radical-left (EUL), as well as the anti-European group (EN), were expected to vote against Santer. In the middle, the liberals (ELDR) stated that they would vote against Santer, as a protest against the continued 'stitch-up' in the European Council between the socialist and conservative government leaders. If this left-right party split held, the vote would be very close.

However, the next day, 21 July, Santer scraped through by 260 votes to 238. As Table 10.3 shows, the vote was broadly along party lines, in that the majority in each political group voted as expected and the groups maintained an average cohesion score of 0.753 in the vote. However, had the vote been completely along left–right party lines, Santer would have lost. A group of socialist MEPs from parties in government who broke from the socialist group whip to support Santer made the difference between losing and winning. In particular, twenty out of twenty-one Spanish socialists voted in favour of Santer on the instruction of their party leader, Prime Minister Felipé Gonzalez, who had agreed to support Santer in the European Council. As a result, the 'pro-Santer' camp was a coalition of MEPs on the right of the parliament plus MEPs on the left whose national parties were in government (Hix and Lord, 1996; Gabel and Hix, 2002a).

Once the members of the Commission had been nominated by the governments, the parties in the parliament realised that the Santer Commission would contain politicians from all the main groups. As a result, the coalition in support of the Commission increased. The three parties on the centre-right (EPP, FE and EDA) who had backed Santer were now joined by the next two groups on the left–right spectrum, the ELDR and PES, respectively. So, in January 1999, a large majority of MEPs, which stretched from the right to the centre-left, voted to invest the new Commission. Only the three small groups to the left of the socialists (ERA, G and EUL) and the anti-European group (EN) remained outside the broad pro-Commission coalition.

But it was not long before the new Commission was embroiled in a political crisis. In March 1996, the British government announced that its scientists had found a probable link between Bovine Spongiform Encephalopathy (BSE) and Creutzfeld Jakob's Disease, a fatal brain-wasting condition in humans, and that all cows aged over thirty months would be slaughtered rather than be allowed to enter the human food chain. The EU agriculture commissioner, Franz Fischler, immediately issued a ban on all exports of British beef. The British government lobbied hard to have the ban lifted, and resorted briefly to a policy of non-cooperation in EU business. The pressure paid off and the policy of non-cooperation was ended following an agreement at the Florence European Council in June 1996, under which the British government agreed to additional measures (including an extension of the planned cattle cull) in exchange for a commitment that there would be a phased lifting of the ban.

In the meantime, in September 1996, the European Parliament set up a BSE Committee of Inquiry, to investigate the behaviour of the

Table 10.3. *MEP voting behaviour by party, member state, and government status*

	Vote 1 (1994)			Vote 2 (1995)			Vote 3 (1997)			Vote 4 (1999)		
	Yes	No	Abst.	Yes	No	Abst.	Yes	No	Abst.	Yes	No	Abst.
Political group												
G	1	17	2	1	21	0	19	0	2	25	0	0
EUL	0	21	0	0	14	16	25	0	0	18	3	0
ERA	0	18	0	0	12	1	12	3	2	4	13	2
PES	45	140	5	177	28	9	17	140	5	37	159	2
ELDR	8	24	6	31	4	13	4	26	2	32	6	0
EPP	152	0	1	159	9	4	7	138	2	70	91	21
EDA/UFE	22	0	1	19	0	3	5	15	1	14	11	2
FE	26	0	0	22	1	0						
EN	0	7	8	0	0	14	12	3	0	14	0	0
NA	6	11	0	8	14	0	17	1	1	18	10	0
Member state												
Luxembourg	6	0	0	6	0	0	0	6	0	0	6	0
Spain	49	7	2	54	0	9	11	41	1	1	52	0
Greece	19	4	0	19	2	2	2	10	1	6	11	3
Italy	42	23	1	53	6	7	5	17	0	9	58	0
Ireland	12	3	0	11	3	0	2	7	0	3	11	0
Portugal	17	5	3	17	3	5	6	13	3	5	19	0
Finland				10	4	1	3	11	0	3	9	3
Denmark	7	2	5	11	0	5	2	8	0	9	4	0
United Kingdom	19	67	0	70	9	6	0	71	5	20	57	3
Austria				17	3	1	5	14	0	11	10	0
Netherlands	10	19	2	20	3	8	1	26	1	13	8	7
Sweden				20	1	1	7	9	0	13	6	2
Germany	48	44	3	61	34	2	8	71	2	86	6	0
Belgium	7	17	1	17	7	0	9	14	0	14	8	3
France	24	47	6	31	28	13	57	8	2	39	28	6
Government												
In government	184	19	0	207	15	14	32	155	2	80	188	6
In opposition	76	219	18	210	88	46	86	171	13	152	105	21
Total	260	238	23	417	103	60	118	326	15	232	293	27
Cohesion												
Political groups	0.752			0.740			0.773			0.641		
Member states	0.559			0.626			0.677			0.562		
In government	0.860			0.816			0.730			0.529		
In opposition	0.546			0.416			0.450			0.320		

Note: The political groups are sorted from left to right, except for the EN and NA. The member-state delegations are sorted from the most pro-Commission delegation to least pro-Commission, on the basis of their voting behaviour in the four votes. The cohesion scores are the mean scores for the political groups and delegations and the total scores for the MEPs from national parties in government and from national parties in opposition (see Chapter 5 for the calculation of the cohesion scores). G = Greens, EUL = European United Left, EN = Europe of Nations, NA = non-attached.

Commission in the developing crisis. The committee reported on 17 February 1997, and criticised the Commission for failing to handle the crisis effectively. The parliament also supported the committee's recommendation for a 'suspended motion of censure', whereby the parliament would vote on a motion of censure if the Commission failed to act on the parliament's recommendations. However, several MEPs felt that this was not strong enough, and José Happart (PES, Belgium) tabled a motion of censure on 17 February 1997. The motion was easily defeated by 188 votes in favour to 326 against, as the leaderships and the majorities of the pro-Commission political groups (PES, ELDR, EPP and UFE) all opposed the censure.[1] Nevertheless, the majorities in the non pro-Commission groups all voted in favour of censure, and seven EPP and seventeen socialist MEPs (almost all from France) voted against their European parties' positions.

A much deeper crisis then developed in 1998. A special report by the European Court of Auditors pointed to some serious irregularities, mismanagement, nepotism and perhaps even fraud in the way the Commission had implemented the 1996 annual EU budget. The European Parliament duly refused to discharge the 1996 budget on 31 March 1998. The Parliament refused again in December 1998 and the main political groups in the parliament tabled a motion of censure for the first plenary session of the New Year. In the meantime, the Commission was asked to provide detailed information on all internal investigations into cases of corruption in the Commission.

On 14 January 1999, the main political groups agreed to withdraw the motion of censure after the socialist group tabled a motion for the European Parliament to establish a Committee of Independent Experts to investigate all the allegations. But seventy-one MEPs led by the green group, immediately tabled a new motion of censure and demanded a vote. The censure motion failed by 232 in favour of censure to 293 votes against and 27 abstentions. This was the largest number of MEPs who had voted in favour of a Commission censure motion in the history of the European Parliament. Also, although the leaderships of the two largest political groups had opposed the censure motion, two of the pro-Commission groups (ELDR and UFE) joined the more extremist groups in backing the censure motion and 107 MEPs defected from the voting instructions issued from the PES and EPP whips.

The Committee of Independent Experts then issued its report on 15 March 1999. Although the report did not find that any individual

---

[1] Two of the pro-Commission political groups, Forza Europa and the European Democratic Alliance, merged in 1995 to form the Union for Europe group.

Commissioner had benefited from fraudulent dealings involving EU funds, it concluded that there were 'instances where Commissioners or the Commission as a whole bear responsibility for instances of fraud, irregularities or mismanagement in their services or areas of special responsibility' (European Parliament, 1999: 137). The report also singled out Santer, Cresson, Marín, Wulf-Mathies and Deus Pinheiro for particular criticism.

The report was leaked to the Commission the day before its official release, and Santer immediately called a meeting of the full Commission on that Sunday evening. Shortly before 1 a.m. the next morning the Commission resigned *en masse*. Apart from the findings of the report, a key factor in the decision to resign was a statement on the evening of 14 March by Pauline Green, the leader of the socialist group, that the socialist group had changed its position and would now vote to censure the Commission. With the socialist group now supporting censure, a censure motion would almost certainly pass the two-thirds threshold. Santer consequently persuaded his colleagues to resign rather than be voted down in the European Parliament. Hence, although no final censure vote was held, in practice the Santer Commission was censured by the European Parliament.

The cohesion scores reported in Table 10.3 suggest that several factors influenced how the MEPs voted in the four votes on the Santer Commission. The political groups were relatively cohesive in all four votes, although they were slightly less cohesive in these votes than on average in all the other votes in the fourth parliament (see Chapter 5). Some press coverage of the second censure vote claimed that there was a north–south split in the parliament, between MEPs from northern (and predominantly Protestant) states, who were more concerned about mismanagement and lack of transparency in the EU, and MEPs from southern (and predominantly Catholic) states, who were less concerned about mismanagement or transparency. However, in all votes, including the censure vote in January 1999, the political groups were on average more cohesive than the member-state delegations of MEPs. The other main factor in the votes was that MEPs from governing parties overwhelmingly supported the Commission in all four votes, although MEPs from opposition parties were less cohesive and tended to split along predictable party lines.

However, it is impossible from these cohesion scores to distinguish the independent effects of these factors. For example, almost all the national parties in government were also members of the pro-Commission political groups. In the next section we consequently use a statistical method to analyse the determinants of MEP voting behaviour in the four votes on the Santer Commission.

10.3   Analysis: MEP behaviour in the investiture and censure of the Commission

10.3.1   Variables

The dependent variable in the analysis is a vote decision by an MEP (Yes or No).[2] To make the vote decisions comparable we coded 1 if the MEP voted 'in favour' of the Commission (Yes in the first and second votes, and No in the third and fourth votes) and 0 if the MEP voted 'against' the Commission (No in the first and second votes, and Yes in the third and fourth votes). We estimate MEP voting behaviour in each of the four votes separately and then estimate two models of MEP voting in all four votes pooled.

We then use seven sets of independent variables to test our argument that European political groups and left–right policy preferences are the main drivers of politics in the European Parliament and to investigate the other key factors shaping MEP behaviour in these votes. First, to measure MEPs' ideological positions we use the scores on the first two dimensions produced by applying the NOMINATE scaling method to all the roll-call votes in the fourth parliament. Given our results from Chapter 9, we treated the scores on the first dimension as MEPs' left–right positions (*Left–right*) and the scores on the second dimension as MEPs' preferences towards European integration (*Anti/Pro-EU*). To capture the conflict between the rather centrist median member of the Santer Commission and the political extremes in the European Parliament, we also include a variable that measures how far an MEP is from the centre of the left–right dimension (*Left–right extremism*), which is calculated as the absolute value of each MEP's score on the first NOMINATE dimension (where minus 1 is the furthest left position and plus 1 is the furthest right position).

Second, we use two variables to capture the effect of the strategic interests of national parties in government. The variable *NP in govt-PM* was coded 1 if an MEP's national party held the office of prime minister (either in a single-party government or a coalition government), and 0 otherwise. And, the variable *NP in govt-junior* was coded 1 if an MEP's national party was a member of a coalition government but did not hold the prime minister's office, and 0 otherwise. Hence, these variables capture the difference between being represented in the European

---

[2] We deleted abstentions. As a robustness check we included abstentions and ran an ordered logit (with Yes = 2, Abstain = 1, and No = 0). The results were identical to the binomial logit. We report the results of the binomial analysis because the coefficients are easier to interpret.

Council, which brings together the heads of government and nominates the Commission President, being a junior member of a government, and being in opposition (in which case an MEP scores 0 on both variables).

As Table 10.4 shows, the make-up of the parties in government changed considerably between 1994 and 1999, from a right-wing majority in the European Council and Council at the time of the first two votes to a left-wing dominated European Council and Council at the time of the third and fourth votes. Following the logic of Lupia and Strøm (1995), as the European Council became increasingly dominated by parties on the left, the MEPs on the centre-left in the European Parliament could be more likely to vote against the Commission, as they could reasonably expect that a new Commission would be closer to their policy preferences than the current Commission. Indeed, that is exactly what happened. After the Santer Commission had been removed, it was replaced in May 1999 by a considerably more left-wing Commission, with twelve politicians from parties on the left and eight politicians from parties on the right (Hix, 2005: 42).

Third, to capture the office-seeking interests of national parties we include a variable indicating whether the national party of the MEP was represented in the Santer Commission (*NP in Commission*).

Fourth, to capture national interests and preferences in the votes we use a continuous variable that measures national governments' level of transparency and corruption (*Transparency*). We use Transparency International's Corruption Perceptions Index (CPI), where higher scores on the CPI index imply a higher level of government transparency.[3] This measure is a proxy for the main national split in the two censure votes, where the member-states with higher levels of government probity were alleged to have been more in favour of punishing the Commission for mismanagement and nepotism.

Fifth, to examine the effect of European political group membership, and to investigate the determinants of variations in MEP voting within each political group, in one of the models with the pooled dataset we include dummy variables for each political group. The non-attached MEPs (NA) were excluded as the baseline category.

Sixth, to analyse the determinants of variations in MEP voting within each member-state delegation of MEPs, in the other model of the pooled dataset we include dummy variables for each member-state delegation.

Finally, because of the different majority thresholds in each of the votes, we include a dummy variable for each vote in the two models with

---

[3] See www.transparency.org

Table 10.4. *Parties in government at the time of the votes*

	Vote 1 (1994)	Vote 2 (1995)	Vote 3 (1997)	Vote 4 (1999)
Bel	CVP, PCS, SP, PS			VLD, PRL/FDF, SP, PS, Ecolo, Agalev
Den		SD, RV		
Fra	RPR, UDF, CDS		PS, PCF, PRS, MDC, Verts	
Ger		CDU, FDP		SPD, G
Gre		PASOK		
Ire		FG, LAB		FF, PD
Ita	FI, CCD, CDU, LN, AN		DS, PPI, RI, UDR, PDCI, FV, SDI	DS, PPI, RI, UDR, PDCI, FV, SDI
Lux		POS, POSL		
Net	CDA, PvdA		PvdA, VVD, D'66	
Por	PSD		PS	
Spa	PSOE		PP	
UK	Con		Lab	
Aus			SPO, OVP	
Fin		KESK, KOK		SDP, KOK, SFP, VAS, VIHR
Swe			SAP	
Left	33 %	47 %	67 %	73 %
Right	67 %	53 %	33 %	26 %

Note: In coalition governments, the party of the Prime Minister is underlined. Left governments are shaded.

the pooled dataset. The variable for the fourth vote was excluded as the baseline category.

10.3.2 Results

Table 10.5 presents the results. The main findings are as follows. First, left–right policy preferences determined MEP voting behaviour in all votes. The more right-wing an MEP, the more likely he or she was to support the Santer Commission, and so vote in favour of investing Santer and the Commission as a whole and vote against the censure of the Commission. This simple left–right preference alignment was not significant in the second censure vote (model 4). However, how extreme an MEP was on the left–right dimension, which captures the distance between an MEP and the median member of the Commission, was significant in the second censure vote as well as in the other three votes. Left–right policy preferences also show up in the two models of the pooled votes. In model 5, left–right positions are captured by the political group dummy variables, and the coefficients on these variables exactly match the left–right line-up of the political groups in the fourth parliament. In model 6, within each member-state delegation, left-wing MEPs generally voted against the Commission while centrist and right-wing MEPs generally supported the Commission.

Second, MEP attitudes towards European integration also made a difference. Specifically, the more pro-European an MEP, the more likely he or she supported the Commission, and this held within each of the European political groups as well as within each of the member-state delegations of MEPs.

Third, in general, MEPs from national parties in government were more likely to support the Santer Commission. However, the two government membership variables were not significant in the first censure vote.

Fourth, the main office-seeking variable, whether an MEP's national party was represented in the Commission, was significant in the two censure votes but not in the two investiture votes. However, this is not surprising since in the investiture process the Commission had not yet been established, while in the two censure votes, the national parties in the Commission risked being removed from executive office. Also, within each political group and each national delegation, in models 5 and 6, respectively, MEPs whose national parties were represented in the Commission were more likely to support the Commission.

Finally, MEPs from member states with higher levels of government transparency were more likely to vote to censure the Commission in

Table 10.5. *Determinants of MEP Voting on the Santer Commission*

	(1) Vote 1 (94)	(2) Vote 2 (95)	(3) Vote 3 (97)	(4) Vote 4 (99)	(5) Pooled	(6) Pooled
Constant	-0.383	3.200**	-2.749**	6.026***	3.553***	-0.431
	(0.33)	(3.00)	(2.31)	(7.00)	(4.47)	(0.39)
Left-right (NOM D1)	5.919***	2.877***	3.169***	0.132	-2.347**	3.083***
	(5.50)	(5.76)	(5.13)	(0.42)	(3.16)	(12.43)
Left-right extremism	2.096	-2.983**	-3.408**	-1.554**	0.586	-0.953*
	(0.96)	(2.77)	(2.78)	(2.03)	(0.74)	(1.77)
Anti/Pro-EU (NOM D2)	2.836***	2.358***	3.660***	1.482***	1.787***	2.274***
	(5.61)	(7.17)	(7.95)	(5.74)	(5.88)	(11.80)
NP in govt-PM	4.890***	0.880**	-0.737	0.974**	1.994***	2.338***
	(6.46)	(2.40)	(1.42)	(2.73)	(11.54)	(11.92)
NP in govt-junior	1.732**	1.280**	-0.389	0.566	1.176***	1.490***
	(3.05)	(1.96)	(0.65)	(1.44)	(4.99)	(5.27)
NP in Commission	-0.213	0.258	1.162**	1.009***	0.675***	0.884***
	(0.41)	(0.72)	(2.83)	(3.73)	(3.88)	(4.57)
Transparency	-0.380**	-0.208*	0.560***	-0.845***	-0.513***	-0.085
	(2.37)	(1.75)	(4.40)	(8.33)	(8.20)	(0.56)
G					-6.262***	
					(4.79)	
EUL					-5.745***	
					(5.11)	

PES					−2.962***	
					(3.48)	
ERA					−2.451***	
					(3.25)	
EN					−1.094	
					(1.58)	
ELDR					−0.070	
					(0.13)	
EPP					0.833*	
					(1.86)	
EDA/UFE					1.658***	
					(3.76)	
FE					1.929*	
					(1.73)	
Member-state dummies	No	No	No	No	No	Yes
Observations	494	520	444	519	1977	1954
Pseudo R-Squared	0.73	0.39	0.57	0.32	0.42	0.51

Note: Dependent variable: vote in favour of the Commission (Yes in votes 1 and 2, No in votes 3 and 4). In model 4, the Luxembourg variable was dropped because it predicts success perfectly and the Greece variable was dropped owing to collinearity. In models 5 and 6, dummy variables for the first, second and third votes are included but not reported (the fourth vote is the baseline category). In model 5, the non-attached MEPs (NA) are the baseline category. Z-statistics in parentheses. Method: Logit regression. *Significant at 10%; **significant at 5%; ***significant at 1%.

January 1999 (in model 4). However, these MEPs were not more likely to vote to censure the Commission in February 1997 (in model 3). Although, MEPs from member states with higher levels of government transparency were more likely to vote against Jacques Santer for Commission President and against investing the Commission as a whole. So, from the start of the Santer Commission, MEPs from 'high-transparency' states were less favourable towards the Commission. This might reflect concerns from the beginning about the way Jacques Santer had been chosen, in a rather grubby and secretive deal in the European Council. However, this might also reflect the fact that citizens, parties and MEPs from high-transparency states (notably Scandinavia and the United Kingdom) are generally less favourable towards the EU than citizens, parties and MEPs from southern Europe.

10.4   Conclusion: government-opposition politics arrives in the European Parliament

The case of the investiture and censure of the Santer Commission illustrates how the main arguments and findings in the rest of the book apply in the area of the European Parliament's control of the EU executive. The case also illustrates that MEPs behave similarly when the political stakes are high as when the political stakes are relatively low, which is often the case in day-to-day legislative politics. Despite the cohesive positions taken by some countries, the European political groups were the dominant actors in the formation and termination of the Santer Commission, and the battles between these groups were predominantly along the left–right dimension of politics.

A centre-right coalition of European parties backed Santer for Commission President, supported by some left-wing MEPs from national parties in government, who had backed Santer in the European Council. Then, once an ideologically broad team of Commissioners had been put together, the pro-Commission coalition was extended to include the next two parties to the left of the initial coalition: the liberals and socialists, respectively. This coalition held together in two censure votes. Then, when the socialists and liberals decided to abandon Santer, in part expecting that the new Commission would be closer to their policy preferences, the Commission resigned before a third censure vote could be held.

The resignation of Santer, in the face of pressure from the European Parliament, had significant implications for the relationship between the Commission and the European Parliament (e.g. Topan, 2002). The next Commission, led by Romano Prodi, was considerably more deferential to the parliament. And, buoyed by its new power over the EU executive, the parliament asserted itself again when Barroso was forced to withdraw the proposed team of Commissioners in October 2004 before the parliament could vote to reject them.

More generally, the battles in the European Parliament over the Santer Commission can be seen as the arrival of government-opposition politics in the European Parliament. For the first time, a coalition of 'governing' political groups, which were represented in the Commission, supported the Commission against a smaller group of 'opposition' parties, mainly to the left of the socialists. However, despite being the largest group in the fourth parliament, the socialists always felt second-class citizens in a Commission led by a Christian democrat. Not surprisingly, it was the socialist group rather than the EPP that eventually withdrew its support.

Government-opposition politics then continued in the Prodi and Barroso Commissions. With the Prodi Commission dominated by left-wing politicians, the socialists behaved in the fourth parliament like a minority government party, supporting virtually all the Commission's initiatives. On the other side of the political divide, the EPP, which was the largest political group in the fifth parliament and was dominated by the German CDU (who did not have a Commissioner), behaved like the main political party in opposition. As a result, unlike the Santer Commission, which had an 'oversized' supporting coalition in the parliament, the period of the Prodi Commission was one of 'divided government': with a centre-left-dominated Commission facing a centre-right-dominated European Parliament.

Then, the situation switched again with the Barroso Commission to a system of more clearly 'united government'. This time, a narrow centre-right majority existed in both the Commission and the European Parliament. Unlike in the period of the Santer Commission, the majority in the socialist group now opposed the Commission, and in an unprecedented step even tried to stop the parliament approving the Commission's work programme in January 2005.

With the arrival of government-opposition politics, the parties in the European Parliament finally have a new incentive to use their organisational muscle to influence the legislative agenda initiated by the Commission.

11   The Takeover Directive

Whereas the case study in the previous chapter looked at the power of the European Parliament to control the EU executive, this chapter looks at the power of the parliament to make legislation. We focus on the Takeover Directive, which is one of the most high-profile pieces of legislation ever to pass through the European Parliament.[1] One reason for the public attention to this particular bill was the dramatic tied vote in the third reading in the parliament in July 2001, which meant that the first attempt to pass the legislation failed. But even without such an unusual event, the Takeover Directive represented a major piece of EU regulation because it aimed to establish common European-wide rules governing shareholders' rights and defensive measures in the event of takeover bids. The bill consequently addressed one of the central differences between the so-called 'Anglo-Saxon' and 'Rhenish' models of capitalism.

To test our argument in this case the chapter is organised as follows. Section 11.1 presents a short history of the Takeover Directive, from its origins in the 1970s to its eventual adoption in April 2004. Section 11.2 then discusses some descriptive evidence of how MEPs voted in three key votes on the legislation, and the findings of the existing research on the passage of this directive in the European Parliament. In Section 11.3 we undertake a statistical analysis of MEP voting behaviour in these three votes. Section 11.4 contains a brief conclusion.

We find, in contrast to some existing research, that European political parties and left–right preferences had a significant influence on MEP voting behaviour throughout the passage of the Takeover Directive. When there are high political stakes, MEPs from one or two member states may vote along national rather than party lines in one or two votes on a piece of legislation. All the other MEPs will vote along party lines, and those MEPs who broke from party lines in some votes will support

---

[1] For example, Lexus Nexus returned 227 articles in major newspapers that mentioned the EU Takeover Directive (the search was undertaken on 28 June 2005).

their European parties' positions in all the other votes on a bill. Hence, in general, political behaviour and policy outcomes in the European Parliament are determined more by European party positions and left–right preferences than by national interests.

11.1   A short history of the Takeover Directive

The Commission proposed the 'thirteenth European Parliament and Council Directive on company law concerning takeover bids' on 7 February 1996.[2] This was the latest of a series of attempts to harmonise member states' takeover rules (cf. Berglöf and Burkart, 2003). Having failed to secure support for a directive in the early 1970s, the Commission tried again in 1989, as part of the programme to complete the single market. However, this attempt was dropped after three years of negotiations in the Council. The German government was strongly opposed to any attempt to impose European-wide standards, which would invariably mean fundamentally changing German takeover practices, for example by introducing the principle of one-share-one-vote. Nevertheless, the Commission announced at the Essen European Council in December 1994 that it would try again, arguing that a common set of rules was essential for establishing legal certainty and for fostering mergers and acquisitions in the single market.

The 1996 proposal was less ambitious than the previous Commission proposals in that it did not propose full harmonisation of national takeover rules. Instead, the member states would be required to ensure that their own rules concerning takeover bids complied with five general principles: (1) that all shareholders should be treated equally; (2) that the persons to whom a bid is addressed must be allowed the necessary time and information to take a sufficiently well-founded decision on the bid; (3) that the management board of the offeree company must act in the interests of the company as a whole and take account of shareholders' interests; (4) that the creation of false markets in the securities of the offeree company is prohibited; and (5) that offeree companies must not be hampered in the conduct of their business for any longer than is reasonably necessary for a bid to purchase their shares. Also, one key provision was a British-style 'neutrality rule', whereby companies would not be allowed to take defensive measures against a takeover bid once a bid had been launched without gaining the specific approval of shareholders for the action.

---

[2] Procedure reference: COD/1995/0341.

Upon receiving the draft legislation, the European Parliament assigned the bill to its Legal Affairs and Internal Market Committee. Nicole Fontaine, a French conservative in the EPP group, won the right to act as the rapporteur on the legislation. In May 1997 the committee approved almost unanimously (minus one vote) the main elements of the Commission proposal, and in June 1997 the European Parliament's plenary approved the Fontaine Report in the first reading of the bill. The parliament nevertheless proposed twenty-two amendments. Most of these were technical rather than substantive. However, the substantive amendments strengthened the protection of minority shareholders in the event of a takeover, specifying that when the board of the company acts in the interests of the company this should include safeguarding jobs, and requiring that the company management consult the workforce before giving its opinion on a bid.

The Commission accepted most of these amendments. Then, in June 2000, the Council reached a 'common position' on the legislation, by unanimity amongst the EU governments. This common position incorporated thirteen amendments proposed by the European Parliament, including most of the substantive ones. A compromise deal between the European Parliament and the Council looked possible.

However, this was not to be. First, in late 2000, German industry started to express concerns about the directive. Following the aggressive takeover in early 2000 of Mannesmann by Vodafone, the British telecommunications company, concerns were raised in Germany that Volkswagen was the potential target of a hostile takeover bid from one of the American car companies, and that the neutrality rule would make it more difficult for Volkswagen or the German government to act against such a bid. The German Chancellor, Gerhard Schröder, was a former member of the supervisory board of Volkswagen and maintained close personal connections with the management of the company. The German government consequently started to speak out against the neutrality rule in the draft directive, despite having supported it in the Council earlier in the year.

Second, following the elections to the European Parliament in June 1999 and the subsequent appointment of Fontaine as the new President of the Parliament, Klaus-Heiner Lehne, a German Christian democrat in the EPP group, became the new rapporteur on the bill. Although Lehne was from the main German opposition party, he was sympathetic to the views of the German government and German industry and started to mobilise support in the parliament to limit the potential liberalising effects of the directive. As Rolf Skog notes (2002: 308): 'the rapporteur, in practice, became a spokesman for VW, BASF and other large companies, which at all costs hoped to avoid the risk that, like Mannesmann, they too might end up in foreign hands'.

In the second reading of the legislation in the European Parliament in December 2000, Lehne managed to persuade the parliament to add several new amendments designed to strengthen the hand of companies facing a hostile takeover bid. In particular, the MEPs supported an amended neutrality rule, which would allow a company to take defensive measures during the period of acceptance of the bid if the measures had been approved by a prior general meeting of the shareholders. In other words, this would replace the British practice with the existing German practice, rather than vice versa (Bergklöf and Burkhart, 2003: 187). The parliament also adopted several amendments to promote workers' rights to information about the implications of a takeover bid, which again could discourage hostile takeover moves.

Under the co-decision procedure, the difference between the texts approved by the Council and the European Parliament at second reading triggered a 'conciliation committee', which was composed of fifteen MEPs and the fifteen deputy ambassadors to the EU of the member states. After several months of negotiations, the conciliation committee eventually reached an agreement in June 2001, via a compromise between the positions of the Council and the European Parliament on the two remaining unresolved issues: defensive measures and workers' information rights.

The conciliation deal needed then, however, to be approved by the Council and the European Parliament in a third reading by a simple 'up or down' vote. The vote in the European Parliament was scheduled for the next plenary session, in July 2001. Three weeks before the plenary, the German government and Klaus-Heiner Lehne came out against the compromise deal. Speaking in the debate in the parliament during the third reading, Lehne argued that the requirement that the board of a company which is the object of a takeover bid refrain from taking defensive action until it has consulted its shareholders could only be justified if there was a 'level playing field' across all member states: in other words, a full harmonisation of national takeover rules. Lehne and the German government maintained that without full harmonisation German firms were at an unfair disadvantage. This directive would prevent German firms faced with a hostile bid from raising new capital, making new acquisitions or selling assets without prior shareholder approval, but would allow golden shares or multiple voting rights, which were illegal in Germany but not in France and Scandinavia.

This was a highly unprecedented move by the German government, as never before in the middle of the adoption of a piece of legislation had a member state turned against a position it previously supported in the Council and then started to mobilise to affect the outcome of the final vote in the European Parliament. But Schröder was undeterred by the criticism from the other member states and the European Commission, and undertook an intensive lobbying campaign of German and other MEPs, with implicit cooperation from the leadership of the German opposition Christian democrats.

The result was a tied vote on 4 July 2001: with 273 MEPs voting in favour, 273 against and 22 abstentions. This meant that the directive was not approved by the European Parliament and so fell at the final hurdle.

After the failure of the directive, the European Commission appointed a high-level group of company law experts, chaired by Dutch law professor Jaap Winters, to examine the objections raised by the opponents and to come up with some solutions. Based on the Winters Report, the Commission initiated a new draft directive in October 2002.[3] The proposal included a new 'breakthrough rule', which aimed to facilitate the success of hostile bids against multiple voting rights, by ensuring that acquiring a majority stake is sufficient for a takeover. But agreement in the Council still proved difficult. The German government insisted that all defensive mechanisms, including multiple voting rights, should either be completely excluded or explicitly allowed. Also, Schröder allegedly secured the support of the British government for this position by agreeing to support British efforts to water down the provisions of a separate piece of legislation – the directive on Temporary Agency Workers (Guerrera and Jennen, 2003). On the other side, the French and Scandinavian governments refused to accept any rules that would deprive their companies of multiple voting rights.

The Council eventually reached a compromise solution in November 2003. Under the compromise, each member state would be free to decide whether to apply the neutrality article and/or the breakthrough rule. In other words, this left all existing national defensive provisions in place. Frits Bolkestein, the Dutch liberal Commissioner responsible for the directive, was so angry with this deal that he threatened to withdraw the directive altogether, but could not gain support from his Commission colleagues for such an action.[4] The European Parliament then

---

[3] Reference COD/2002/0240.

[4] At exactly this time the Commission was preparing to refer the Council to the European Court of Justice for breach of the Stability and Growth Pact. For this reason, many Commissioners were reluctant to start a second major inter-institutional conflict by withdrawing a piece of legislation for the first time in the history of the EU.

approved the new directive on 16 December 2003 and the Council adopted the final legislative act on 22 December 2003.

11.2 Explaining MEP voting on the Takeover Directive: nationality or party?

Table 11.1 shows the outcome of three key votes on the Takeover Directive. The first vote was on an amendment proposed in the Lehne Report in the second reading of the bill in the parliament, on 13 December 2000. There was no roll-call vote on Lehne's proposed amendment of the neutrality rule. However, there was a roll-call vote on Amendment 6 in the Lehne Report, which related to the definition of 'control' of a company. This amendment proposed that a shareholder holding 30 per cent of the shares can exercise control unless another shareholder controls 5 per cent or more of the shares. In practice this amendment would impose a new harmonised rule, which would establish a blocking power of minority shareholders in all member states, and hence discourage hostile takeover bids (Bergklöf and Burkhart, 2003). A majority of those MEPs taking part in the vote supported this amendment, but the number of MEPs voting in favour of the amendment did not reach the 'absolute majority' threshold (of 314 out of all 626 MEPs), which is required for amendments to be passed in the second reading of the co-decision procedure. Hence, although this amendment did not pass, the issues at stake in this roll-call vote are a good approximation of the main differences in the parliament in the second reading of the bill.

Table 11.1. *Three key votes on the Takeover Directive*

	Vote 1	Vote 2	Vote 3
Date	13 December 2000	4 July 2001	16 December 2003
Subject	Amendment on minority shareholders' rights (2nd reading)	Approve legislation (3rd reading)	Approve legislation (new 1st reading)
Yes	311	273	325
No	219	273	221
Abstain	8	22	7
Total	538	568	553
Result	Fail*	Fail	Pass

*Note: Amendments to legislation in the second reading of the co-decision procedure require an absolute majority of component members of the European Parliament to pass: 314 out of 626 MEPs.

The second vote was the vote in the third reading in the parliament on 4 July 2001, to approve the agreement in the conciliation committee and finally pass the directive into law. As discussed, this vote was a tie, which meant that the directive was not approved by the European Parliament. The third vote was the vote on 16 December 2003 in the first reading of the re-proposed directive in the European Parliament, to approve the deal in the Council and pass the revised legislation into law. In other words, with this vote the European Parliament finally passed the EU Takeover Directive.

Table 11.2 shows the breakdown of MEP behaviour in these three votes by European political group, member state and national party position in the Council vis-à-vis the directive. These descriptive data illustrate quite different voting patterns in each of the votes. In the first and third votes, political groups were more cohesive than national delegations. In the second vote, in contrast, member-state delegations were more cohesive than political groups. And in the third vote, MEPs from parties that supported the directive in the Council were more cohesive than the member-state delegations. Whereas all the parties in government supported the directive at the time of the first vote, at the time of the second vote the government parties in Germany (the social democrats and greens) were the only governing parties who openly opposed the agreement in the Council, and at the time of the third vote the Spanish government party (the conservatives) was the only party in government that abstained in the Council.

Two recent papers have attempted to explain how the MEPs voted on the Takeovers Directive (Callaghan and Höpner, 2004; Ringe, 2005). Although the papers use slightly different variables, the key claim in both papers is that national interests, and particularly different 'models of capitalism', explain the outcome more than European party positions or left–right ideological preferences of the MEPs.

Callaghan and Höpner find that in the tied vote in July 2001, 'the relative importance of nationality and party group affiliation varied systematically depending on the party group in question' (2004: 2). As Table 11.2 shows, the smaller European parties voted along ideological lines, with the liberals (ELDR) and Gaullists and allies (UEN) supporting the directive and the greens (G/EFA) and radical-left (EUL/NGL) opposing the directive. Meanwhile, the two largest groups – the Christian democrats and conservatives (EPP) and socialists (PES) – were spilt down the middle along national lines. While MEPs in these two groups from the Anglo-Saxon economies (Britain and Ireland) generally supported the directive, the MEPs from the Rhenish economies (Germany, Austria, Belgium and the Netherlands) generally

Table 11.2. *MEP voting behaviour by party, member state, and council position*

	Vote 1 (2000)			Vote 2 (2001)			Vote 3 (2003)		
	Yes	No	Abst.	Yes	No	Abst.	Yes	No	Abst.
Political group									
EUL/NGL	30	3	2	1	30	7	2	43	0
G/EFA	5	29	4	8	31	2	9	35	0
PES	115	47	0	80	84	0	29	120	2
ELDR	0	47	0	45	0	0	43	1	0
UEN	1	23	1	16	0	0	21	1	0
EPP-ED	153	46	1	98	119	4	203	2	2
EDD	4	10	0	9	5	3	3	11	0
NA	3	14	0	16	4	6	15	8	3
Member state									
United Kingdom	1	80	0	72	6	0	65	14	0
Ireland	5	9	0	10	2	0	12	2	0
Sweden	8	11	0	19	0	3	13	6	0
Finland	7	9	0	11	2	1	9	5	0
Denmark	9	6	0	13	0	1	8	6	0
Portugal	17	3	0	19	1	2	12	9	0
Luxembourg	4	2	0	5	1	0	3	3	0
France	26	46	5	45	26	10	25	47	3
Italy	40	15	2	32	36	3	47	22	2
Netherlands	14	11	0	9	22	0	17	11	0
Belgium	11	12	0	5	16	0	11	13	0
Spain	49	7	0	26	31	1	32	23	0
Austria	14	4	1	4	14	1	10	7	0
Germany	84	3	0	1	95	0	53	37	2
Greece	22	1	0	2	21	0	8	16	0
Position in Council									
In Council coalition	103	84	3	121	74	4	157	20	0
Not in Council coalition	208	135	5	152	199	18	168	201	7
Total	311	219	8	273	273	22	325	221	7
Cohesion									
Political groups		0.728			0.598			0.838	
Member states		0.580			0.674			0.450	
In Council coalition		0.397			0.412			0.579	

Note: The political groups are sorted from left to right, except for the EDD and NA. The member-state delegations are sorted from the most in favour of the directive to the least in favour of the directive, basis of their voting behaviour in the three votes. The cohesion scores are the mean scores for the political groups and delegations and the total scores for the MEPs from national parties in government who supported the directive in the EU Council – which is all parties in government in the first vote, all parties in government except for the German SPD and Greens in the second vote, and all parties in government except for the Spanish PP in the third vote (see Chapter 5 for the calculation of the cohesion scores).

opposed the directive. For example, one variable that predicts MEP voting behaviour in this vote is the La Porta et al. index of shareholder protection, where the higher the existing level of shareholder protection in a member state the more likely the MEPs from that state were to have voted in favour of the directive in July 2001 (La Porta et al., 1998).

Ringe (2005) looks at voting behaviour in the tied vote as well as in a vote on the first reading of the directive, in October 1997, during the fourth parliament. He finds that left–right ideological preferences influenced MEP behaviour in both votes. However, a far more significant determinant of behaviour in both votes was the specific model of capitalism in the member state of the MEP. Specifically, as the descriptive data in Table 11.2 suggest, MEPs from liberal market economies (United Kingdom and Ireland) and nationally coordinated economies (Denmark, Finland and Sweden) supported the directive, MEPs from partial or family-oriented coordinated market economies (France, Italy, Spain, Greece and Portugal) were split and MEPs from sectorally coordinated economies (Germany, Austria, Belgium, Netherlands and Luxembourg) opposed the directive (Kitschelt et al., 1999; cf. Hall and Soskice, 2001). Ringe also confirms the inference from Table 11.2 that MEPs from parties in government supported the directive more than MEPs from parties in opposition.

In other words, existing research suggests that national interests had a significant influence on voting in the European Parliament on the Takeover Directive. However, this research has mainly focussed on the high-profile tied vote in July 2001. The descriptive results in Table 11.2 suggest that national interests were not so influential in the two other key votes we have identified. So, to draw more general inferences about the politics of the Takeover Directive in the European Parliament we need to undertake a statistical analysis of MEP voting behaviour in all three votes.

11.3   Analysis of MEP behaviour on the Takeover Directive

11.3.1   Variables

Because the voting patterns were relatively different in each of the three votes, we look at MEP behaviour in each vote separately rather than pooling the vote decisions from all three votes. Nevertheless, to make the results more easily comparable, we recoded the vote decisions in the first vote, so that the direction of the dependent variable is the same in each vote. Thus, the dependent variable is 'support for the Directive', where a No vote in the first vote and a Yes vote in the second and third votes takes the value 1, and a Yes vote in the first vote and No vote in the second and third votes takes the value 0. We ignore the abstentions.[5]

We use five sets of independent variables to explain MEP support for the Takeover Directive in all three votes. First, as in the previous chapter, to measure MEPs' ideological positions we use the scores on the first two dimensions produced by applying the NOMINATE scaling method to all the roll-call votes in the fifth parliament. Given our results from Chapter 9, we treat the scores on the first dimension as MEPs' left–right positions (*Left–right*) and the scores on the second dimension as MEPs' preferences towards European integration (*Anti/Pro-EU*).

Second, to capture member state interests in the legislation, we use a continuous variable representing the mean value of annual cross-border merger and acquisition deals in the 1990s in each member state as a percentage of the total stock market capitalisation of that state (*M&A volume*) (Evenett, 2003). Member states with more liberal takeover rules (such as the United Kingdom, Luxembourg, Sweden and the Netherlands) tended to have a higher annual volume of mergers and acquisitions, whereas member states with more restrictive takeover rules (such as France, Germany, Italy, Portugal and Greece) tended to have a lower annual volume of mergers and acquisitions. Hence, this is a reasonable proxy for the main national interest affected by the directive: the existing national rules governing takeovers. It is also a continuous variable instead of a dummy variable, such as the models of capitalism variables used by Ringe (2005), or an ordinal variable, such as the La Porta et al. index used by Callaghan and Höpner (2004). However, as this variable is based on OECD data, it does not include an estimate for Ireland.

Third, we use a variable to capture the effect of the strategic interests of national parties in government during the passage of the Takeover Directive (*Council coalition*). On the basis of the newspaper reports about the coalition that backed the directive in the Council, we assume that all the national parties in government supported the directive at the time of the vote, that all the parties in government except the two German governing parties (the social democrats and greens) supported the directive at the time of the second vote, and that all the parties in government except the Spanish conservatives (who abstained in the Council on the re-proposed directive) supported the directive at the time of the third vote. Hence, the MEPs from all parties who supported the directive at the time of the vote take the value 1, and the MEPs from all the other parties take the value 0. As Table 11.3 shows, there was

---

[5] We also used an ordered logit analysis to incorporate abstention votes. The results when including abstention votes were qualitatively identical.

Table 11.3. *Parties in government at the time of the votes*

	Vote 1 (2000)	Vote 2 (2001)	Vote 3 (2003)
Aus		OVP, FPO	
Bel	VLD, PRL/FDF, SP, PS, Ec, Ag		VLD, MR(PRL/FDF), PS, SP.A, Spirit
Den	SD, RV		V, KF
Fin	SDP, KOK, SFP, VAS, VIHR		KESK, SDP, SFP
Fra	PS, PCF, PRS, MDC, Verts		UMP, UDF
Ger		SPD, G	
Gre		PASOK	
Ire		FD, PD	
Ita	DS, PPI, RI, UDR, PDCI, FV, SDI	FI, AN, UDC, LN, NPSI	
Lux		PCS, DP	
Net	PvdA, VVD, D'66		CDA, VVD, D'66
Por	PS		PSD
Spa		PP	
Swe		SAP	
UK		Lab	
Left	67 %	60 %	27 %
Right	33 %	40 %	73 %

Note: Left governments are shaded.

considerable change in the make-up of the Council between the time of our first vote in December 2000 and our third vote in December 2003. Whereas the Council was dominated by governments on the centre-left in the first two votes, by the time of the third vote the Council was dominated by governments on the centre-right.

Fourth, to examine the effect of European political group membership, and to investigate the determinants of variations in MEP voting within each political group, in a separate model for each vote we include dummy variables for each political group. The dummy variable for non-attached MEPs (NA) was excluded as the baseline category.

Finally, to examine the effect of individual member states, and to analyse the determinants of variations in MEP voting within each member-state delegation of MEPs, in a separate model for each vote we include dummy variables for member states' delegations of MEPs. The variables for Luxembourg and Portuguese MEPs were excluded as the baseline category, as the behaviour of the MEPs from these two states tended to be predicted perfectly by the other variables.

11.3.2. Results

Table 11.4 presents the results. The main findings are as follows. First, national interests mattered, but less in the third vote than in the first two votes. Interestingly, the *M&A volume* variable, which captures national interests, does not explain variations in the voting behaviour of the MEPs within the European political groups in the first vote, but does explain differences within the European parties in the second and third votes.[6] A similar result is found when looking at the significance of the individual member state dummy variables. Three of these variables are significant in the first vote, with the British, French and Finnish MEPs more likely to support the directive than the baseline group, controlling for other factors. Eight of the ten member-state variables are significant in the second vote. And only two of the member-state variables are significant in the third vote, with Greek and French MEPs most likely to oppose the directive, controlling for other factors.

Second, ideological and party preferences did, in fact, make a difference, and mattered in all three votes. The first vote did not split clearly along left–right lines, as measured by the first dimension of NOMINATE scores of the MEPs. The coalition in favour of the amendment was the two largest parties (EPP and PES) and the radical-left against the liberals,

---

[6] We also estimated the same models using the La Porta et al. index of shareholder rights instead of our continuous variable and the results were not substantially different.

Table 11.4. Determinants of MEP Voting on the Takeover Directive

	Vote 1 (2000)			Vote 2 (2001)			Vote 3 (2003)		
	(1)	(2)	(3)	(4)	(5)	(6)	(7)	(8)	(9)
Constant	-1.442***	-4.601***	-1.999**	-0.716***	-0.900	2.621**	-0.554*	-0.634	0.535
	(6.65)	(3.72)	(2.76)	(4.09)	(1.29)	(2.41)	(1.96)	(0.72)	(0.48)
Left-right (NOM D1)	0.260	12.635***	0.215	0.785***	-1.034	1.335***	4.833***	4.428**	5.919***
	(1.28)	(4.87)	(0.77)	(4.45)	(0.93)	(5.11)	(11.32)	(2.44)	(10.29)
Anti/Pro-EU (NOM D2)	-3.648***	-10.500***	-3.532***	-1.347***	-7.671***	-0.066	-1.028**	1.686	-2.671***
	(9.61)	(6.58)	(6.51)	(4.79)	(7.62)	(0.16)	(2.22)	(1.51)	(3.91)
M&A volume	0.216***	-0.006	0.101	0.104**	-0.105*	-0.102	0.114	0.216**	-0.179
	(3.87)	(0.07)	(0.86)	(2.13)	(1.72)	(0.65)	(1.54)	(2.15)	(0.69)
Council coalition	1.163***	0.822*	0.830**	1.090***	0.878***	0.376	1.435***	2.984***	2.670***
	(4.35)	(1.82)	(2.50)	(5.34)	(3.70)	(1.46)	(4.28)	(4.73)	(4.73)
EUL/NGL		7.319**			-7.331***			0.750	
		(2.72)			(4.28)			(0.39)	
G/EFA		13.576***			-2.987**			1.734	
		(4.79)			(2.23)			(0.84)	
PES		10.381***			4.045***			-3.514**	
		(4.88)			(3.80)			(2.09)	
ELDR								2.644	
								(2.04)	
UEN								1.194	
								(0.98)	
EPP-ED		-5.339***			1.684			1.414	
		(3.57)			(1.90)			(1.11)	
EDD		1.680			-2.763**			-1.384	
		(0.40)			(2.94)			(1.56)	
Austria			-0.258			-3.763***			1.704

Belgium			0.760			−3.369***		−1.539
			(0.96)			(3.40)		(0.90)
Denmark			0.289					0.846
			(0.36)					(0.60)
Finland			1.459*			−0.946		−1.180
			(1.77)			(0.78)		(0.79)
France			1.656**			−1.903**		−3.804**
			(2.51)			(2.04)		(2.95)
Germany			−1.438*			−7.438***		−1.177
			(1.69)			(5.50)		(1.10)
Greece			−1.381			−5.199***		−2.181*
			(1.08)			(4.00)		(1.65)
Italy			0.581			−3.180***		0.015
			(0.81)			(3.18)		(0.01)
Netherlands			0.998			−3.403***		0.077
			(1.40)			(3.89)		(0.05)
Spain			−0.022			−2.910**		1.310
			(0.03)			(2.97)		(1.21)
Sweden			1.133					1.757
			(1.37)					(0.98)
United Kingdom			5.821***			−0.118		0.620
			(5.01)			(0.13)		(0.55)
Observations	516	452	516	534	478	502	527	527
Pseudo R-squared	0.23	0.55	0.48	0.10	0.27	0.42	0.55	0.64

Note: Dependent variables: No in Vote 1, Yes in votes 2 and 3. Absolute Z-statistics in parentheses. ELDR and UEN were dropped in models 2 and 3. Denmark and Sweden were dropped in model 6 because of multi-collinearity. Method: Logit regression. *Significant at 10%; **significant at 5%; ***significant at 1%.

greens and Gaullists. This conflict was captured by the second dimension of NOMINATE coordinates. In general, this dimension represents anti/pro-European integration preferences. But, in this case, this dimension also captures the conflict between MEPs from parties representing producers and workers (in the EPP, PES and EUL/NGL) against MEPs representing consumers and minority shareholders (in the ELDR, G/EFA and UEN).

In the second and third votes, the influence of left–right positions is clearer. The further right an MEP, the more likely he or she voted in favour of the directive in both votes. Moreover, this was true on average within each member state's delegation of MEPs (as the results in models 6 and 9 show).

Finally, the interests of national parties in government were significant in all three votes. Indeed, whether or not an MEP's national party was part of the coalition in the Council in favour of the directive was the main determinant of variations in voting behaviour within the European parties in all three votes. So, in the second vote, the splits in the two biggest political groups were less a result of national interests than a split between parties in government who supported the directive in the Council and parties in opposition.

For example, of the ten socialist parties in government in July 2001 that had supported the directive in the Council, the majority of MEPs from only two parties (the Dutch PvdA and Greek PASOK) voted against the directive. Then, when several of these parties were in opposition in december 2003, the MEPs from these parties were freer to vote along ideological lines and support the position of their European party, and so vote against the directive. Only the MEPs from the Swedish and British socialist parties in government (SAP and Labour) broke from the PES group position in the third vote. In fact, in the third vote, the German social democrats, whose prime minister now supported the re-proposed directive in the Council, chose to vote with their political group and against the position of their government.

11.4   Conclusion: parties and ideology matter, even when national interests interfere

Even on one of the most high-profile pieces of EU legislation to pass through the European Parliament, and on an issue where there was a clear clash of national interests, the left–right policy preferences of MEPs and the positions the European parties took on this issue had a clear and predictable influence on the voting behaviour of the MEPs on the legislation. The central issue in the Takeover Directive was whether an Anglo-Saxon model of takeovers, which reduced the possibility of blocking hostile takeover bids, should be imposed throughout the EU. This clearly pitted British economic interests against German industrial interests. As a result, while British MEPs overwhelmingly voted in favour of the directive at all stages of the passage of the legislation, German MEPs overwhelmingly voted against the directive.

However, the main issue in the directive was also a battle between rival ideological conceptions of the role of EU regulation. On one side, right-wing parties and MEPs favoured a gradual liberalisation of the more highly regulated continental models of capitalism. On the other side, left-wing parties and MEPs favoured protecting workers and national industrial 'champions'. Hence, while MEPs in the European conservative and liberal parties tended to support the Takeover Directive, MEPs in the European socialist, green and radical-left parties tended to oppose the directive.

In other words, the case of the Takeover Directive is an exception that proves a general rule. When there are high political stakes on a legislative issue before the European Parliament, MEPs from one or two member states may vote along national rather than party lines in one or two votes on the legislation in question. This is not generally the case, even when there are high political stakes. Even if some MEPs vote along national lines in a particular vote, all the other MEPs invariably vote along European party lines. Moreover, those MEPs who broke from trans-national party lines in some votes will vote with their European parties in all the other votes on the legislation. This was exactly the situation with the Takeover Directive. For example, in the second vote we analysed, all the German MEPs voted against the directive. But in the final vote on the re-proposed legislation in 2003, the German social democrats and greens followed the position of the socialist group rather than their government, and voted against the directive.

Similarly, when legislation passes through the European Parliament, MEPs from parties who supported the legislation in the other chamber of the EU's bicameral system – the Council – tend to vote in favour of the legislation. However, the make-up of the Council is rarely stable for a long period. This is because national election timetables differ, and while some national parties in government win re-election, others are defeated. As a result, in any one legislative vote in the European Parliament, the effect of being in government can be identified in the voting behaviour of MEPs, particularly in the two largest political groups, which contain most of the main parties of government. But because the coalition in the Council changes even in the passage of a single piece of legislation, the government–opposition effect is swamped by the more stable structure of the European parties and the more stable left–right dimension of politics in the European Parliament.

Conclusion

We have analysed in this book for the first time all roll-call votes by MEPs in the five elected European Parliaments since 1979. This research has delivered important insights both from the point of view of political science in general and from the point of view of the study of European Union institutions.

The European Parliament is a unique object of study. It has elected representatives from all the main party families in Europe (conservatives, socialists, liberals, greens, variants of the extreme left and extreme right as well as anti-Europeans) from a growing number of countries (9 in 1979, 10 since 1981, 12 since 1986, 15 since 1995, and 25 since 2004). It has the potential to be the most fragmented parliament in the world. Studying the European Parliament is a good test of two opposing views of democracy: the citizen-delegate view on the one hand, according to which fragmentation is desirable because it allows a close connection between representatives and their home constituency; and the party-based view on the other, according to which it is desirable for elected representatives to group into disciplined political parties. The European Parliament clearly follows the model of party-based democracy.

In its young life, the European Parliament has evolved quickly towards a robust party system, as has been the case in the history of most legislatures. The European Parliament is a particularly interesting case to study the formation of a party system. Indeed, we have argued that parties solve external collective-action problems, such as mobilising the electorate and providing electoral reliability, but also that parties solve internal collective action problems within the legislature, in order to increase the predictability of voting patterns, reduce the dimensionality of politics, enhance the quality of legislation by adequate specialisation and more efficient and comprehensive provision of public goods. In the case of the European Parliament, the external aspect is still largely missing because the electoral connection between voters and the European Parliament operates not via the European parties but via national parties. The European Parliament is thus an interesting case of party formation for the sole purpose of solving collective action problems internal to the legislature.

The study of the European Parliament also raises a fundamental question in political science: whether parties form along national lines or according to broad ideological families. We put forward the idea that parties should form along ideological socio-economic lines and not along national lines because of the nature of differences related to the resolution of legislative conflicts between opposing groups. Conflicts between well-recognised territorial groups can be solved by federalism, such as a mix of centralisation and decentralisation of powers and strongly reducing conflicts between territorial groups while preventing too large inefficiencies such as protectionism by maintaining some centralisation of competences. Conflicts between socio-economic groups, meanwhile, cannot be solved by decentralising legislative power to sectors or social groups because of the destructive externalities that would be involved. Therefore, such conflicts should shape legislative activities, leading to the formation of parties along socio-economic and ideological interest. This, we argue, is the main reason that in democracies where borders have stabilised and an adequate mix of centralisation and decentralisation of government has been found (which is the case in most advanced democracies), parties form not along territorial lines but along the traditional left-right dimension of politics.

These theoretical ideas have been confirmed in our study of the European Parliament. We show that parties have formed around the traditional socio-economic and ideological cleavages. Moreover, parties have become more cohesive over time as the European Parliament has seen its powers increase in the last twenty-five years. Coalitions between parties are also very much along ideological lines. Using established scaling methods and econometric analysis, we have identified two main dimensions in the European Parliament: the first dimension is the traditional left–right axis and the second dimension is a mixture of attitudes towards European integration (in favour and against) and government-opposition status in the EU institutions (depending on the representation of the European political groups and national parties in the Council and Commission).

As stated, party formation has occurred mostly to solve the internal collective action problems within the European Parliament. Increased powers to the European Parliament have given national parties an increased incentive to act jointly and present a cohesive front to compete with other European parties to be on the winning side, and so shape policy outputs from the EU. We find evidence of the ability of the

European parties to discipline their MEPs. Participation in votes is larger for close votes, indicating the capacity of the European parties to mobilise their backbenchers. We find that a European party is no less cohesive when facing hostile amendments on bills it sponsors (on which it has the rapporteurship) than on other items on the agenda. Recent theories of agenda-setting have emphasised that party leaders can use control over the agenda to allow only bills that will not divide their party members. We find some evidence for these theories. But we also find evidence for the fact that the European parties are able to discipline their members even when they do not control the agenda.

The main channel of cohesion of European parties is the action of national parties to overcome their own collective-action problems. In the literature on the European Parliament, the national parties have sometimes been opposed to the European parties and there have often been high-profile conflicts between certain national parties and European parties. However, most of the time, the national parties within a European political group operate to find a consensus position to compete with the other European political groups. Once consensus is reached, national parties are the main channel for disciplining the MEPs. MEPs tend to vote with their European political group, independently of their own ideological positions. However, the ideological distance between an MEP's national party and his or her European party can sometimes cause the MEP to deviate from the European party line.

The findings in this book also have important implications for the future of parties and politics in the European Parliament. They imply a very positive message concerning the functioning of the party system in the European Parliament. Further allocation of power to the only elected body in the EU should increase the cohesion of the party system as it has done in the past. Competition between the European parliamentary parties should then increase and produce healthy democratic outcomes. Another implication is that the traditional left–right debates should become more and more part of EU political debates.

However, it is also important to emphasise that the EU is still a very imperfect democracy. As we mentioned throughout this book, unlike in other democracies, the connection between the European electorate and European parties is weak. Voters rarely make choices in European Parliament elections on the basis of the positions and behaviour of the MEPs and European parties. Also, participation in European Parliament elections has declined and one urgently needs to overcome this by giving more life to the European parties. What would it take to connect the European parties and the party system in the European Parliament to the voters?

Following our theoretical discussions in Chapter 2, two things need to be done to establish a clear connection between voters and the European Parliament: (1) voters need to be able to identify and use European-wide 'brand labels'; and (2) the European parties must work directly to mobilise the electorate to participate in European elections. Any change short of achieving these two objectives would be insufficient to provide an electoral connection between the European parties and their electorate. This would allow campaigns and platforms to be truly pan-European and not simply protest votes against incumbent national governments as is the case now. Control over the electoral process by the European parties would also give them more instruments to directly discipline their MEPs, without having to resort to the channel of national parties.

Such changes can occur along two possible paths: the parliamentary and the presidential model. It is worthwhile to briefly sketch what directions these would be.

In the parliamentary model, elections to the European Parliament should become a more direct contest for the control of the Commission. Right now, the President of the Commission is proposed by the European Council, and individual member states, until recently, decided unilaterally who their representative in the Commission would be. The European Parliament has shown in the case of the confirmation of the Barroso Commission, outlined in the Introduction to this book, that it was able to veto the will of the member states. However, the process of the formation of the Commission is still quite far from the traditional parliamentary model. A few changes would, however, go a long way in the direction of the European model.

First of all, as stated earlier, electoral campaigns for the European elections should be under the control of the European parties, with their party labels, their platforms and their campaigns.

Second, the European parties should take the initiative away from the Council by announcing before the election their candidates for the Presidency of the Commission. In effect, this would replicate the German system, where each party announces its candidate for Chancellor before each Bundestag election. This would give incentives to European parties to choose a candidate who would have a broad appeal amongst the European electorate. This would strongly reduce the initiative of the European Council, which would then not dare veto for the President of the Commission the candidate of the party who won the European elections. The campaign would become more 'personalised' and might have a more mobilising effect on voters. The elected president would then have more clout to negotiate with individual governments on the choice of the composition of the Commission, the latter knowing that the European Parliament can impose its veto right.

The presidential model would be somewhat different, but would also be based around elections. This would involve a separate (though possibly simultaneous) election for the Presidency of the Commission. The best system for such an election would be a run-off, following the French model, so as to allow the elected president to be elected with a majority of votes. In the first round, candidates of parties or of cartels of parties would present themselves to the European electorate. The two candidates who receive the most votes would then compete in the second round. An original institutional twist related to the multinational character of Europe might be that before the second round each of the two candidates presents his or her candidates for vice-presidents, or possibly even his or her whole team of Commissioners. The second round would then not simply be between two candidates but between two teams. This would give the candidates for the presidency a strong incentive to select competent and well-respected politicians with a right national mix.

This is not the place to discuss at length the pros and cons of movements towards the presidential or parliamentary model. It is likely, though not certain, that the parliamentary model would seem more appealing to European citizens. However, in both models, the European party system would be strengthened by creating a direct connection to the European electorate. For example, the United States and Britain both had parliamentary-based parties before the development of electoral parties. What promoted electoral parties in both cases was the battle for executive office. In the American presidential system, the electoral-based parties that were formed in the 1820s and 1830s to fight presidential elections were more clearly connected to the citizens than the political factions that had formed in the early US Congresses, and gradually developed as powerful political organisations both inside and outside the US Congress (Aldrich, 1995). Similarly, in the British parliamentary system, once the Cabinet became accountable to the House of Commons instead of the King in the late 1800s, electoral party machines began to be formed to win a majority in the parliament and so form the government (Cox, 1987). Hence, regardless of whether the EU evolves towards a presidential or a parliamentary model, a contest for control of the Commission would almost certainly further strengthen the parties in the European Parliament as well as establish a connection between European parties and EU citizens.

In conclusion, our research suggests that European democracy would be well served by giving more powers to the European Parliament.

Bibliography

Aldrich, John H. (1995) *Why Parties? The Origin and Transformation of Political Parties in America*, Chicago, IL: The University of Chicago Press.

Alesina, Alberto and Howard Rosenthal (1995) *Partisan Politics, Divided Government, and the Economy*, Cambridge: Cambridge University Press.

Alesina, Alberto and Enrico Spoloare (2003) *The Size of Nations*, Cambridge, MA: MIT Press.

Alesina, Alberto, Ignazio Angeloni and Ludger Schuknecht (2001) 'What Does the European Union Do?', NBER Working Paper No. 8647.

Amorim Neto, Octavio, Gary W. Cox and Mathew D. McCubbins (2003) 'Agenda Power in Brazil's Câmara dos Deputados, 1989–98', *World Politics*, vol. 55, no. 4, pp. 550–78.

Andeweg, Rudy (1995) 'The Reshaping of National Party Systems', in Jack Hayward (ed.) *The Crisis of Representation in Europe*, London: Frank Cass.

Arrow, Kenneth, J. (1951) *Social Choice and Individual Values*, New York, NY: Wiley.

Aspinwall, Mark (2002) 'Preferring Europe: Ideology and National Preferences on European Integration', *European Union Politics*, vol. 3, pp. 81–112.

Attinà, Fulvio (1990) 'The Voting Behaviour of the European Parliament Members and the Problem of Europarties', *European Journal of Political Research*, vol. 18, pp. 557–79.

Attinà, Fulvio (1992) 'Parties, Party Systems and Democracy in the European Union', *International Spectator*, vol. 27, pp. 67–86.

Banzhaf, John F. (1965) 'Weighted Voting Doesn't Work: A Mathematical Analysis', *Rutgers Law Review*, vol. 19, pp. 317–43.

Bardi, Luciano (1992) 'Transnational Party Federations in the European Community', in Richard S. Katz and Peter Mair (eds.) *Party Organizations: A Handbook on Party Organizations in Western Democracies*, London: Sage.

Bardi, Luciano (1994) 'Transnational Party Federations, European Parliamentary Party Groups, and the Building of Europarties', in

Richard S. Katz and Peter Mair (eds.) *How Parties Organize: Change and Adaptation in Party Organizations in Western Democracies*, London: Sage.

Baron, David P. and John A. Ferejohn (1989) 'Bargaining in Legislatures', *American Journal of Political Science*, vol. 83, pp. 1181–206.

Bartolini, Stefano (2000) *The Political Mobilization of the European Left, 1860–1980: The Class Cleavage*, Cambridge: Cambridge University Press.

Bartolini, Stefano (2005) *Restructuring Europe: Centre Formation, System Building, and Political Structuring between the Nation State and the European Union*, Oxford: Oxford University Press.

Bartolini, Stefano and Peter Mair (1990) *Identity, Competition, and Electoral Availability: The Stability of European Electorates, 1885–1985*, Cambridge: Cambridge University Press.

Benoit, Kenneth R. and Michael J. Laver (2005) *Party Policy in Modern Democracies*, London: Routledge.

Berglöf, Erik and Mike Burkart (2003) 'European Takeover Regulation', *Economic Policy*, vol. 18, no. 1, pp. 171–213.

Bergman, Torbjörn, Wolfgang C. Müller and Kaare Strøm (2000) 'Parliamentary Democracy and the Chain of Delegation', *European Journal of Political Research* Vol. 37, no. 3, pp. 255–260.

Bindseil, Ulrich and Cordula Hantke (1997) 'The Power Distribution in Decision-Making among EU Member States', *European Journal of Political Economy*, vol. 13, no. 2, pp. 171–185.

Black, Duncan (1958) *The Theory of Committees and Elections*, Cambridge: Cambridge University Press.

Bobbio, Norberto (1996 [1995]) *Left and Right: The Significance of a Political Distinction*, trans. A. Cameron, Cambridge: Polity.

Bolingbroke, Henry St. John (1971 [1738]) *The Idea of a Patriot King*, Menston: Scholar Press.

Bolton, Patrick and Mathias Dewatripont (2005) *Contract Theory*, Cambridge, MA: MIT Press.

Bolton, Patrick and Gérard Roland (1997) 'The Breakup of Nations: A Political Economy Analysis', *The Quarterly Journal of Economics*, vol. 112, no. 4, pp. 1057–90.

Bourguignon-Wittke, Roswitha, Eberhard Grabitz, Otto Schmuck, Sabine Steppat and Wolfgang Wessels (1985) 'Five Years of the Directly Elected European Parliament: Performance and Prospects', *Journal of Common Market Studies*, vol. 24, no. 1, pp. 39–59.

Bowler, Shaun and David Farrell (1993) 'Legislator Shirking and Voter Monitoring: Impacts of European Parliament Electoral Systems upon Legislator/Voter Relationships', *Journal of Common Market Studies*, vol. 31, no. 1, pp. 45–69.

Bowler, Shaun, David M. Farrell and Richard S. Katz (eds.) (1999) *Party Discipline and Parliamentary Government*, Columbus, OH: Ohio State Press.

Brancati, Dawn (2007) 'The Origins of Regional Parties', *British Journal of Political Science* (forthcoming).

Brzinski, Joanne Bay (1995) 'Political Group Cohesion in the European Parliament, 1989–1994', in Carolyn Rhodes and Sonia Mazey (eds.) *The State of the European Union, Vol. 3*, London: Longman.

Budge, Ian, Hans-Dieter Klingemann, Andrea Volkens, Judith Bara and Eric Tanenbaum (2001) *Mapping Policy Preferences: Estimates for Parties, Electors, and Governments 1945–1998*, Oxford: Oxford University Press.

Callaghan, Helen and Martin Höpner (2004) 'Parties or Nations? Political Cleavages over EU Efforts to Create a Single European Market for Corporate Control', paper presented at the Annual Meeting of the American political Science Association, September 1994, Chicago.

Cameron, Charles M. (2000) *Veto Bargaining: Presidents and the Politics of Negative Power*, Cambridge: Cambridge University Press.

Campbell, Angus, Philip E. Converse, Warren E. Miller and Donald E. Stokes (1960) *The American Voter*, New York, NY: Wiley.

Caramani, Daniele, (2004) *The Nationalization of Politics: The Formation of National Electorates and Party Systems in Western Europe*, Cambridge: Cambridge University Press.

Carrubba, Clifford J., Matthew Gabel, Lacey Murrah, Ryan Clough, Elizabeth Montgomery and Rebecca Schambach (2006) 'Off the Record: unrecorded Legislative votes, selection Bias and and Roll-Call Votes Analysis', *British Journal of Political Science*, vol. 36, no. 4, pp. 691–704.

Castanheira, Micael (2003) 'Voting for Losers', *Journal of the European Economic Association*, vol. 1, no. 5, pp. 1207–38.

Chandler, William, Gary W. Cox and Mathew D. McCubbins (2005) 'Agenda Control in the German Bundestag, 1987–2002', mimeo, University of California, San Diego, CA.

Chhibber, Pradeep and Kenneth Kollman (2004) *The Formation of National Party Systems: Federalism and Party Competition in Britain, Canada and the US*, Princeton, NJ: Princeton University Press.

Claeys, Paul-Henri and Nicole Loeb-Mayer (1979) 'Trans-European Party Groupings: Emergence of New and Alignment of Old Parties in the Light of the Direct Elections to the European Parliament', *Government and Opposition*, vol. 14, no. 4, pp. 455–78.

Corbett, Richard (1988) *The European Parliament's Role in Closer EU Integration*, London: Palgrave.

Corbett, Richard, Francis Jacobs and Michael Shackleton (2005) *The European Parliament*, 6th edition, London: John Harper Publishing.

Cowen, Michael and Liisa Laakso (eds.) (2002) *Multi-Party Elections in Africa*, Oxford: James Currey.

Cox, Gary W. (1987) *The Efficient Secret: The Cabinet and the Development of Political Parties in Victorian England*, Cambridge: Cambridge University Press.

Cox, Gary W. and Mathew D. McCubbins (1993) *Legislative Leviathan: Party Government in the House*, Berkeley, CA: University of California Press.

Cox, Gary W. and Mathew D. McCubbins (2002) 'Agenda Power in the U.S. House of Representatives, 1877 to 1986', in David W. Brady and Mathew D. McCubbins (eds.) *Party, Process, and Political Change in Congress: New Perspectives on the History of Congress*, Stanford, CA: Stanford University Press.

Cox, Gary W. and Mathew D. McCubbins (2005) *Setting the Agenda: Responsible Party Government in the U.S. House of Representatives*, Cambridge: Cambridge University Press.

Cox, Gary W., Mikitaka Masuyama and Mathew D. McCubbins (2000) 'Agenda Power in the Japanese House of Representatives' *Japanese Journal of Political Science*, vol. 1, no. 1, pp. 1–21.

Crombez, Christophe (2001) 'Institutional Reform and Co-Decision in the European Union', *Constitutional Political Economy*, vol. 11, no. 1, pp 41–57.

Dahl, Robert A. (1956) *A Preface to Democratic Theory*, Chicago, IL: University of Chicago Press.

Dahrendorf, Ralf (1959) *Class and Class Conflict in Industrial Society*, London: Routledge.

Dalton, Russell J., Scott Flanagan and Paul A. Beck (1984) *Electoral Change in Advanced Industrial Democracies: Realignment or Dealignment?* Princeton, NJ: Princeton University Press.

Diermeier, Daniel and Timothy J. Feddersen (1998) 'Cohesion in Legislatures and the Vote of Confidence Procedure', *American Political Science Review*, vol. 92, pp. 611–21.

Diermeier, Daniel and Antonio Merlo (2000) 'Government Turnover in Parliamentary Democracies', *Journal of Economic Theory*, vol. 94, no. 1, pp. 46–79.

Diermeier, Daniel and Randolf T. Stevenson (1999) 'Cabinet Survival and Competing Risks', *American Journal of Political Science*, vol. 43, pp. 1051–98.

Diermeier, Daniel and Randolf T. Stevenson (2000) 'Cabinet Termination and Critical Events', *American Political Science Review*, vol. 94, pp. 627–40.

Downs, Anthony (1957) *An Economic Theory of Democracy*, New York, NY: Harper and Row.

Duverger, Maurice (1954 [1951]) *Political Parties: Their Organization and Activities in the Modern State*, New York, NY: Wiley.

Eijk, Cees van der and Mark Franklin (eds.) (1996) *Choosing Europe? The European Electorate and National Politics in the Face of Union*, Ann Arbor, MI: University of Michigan Press.

Enelow, James M. and Melvin J. Hinich (1984) *The Spatial Theory of Voting: an Introduction*, Cambridge: Cambridge University Press.

Epstein, David and Sharyn O'Halloran (1999) *Delegating Powers: A Transaction Cost Politics Approach to Policy Making Under Separate Powers*, Cambridge: Cambridge University Press.

European Parliament (1999) *The Committee of Experts' Report on Fraud, Mismanagement and Nepotism in the European Commission*, Brussels: European Parliament.

Evenett, Simon J. (2003) 'The Cross-Border Mergers and Acquisitions Wave of the late 1990s', in Robert E. Baldwin and L. Alan Winters (eds.) *Challenges to Globalization: Analyzing the Economics*, Chicago, IL: University of Chicago Press.

Fearon, James D. (1999) 'Electoral Accountability and the Control of Politicians: Selecting Good Types versus Sanctioning Poor Performance', in Bernard Manin, Adam Przeworski and Susan Stokes (eds.) *Democracy, Accountability, and Representation*, Cambridge: Cambridge University Press.

Ferejohn, John (1986) 'Incumbent Performance and Electoral Control', *Public Choice*, vol. 50, pp. 5–26.

Ferejohn, John and Morris Fiorina (1974) 'The Paradox of Not Voting: A Decision Theoretic Analysis', *American Political Science Review*, vol. 68, pp. 525–36.

Figueiredo, Argelina Cheibub and Fernando Limongi (2000) 'Presidential Power, Legislative Organization, and Party Behavior in Brazil', *Comparative Politics*, vol. 32, no. 2, pp. 151–70.

Finer, Samuel E. (1987) 'Left and Right', in Vernon Bogdanor (ed.) *The Blackwell Encyclopaedia of Political Institutions*, Oxford: Blackwell.

Fitzmaurice, John (1975) *The Party Groups in the European Parliament*, Farnborough: Saxon House.

Flanagan, Scott C. (1987) 'Value Change in Industrial Societies', *American Political Science Review*, vol. 81, no. 4, pp. 1303–18.

Franklin, Mark, Tom Mackie and Henry Valen (eds.) (1992) *Electoral Change: Responses to Evolving Social and Attitudinal Structures in Western Countries*, Cambridge: Cambridge University Press.

Gabel, Matthew J. and Christopher J. Anderson (2002) 'The Structure of Citizen Attitudes and the European Political Space', *Comparative Political Studies*, vol. 35, no. 8, pp. 893–913.

Gabel, Matthew J. and Simon Hix (2002a) 'The European Parliament and Executive Politics in the EU: Voting Behaviour and the Commission President Investiture Procedure', in Madeleine Hosli, Adrian Van Deemen and Mika Widgrén (eds.) *Institutional Challenges in the European Union*, London: Routledge.

Gabel, Matthew J. and Simon Hix (2002b) 'Defining the EU Political Space: An Empirical Study of the European Elections Manifestos, 1979–1999', *Comparative Political Studies*, vol. 35, pp. 934–64.

Grant, Ruth (1977) 'The Origins of American Political Parties: Antifederalists and Jeffersonian Republicans', mimeo, University of Chicago.

Grosclose, Tim and James M. Snyder Jr. (1996) 'Buying Supermajorities', *American Political Science Review*, vol. 90, pp. 303–315.

Guerrera, Francesco and Birgit Jennen (2003) 'UK in deal with Germany over Takeover Code', *The Financial Times*, 3 February 2003, p. 10.

Hall, Peter and David Soskice (eds.) (2001) *Varieties of Capitalism: The Institutional Foundations of Comparative Advantage*, Oxford: Oxford University Press.

Hallstein, Walter (1972) *Europe in the Making*, London: Allen and Unwin.

Henig, Stanley (ed.) (1979) *Political Parties in the European Community*, London: Allen and Unwin.

Herbst, Jeffrey (2000) *States and Power in Africa: Comparative Lessons in Authority and Control*, Princeton, NJ: Princeton University Press.

Hix, Simon (1994) 'The Study of the European Community: The Challenge to Comparative Politics', *West European Politics*, vol. 17, no. 1, pp. 1–30.

Hix, Simon (1999) 'Dimensions and Alignments in European Union Politics: Cognitive Constraints and Partisan Responses', *European Journal of Political Research*, vol. 35, pp. 69–106.

Hix, Simon (2001) 'Legislative Behaviour and Party Competition in European Parliament: An Application of Nominate to the EU', *Journal of Common Market Studies*, vol. 39, pp. 663–88.

Hix, Simon (2002a) 'Constitutional Agenda-Setting Through Discretion in Rule Interpretation: Why the European Parliament Won at Amsterdam', *British Journal of Political Science*, vol. 32, no. 2, pp. 259–80.

Hix, Simon (2002b) 'Parliamentary Behavior with Two Principals: Preferences, Parties, and Voting in the European Parliament', *American Journal of Political Science*, vol. 46, no. 3, pp. 688–98.

Hix, Simon (2004) 'Electoral Institutions and Legislative Behavior: Explaining Voting Defection in the European Parliament', *World Politics*, vol. 56, no. 1, pp. 194–223.

Hix, Simon (2005) *The Political System of the European Union*, 2nd edition, London: Palgrave.

Hix, Simon and Christopher Lord (1996) 'The Making of a President: The European Parliament and the Confirmation of Jacques Santer as President of the Commission', *Government and Opposition*, vol. 31, no. 1, pp. 62–76.

Hix, Simon and Christopher Lord (1997) *Political Parties in the European Union*. Basingstoke: Macmillan.

Hix, Simon, Amie Kreppel and Abdul Noury (2003) 'The Party System in the European Parliament: Collusive or Competitive?', *Journal of Common Market Studies*, vol. 41, no. 2, pp. 309–31.

Hix, Simon, Abdul Noury and Gérard Roland (2005) 'Power to the Parties: Cohesion and Competition in the European Parliament, 1979–2001', *British Journal of Political Science*, vol. 35, no. 2, pp. 209–34.

Hoffmann, Stanley (1966) 'Obstinate or Obsolete? The Fate of the Nation-State and the Case of Western Europe', *Daedalus*, vol. 95, pp. 862–914.

Hooghe, Liesbet and Gary Marks (1999) 'The Making of a Polity: The Struggle Over European Integration', in Herbert Kitschelt, Peter Lange, Gary Marks and John Stephens (eds.) *Continuity and Change in Contemporary Capitalism*, Cambridge: Cambridge University Press.

Hooghe, Liesbet, Gary Marks and Carole Wilson (2002) 'Does Left/ Right Structure Party Positions on European Integration?', *Comparative Political Studies*, vol. 35, pp. 965–989.

Hosli, Madeleine O. (1997) 'Voting Strength in the European Parliament', *European Journal of Political Research*, vol. 31, pp. 351–66.

Hoyland, Bjorn (2005) *Government and Opposition in EU Legislative Politics*, Ph.D. thesis, London: London School of Economics and Political Science.

Hotelling, Harold (1929) 'Stability in Competition', *Economic Journal*, vol. 39, pp. 41–57.

Huber, John D. (1996a) *Rationalizing Parliament: Legislative Institutions and Party Politics in France*, Cambridge: Cambridge University Press.

Huber, John D. (1996b) The Vote of Confidence in Parliamentary Democracies', *American Political Science Review*, vol. 80, no. 4, pp. 1131–50.

Ignazi, Piero (1992) 'The Silent Counter-Revolution: Hypotheses on the Emergence of Extreme-Right Parties in Europe', *European Journal of Political Research*, vol. 22, no. 1, pp. 3–34.

Inglehart, Ronald (1977) *The Silent Revolution: Changing Values and Political Styles among Western Publics*, Princeton, NJ: Princeton University Press.

Inglehart, Ronald (1990) *Culture Shift in Advanced Industrial Society*, Princeton, NJ: Princeton University Press.

Jensen, Michael and William Meckling (1976) 'Theory of the Firm: Managerial Behaviour, Agency Cost and Capital Structure', *Journal of Financial Economics*, vol. 3, pp. 305–60.

Karvonen, Lauri and Stein Kuhnle (eds.) (2001) *Party Systems and Voter Alignments Revisited*, London: Routledge.

Katz, Richard S. and Peter Mair (1995) 'Changing Models of Party Organization and Party Democracy: The Emergence of the Cartel Party', *Party Politics*, vol. 1, no. 1, pp. 5–28.

Key, Valdimar O. (1961) *Public Opinion and American Democracy*, New York, NY: Knopf.

Kiewiet, D. Roderick and Matthew D. McCubbins (1991) *The Logic of Delegation: Congressional Parties and the Appropriations Process*, Chicago, IL: University of Chicago Press.

King, Anthony (1969) 'Political Parties in Western Democracies: Some Sceptical Reflections', *Polity*, vol. 2, no. 2, pp. 111–41.

Kitschelt, Herbert (1994) *The Transformation of European Social Democracy*, Cambridge: Cambridge University Press.

Kitschelt, Herbert (1995) *The Radical Right in Western Europe: A Comparative Analysis*, Ann Arbor, MI: University of Michigan Press.

Kitschelt, Herbert, Peter Lange, Gary Marks and John D. Stephens (eds.) (1999) *Continuity and Change in Contemporary Capitalism*, Cambridge: Cambridge University Press.

Krehbiel, Keith (1993) 'Where's the Party?', *British Journal of Political Science*, vol. 23, pp. 235–66.

Krehbiel, Keith (1998) *Pivotal Politics: A Theory of U.S. Lawmaking*, Chicago, IL: University of Chicago Press.

Kreppel, Amie (2000) 'Rules, Ideology and Coalition Formation in the European Parliament: Past, Present and Future', *European Union Politics*, vol. 1, pp. 340–62.

Kreppel, Amie (2002a) 'Moving Beyond Procedure: An Empirical Analysis of European Parliament Legislative Influence', *Comparative Political Studies*, vol. 35, no. 7, pp. 784–813.

Kreppel, Amie (2002b) *The European Parliament and Supranational Party System: A Study in Institutional Development*, Cambridge: Cambridge University Press.

Kreppel, Amie and Simon Hix (2003) 'From "Grand Coalition" to Left-Right Confrontation: Explaining the Shifting Structure of Party Competition in the European Parliament', *Comparative Political Studies*, vol. 36, pp. 75–96.

Kreppel, Amie and George Tsebelis (1999) 'Coalition Formation in the European Parliament', *Comparative Political Studies*, vol. 32, pp. 933–66.

La Porta, Rafael, Florencio Lopez-de-Silanes, Andrei Shleifer and Robert Vishny (1998) 'Law and Finance', *Journal of Political Economy*, vol. 106, no. 6, pp. 1113–55.

Lane, Jan-Erik Reinert Maeland and Sven Berg (1995) 'The EU Parliament: Seats, States and Political Parties', *Journal of Theoretical Politics*, vol. 7, pp. 395–400.

LaPalombara, Joseph and Myron Weiner (1966) 'The Origin and Development of Political Parties', in Joseph LaPalombara and Myron Weiner (eds.) *Political Parties and Political Development*, Princeton, NJ: Princeton University Press.

Laver, Michael (1998) 'Models of Government Formation', *Annual Review of Political Science*, vol. 1, pp. 1–25.

Laver, Michael (2002) 'Government Termination', *Annual Review of Political Science*, vol. 6, pp. 23–40.

Laver, Michael J. and W. Ben Hunt (1992) *Policy and Party Competition*, London: Routledge.

Laver, Michael and Norman Schofield (1990) *Multiparty Government: The Politics of Coalition in Europe*, Oxford: Oxford University Press.

Laver, Michael J., Kenneth R. Benoit and John Garry (2003) 'Extracting Policy Positions from Political Texts Using Words as Data', *American Political Science Review*, vol. 97, pp. 311–31.

Levitt, Steven D. (1996) 'How Do Senators Vote? Disentangling the Role of Voter Preferences, Party Affiliation, and Senator Ideology', *The American Economic Review*, vol. 86, no. 3, pp. 425–41.

Lipset, Seymour M. (1959) *Political Man*, London: Heinemann.

Lipset, Seymour M. and Stein Rokkan (1967) 'Cleavage Structures, Party Systems and Voter Alignments: An Introduction', in Seymour M. Lipset and Stein Rokkan (eds.) *Party Systems and Voter Alignments: Cross-national Perspectives*, New York, NY: Free Press.

Lupia, Arthur and Kaare Strøm (1995) 'Coalition termination and the Strategic Timing of Legislative Elections', *American Political Science Review*, vol. 89, pp. 648–65.

MacDonald, Stuart E., Ola Listaug and George Rabinowitz (1991) 'Issues and Party Support in Mulitparty Systems', *American Political Science Review*, vol. 85, pp. 1107–31.

MacRae, Duncan, Jr. (1967) *Parliament, Parties, and Society in France 1946–1958*, New York, NY: St. Martin's Press.

Magnette, Paul (2001) 'Appointing and Censuring the Commission: the Adaptation of Parliamentary Institutions to the Community Context', *European Law Journal*, vol. 7, no. 3, pp. 289–307.

Majone, Giandomenico (1993) 'The European Community between Social Policy and Social Regulation', *Journal of Common Market Studies*, vol. 31, no. 2, pp. 153–70.

Majone, Giandomenico (1996) *Regulating Europe*, London: Routledge.

Majone, Giandomenico (2002) 'The European Commission: The Limits of Centralization and the Perils of Parliamentarization', *Governance*, vol. 15, no. 3, pp. 375–92.

Marks, Gary and Marco Steenbergen (2002) 'Introduction: Understanding Political Contestation in the European Union', *Comparative Political Studies*, vol. 35, pp. 879–92.

Marks, Gary and Marco Steenbergen (2004) *Marks/Steenbergen Party Dataset*, Chapel Hill, NC: University of North Carolina Chapel Hill, available at: www.unc.edu/~gwmarks/data.htm

Marks, Gary and Carole J. Wilson (2000) 'The Past in the Present: A Cleavage Theory of Party Response to European Integration', *British Journal of Political Science*, vol. 30, no. 3, pp. 433–59.

Marks, Gary, Carole J. Wilson and Leonard Ray (2002) 'National Political Parties and European Integration', *American Journal of Political Science*, vol. 46, pp. 585–94.

Marquand, David (1978) 'Towards a Europe of the Parties', *Political Quarterly*, vol. 49, pp. 425–45.

Mattila, Miko (2004) 'Contested Decisions: Empirical Analysis of Voting in the EU Council of Ministers', *European Journal of Political Research*, vol. 43, pp. 29–50.

Mattila, Miko and Jan-Eric Lane (2001) 'Why Unanimity in the Council? A Roll Call Analysis of Council Voting', *European Union Politics*, vol. 2, pp. 31–52.

Mayhew, David (1974) *Congress: The Electoral Connection*, New Haven, CT: Yale University Press.

McCubbins, Mathew D. and Thomas Schwartz (1984) 'Congressional Oversight Overlooked: Police Patrols versus Fire Alarms', *American Journal of Political Science*, vol. 28, no. 1, pp. 165–79.

McKelvey, Richard D. (1976) 'Intransitivities in Multidimensional Voting Models and Some Implications for Agenda Control', *Journal of Economic Theory*, vol. 12, no. 3, pp. 472–82.

Moravcsik, Andrew (1991) 'Negotiating the Single European Act: National Interests and Conventional Statecraft in the European Community', *International Organization*, vol. 45, no. 1, pp. 19–56.

Moravcsik, Andrew (1998) *The Choice for Europe: Social Purpose and State Power from Messina to Maastricht*, Ithaca, NY: Cornell University Press.

Moravcsik, Andrew (2002) 'In Defense of the "Democratic Deficit": Reassessing the Legitimacy of the European Union', *Journal of Common Market Studies*, vol. 40, no. 4, pp. 603–34.

Müller, Wolfgang C. and Strøm Kaare (eds.) (2000) *Coalition Governments in Western Europe*, Oxford: Oxford University Press.

Neumann, Sigmund (1956) 'Toward a Comparative Study of Political Parties', in Sigmund Neumann (ed.) *Modern Political Parties*, Chicago, IL: University of Chicago Press.

Niedermeyer, Oskar (1983) *Europäische Parteien? Zur grenzüberschreitenden Interaktion politischer Parteien im Rahmen der Europäischen Gemeinschaft*, Frankfurt: Campus.

Noury, Abdul (2002) 'Ideology, Nationality and Euro-Parliamentarians', *European Union Politics*, vol. 3, no. 1, pp. 33–58.

Noury, Abdul (2004) 'Abstention in Daylight: Stategic Calculus of Voting in the European Parliament', *Public Choice*, vol. 212, pp. 179–211.

Noury, Abdul and Gérard Roland (2002) 'More Power to the European Parliament?', *Economic Policy*, vol. 17, no. 35, pp. 280–319.

Nurmi, Hannu (1997) 'The Representation of Voter Groups in the EP', *Electoral Studies*, vol. 16, pp. 317–27.

Oates, William E. (1972) *Fiscal Federalism*, New York, NY: Harcourt Brace Jovanovich.

Persson, Torsten, Gérard Roland and Guido Tabellini (2000) 'Comparative Politics and Public Finance', *Journal of Political Economy*, vol. 108, pp. 1121–61.

Piketty, Thomas (2000) 'Voting as Communicating', *Review of Economic Studies*, vol. 67, pp. 169–91.

Pollack, Mark A. (1995) 'Regional Actors in an Intergovernmental Play: The Making and Implementation of EC Structural Policy', in Carolyn Rhodes and Sonia Mazey (eds.) *The State of the European Union, vol. 3*, London: Longman.

Poole, Keith T. (2005) *Spatial Models of Parliamentary Voting*, Cambridge: Cambridge University Press.

Poole, Keith T. and Howard Rosenthal (1997) *A Political-Economic History of Roll Call Voting*, Oxford: Oxford University Press.

Pridham, Geoffrey and Pippa Pridham (1981) *Transnational Party Co-operation and European Integration: The Process Towards Direct Elections*, London: Allen and Unwin.

Quanjel, Marcel and Menno Wolters (1993) 'Growing Cohesion in the European Parliament', paper presented at the Joint Sessions of the ECPR, April 1993, Leiden.

Rae, Douglas W. (1967) *The Political Consequences of Electoral Laws*, New Haven, CT: Yale University Press.

Raunio, Tapio (1997) *The European Perspective: Transnational Party Groups in the 1989–1994 European Parliament*, London: Ashgate.

Reif, Karlheinz and Hermann Schmitt (1980) 'Nine Second-Order National Elections: A Conceptual Framework for the Analysis of European Election Results', *European Journal of Political Research*, vol. 8, no. 1, pp. 3–45.

Rice, Stuart A. (1928) *Quantitative Methods in Politics*, New York, NY: Knopf.

Riker, William H. (1962) *The Theory of Political Coalitions*, New Haven, CT: Yale University Press.

Riker, William H. (1980) 'Implications for the Disequilibrium of Majority Rule for the Study of Institutions', *American Political Science Review*, vol. 74, no. 2, pp. 432–46.

Riker, William H. (1986) *The Art of Political Manipulation*, New Haven, CT: Yale University Press.

Riker, William H. and Peter C. Ordeshook (1968) 'A Theory of the Calculus of Voting', *American Political Science Review*, vol. 62, pp. 25–42.

Ringe, Nils (2005) 'Policy Preference Formation in Legislative Politics: Structures, Actors, and Focal Points', *American Journal of Political Science*, vol. 49, no. 4, pp. 731–45.

Rittberger, Berthold (2003) 'The Creation and Empowerment of the European Parliament', *Journal of Common Market Studies*, vol. 41, no. 2, pp. 203–25.

Rittberger, Berthold (2005) *Building Europe's Parliament: Democratic Representation Beyond the Nation State*, Oxford: Oxford University Press.

Rohde, David W. (1991) *Parties and Leaders in the Postreform House*, Chicago, IL: University of Chicago Press.

Rokkan, Stein (1999) *State Formation, Nation-Building, and Mass Politics in Europe: The Theory of Stein Rokkan*, selected and rearranged by Peter Flora, Stein Kuhnle and Derek Urwin, Oxford: Oxford University Press.

Romer, Thomas and Howard Rosenthal (1978) 'Political Resource Allocation, Controlled Agendas, and the Status Quo', *Public Choice*, vol. 33, pp. 27–43.

Rosenthal, Howard and Erik Voeten (2004) 'Analyzing Roll Calls with Perfect Spatial Voting: France 1946–1958', *American Journal of Political Science*, vol. 48, no. 3, pp. 620–32.

Sartori, Giovanni (1976) *Parties and Party Systems: A Framework for Analysis, Volume 1*, Cambridge: Cambridge University Press.

Scarrow, Susan (1997) 'Political Career Paths and the European Parliament', *Legislative Studies Quarterly*, vol. 22, pp. 253–63.

Scharpf, Fritz (1999) *Governing in Europe: Effective and Democratic?* Oxford: Oxford University Press.

Schattschneider, Elmer E. (1942) *Party Government*, New York, NY: Rinehart.

Schattschneider, Elmar E. (1960) *The Semi Sovereign People: A Realist's View of Democracy in America*, New York, NY: Holt, Rinehart and Winston.

Schlesinger, Joseph A. (1984) 'On the Theory of Party Organization', *Journal of Politics*, vol. 46, pp. 369–400.

Schonhardt-Bailey, Cheryl (2003) 'Ideology, Party and Interests in the British Parliament of 1841–1847', *British Journal of Political Science*, vol. 33, no. 2, pp. 581–605.

Schumpeter, Joseph (1943) *Capitalism, Socialism and Democracy*, London: Allen and Unwin.

Scully, Roger M. (1997a) 'Policy Influence and Participation in the European Parliament', *Legislative Studies Quarterly*, vol. 12, pp. 233–52.

Scully, Roger M. (1997b) 'The EP and the Co-Decision Procedure: A Reassessment', *Journal of Legislative Studies*, vol. 3, no. 3, pp. 58–73.

Shapley, Lloyd S. and Martin Shubik (1954) 'A Method for Evaluating the Distribution of Power in a Committee System', *American Political Science Review*, vol. 48, pp. 787–92.

Shugart, Matthew S. and John M. Carey (1992) *Presidents and Assemblies: Constitutional Design and Electoral Systems*, Cambridge: Cambridge University Press.

Skog, Rolf (2002) 'The Takeover Directive: An Endless Saga?', *European Business Law Review*, vol. 13, no. 4, pp. 301–12.

Strøm, Kaare (1990) *Minority Government and Majority Rule*, Cambridge: Cambridge University Press.

Tirole, Jean (1989) *The Theory of Industrial Organization*, Cambridge, MA: MIT Press.

Topan, Angelina (2002) 'The Resignation of the Santer-Commission: The Impact of "Trust" and "Reputation"', *European Integration Online Papers*, vol. 6, paper 14, http://eiop.or.at/eiop/texte/2002–014.htm

Tsebelis, George (1994) 'The Power of the European Parliament as a Conditional Agenda-Setter', *American Political Science Review*, vol. 88, no. 1, pp. 128–42.

Tsebelis, George (1996) 'Maastricht and the Democratic Deficit', *Aussenwirtschaft*, vol. 52, no. 1/2, pp. 29–56.

Tsebelis, George (2002) *Veto Players: How Political Institutions Work*, Princeton, NJ: Princeton University Press/Russell Sage Foundation.

Tsebelis, George and Geoffrey Garrett (2000) 'Legislative Politics in the European Union', *European Union Politics*, vol. 1, no. 1, pp. 9–36.

Tsebelis, George and Geoffrey Garrett (2001) 'The Institutional Foundations of Intergovernmentalism and Supranationalism in the European Union', *International Organization*, vol. 55, pp. 357–90.

Tsebelis, George and Jeannette Money (1997) *Bicameralism*, Cambridge: Cambridge University Press.

Tsebelis, George, Christian B. Jensen, Anastassios Kalandrakis and Amie Kreppel (2001) 'Legislative Procedures in the European Union: An Empirical Analysis', *British Journal of Political Science*, vol. 31, no. 4, pp. 573–99.

Tullock, Gordon (1967) 'Welfare Costs of Tariffs, Monopolies and Theft', *Western Economic Journal*, vol. 5, pp. 224–32.

Van Oudenhove, Guy (1965) *Political Parties in the European Parliament: The First Ten Years (September 1952–September 1962)*, Leyden: A.W. Sijthoff.

Voeten, Erik (2000) 'Clashes of The Assembly', *International Organization*, vol. 54, pp. 185–214.

Weber, Max (1946 [1918]) 'Politics as a Vocation', in Hans H. Gerth and C. Wright Mills (eds.) *From Max Weber: Essays in Sociology*, Oxford: Oxford University Press.

Westlake, Martin (1994) *A Modern Guide to the European Parliament*, London: Pinter.

Williams, Shirley (1991) 'Sovereignty and Accountability', in Robert O. Keohane and Stanley Hoffmann (eds.) *The New European Community*, Boulder, CO: Westview.

Zellentin, Gerda (1967) 'Form and Function of the Opposition in the European Communities', *Government and Opposition*, vol. 2, no. 3, pp. 416–35.

Index

235